POSTMAN'S HORN

POSTMAN'S HORN

AN ANTHOLOGY OF THE LETTERS OF LATTER SEVENTEENTH CENTURY ENGLAND

BY

ARTHUR BRYANT

AUTHOR OF 'KING CHARLES II,' 'SAMUEL PEPYS'
'THE NATIONAL CHARACTER,' 'GEORGE V'
AND 'THE AMERICAN IDEAL'

GREENWOOD PRESS, PUBLISHERS
WESTPORT, CONNECTICUT

Originally published in 1936
by Longmans, Green and Co., London

First Greenwood Reprinting 1970

Library of Congress Catalogue Card Number 77-109713

SBN 8371-4203-2

Printed in the United States of America

CONTENTS

CHAP.   PAGE

'I.   Nursery and School   1

II.   Undergraduates and Dons   31

III.   ' A Flame that so torments me '   ...   66

IV.   Courtship and Weddings   79

V.   Marriage   109

VI.   Woman's Business   129

VII.   Sport   153

VIII. Men of the World   165

IX.   Food and Fellowship   192

X.   Travelling   202

XI.   Friendship   225

XII.   Growing Old   236

XIII. Religion   247

XIV.   Disease, Death and Burial   267

       Notes   297

INTRODUCTION

Long ago dwellers near the highway, in remote houses and hamlets, would sometimes hear borne to them from afar the sound of the postman's horn. A day later, perhaps, the boy from the manor house, riding back with brass-bound satchel from the nearest posting town, would bring a letter. The recipient would scan the superscription—

> ' These
> for my loving wife,
> Madame Wynnington,
> at the Birches in Cheshire.
> Warrington bag '—

then break the crested seal at the back and unfold the sheet. The next moment would tell her that which there was no telegram or telephone to bring tidings—of loved one well or ill, business accomplished or undone, a speedy homecoming or a further spell of absence. She would sigh, refold the sheet, and slip it into bosom or bureau, many times to be taken out again, unfolded and reread.

But the day would come when it would be read no more. In nine cases out of ten it would be burnt or torn to fragments by friendly or unfriendly hands. In the tenth it would survive. Stored in attic or muniment room in some ancient house, wedged between the folios of more serious documents—conveyances of land, wills, marriage settlements—or tied up in some bundle marked by the family solicitor *Of no importance*, it would linger on long after all memory had been lost of those whose life it told. Outside, in park and garden, spring would follow winter, and autumn summer; but in the muniment room the leaves would only turn a fainter sere. Yet one day some curious chatelaine or wandering antiquary would stumble on hidden treasure. Trembling, excited fingers would again unfold the leaves to reveal to eyes, gazing over dead men's shoulders, a life which had once been as real and vital as their own.

All over the land the country houses of England hid such treasure. The historians were utterly unaware of this wealth of material, often rotting in old boxes or consumed by rat or worm, and even had they known of it, would almost certainly have dismissed it as idle rubbish. It was the business of history, as then interpreted, to concern itself with matters of great moment ; with King, treaties, battles and parliaments. The Muse Clio was a lady and did not drink small beer. Not till Sir Walter Scott had taught a new generation to believe in the humanity of its ancestors did Macaulay and Carlyle make the first tentative use of the domestic correspondence of the past to point a moral and adorn a tale. Yet even then more than half a century elapsed before many private muniment rooms first yielded to the living the secrets of the dead. Some still withheld them until the post-war taxation of our own hasty day consigned them and the houses that contained them to the dealer and the estate-breaker.

Since the middle of the nineteenth century, however, the opportunities of the scholar for exploring the every-day background of our social history have steadily increased. To-day, thanks to the labours of the Royal Commission on Historical Manuscripts, first begun in 1869 and continued year by year ever since, of the Camden Society and of similar learned bodies, as well as of privately edited collections like the *Verney Memoirs* and *Chronicles of Erthig*, it is possible for a student to acquaint himself with many thousands of sixteenth-, seventeenth-

and eighteenth-century letters without having recourse to a single unprinted manuscript. Many hundreds of thousands more, it is true, wait to be explored both in private houses and in the public repositories at the British Museum, Record Office and Bodleian Library. But the truths they tell are in a sense already told and in print for those who seek them. One can appraise a great vintage without drinking the whole of it.

Yet knowledge of the vintage itself is indispensable. The only way in which a man can comprehend the modes of thought and behaviour of a vanished society is by making himself familiar with its everyday correspondence. And without that, historical research is a delusion, for the politics, economics, literature and philosophy of any given age alike rest on the social feelings and behaviour of the great mass of living beings who comprise it. It is not only popular books like Lytton Strachey's *Elizabeth and Essex* which are made unreal by their author's ignorance of ancient conventions of speech and action, but the works of more academic writers. To anyone who has made an intimate study of the domestic correspondence of the seventeenth century it is impossible not to be struck by the difference in outlook between those scholars who have familiarised themselves with the tone of Carolean common thought and those who have not. ' In an age dependent less on the principles than on the personalities of the great,' a brilliant American student of the period has written, ' it is necessary that we come to know the figures of that age.' We can only do so by acquainting ourselves with their lives as a whole' and not merely with their political ideals and pursuits, and by studying the growth of their thought and character against the back-ground of common social environment. It is the weakness of one of our chief schools of historical research that it emphasises the importance of proving political and economic theses by a process of laborious accumulation (preferably from unpublished manuscript sources) of all the facts which appear to support the thesis to the exclusion of all other material. In pursuit of this learned game— for it is really nothing more—great masses of manuscript are hastily turned over, of which only the fraction expected to help the search is examined. The remainder is passed over virtually unread.[1] Fortunately the younger generation of English scholars is showing signs of adopting a less exclusive and more catholic attitude.

Nothing is more misleading than judgments formed on the politics of a foreign country by those who have never visited it. The historian can never travel in person through the land of his study, and therefore is in danger of missing those tiny *minutiæ* of daily life that guide men in forming their thought and conduct. Yet something, at least, of that common background to a past existence can be recaptured through its letters. Probably the best foundation for knowledge of a social epoch is a continuous and detailed perusal of a typical family correspondence. The examination and transcription of one such first became the lot of the present writer a dozen years ago through the kindness of Sir Walter Shakerley: from that vast collection, the Shakerley MSS., several letters are here printed for the first time. To work day by day through such a correspondence, pursuing no thesis and seeking only the common mind of a vanished age, is to breathe the air of

[1] A curious example of this is provided on page 570 of Mr. David Ogg's learned work, *England in the Reign of Charles II.* Giving illustrations of the care taken to track down the alleged Popish plotters, the author concludes a well-referenced paragraph with the sentence : ' Even Pepys's nag came on the scene ; for a man was sent to Gravesend to apprehend a suspicious character enquiring after it.' This, while giving the appearance of great familiarity with obscure historical detail, shows how cursory an inspection of the sources cited is thought necessary even by so experienced a scholar and teacher as Mr. Ogg, for a minute's reading would have shown him it was not Pepys's nag that was being watched but that of an escaping suspect —actually an agent of Lord Shaftesbury's—who was being pursued by Pepys's orders.

life. The quiet days and weeks and months of that revealing study naturalise, as it were, the visitor from another age. Squire and chatelaine, sober merchant and ne'er-do-well younger son, the gamekeeper and the steward, parson, physician and traveller, the yeoman farmers and peasants who never wrote themselves but who stray, vital and boisterous like Smug the joiner and Bottom the weaver, across the life-histories of their 'betters,' greet him as a friend. Learning to share their daily thoughts and feelings, the scholar ceases to see the past through the eyes of the present, and acquires that balanced vision which is so much better an historical guide than opinions based on abstract reason, because it is founded on the instincts and even the very prejudices of those who once lived.

For those who have little time for scholarship, I have compiled this anthology of the domestic correspondence of a great and formative age of English history in grateful recollection of those calm and lamp-lit evenings that first taught me that the past was real. It makes no attempt to be comprehensive, and those familiar with the material upon which I have drawn will inevitably deplore many omissions. Its theme throughout is everyday life, whether as lived in the court, the city, or—as in nine cases out of ten—in the country. For that reason I have excluded letters relating to public affairs and the progress of business and science, and have reserved them for a further volume in which I hope to illustrate the changes in public opinion from 1660-1700 in chronological sequence. The subject of the present book being private and not public opinion, a chronological treatment seemed less suitable than one which grouped the material under the changing scenes of ordinary human life from the cradle to the grave.

With a few exceptions the letters all belong to the period between the Restoration and the death of William III. For that reason I have avoided the temptation to include any of Dorothy Osborne's delightful but far from representative love letters. Nor have I made any attempt to choose letters for their literary merit. A careful selection of its finest epistolary gems would give a very different impression of the stylistic abilities and mental outlook of the age. But it would be a false one.

Spelling and punctuation I have modernised, in order to avoid a false sense of 'quaintness.' Indeed, with some of my lady correspondents, if their products were to be even intelligible to the reader, something of the kind was inevitable; for what can the modern eye make of a whole page without a single stop, or of such bewildering letter groupings as '*Iasph nove*' for 'Ladyship know,' '*Cetemaster stoufe*' for 'Kidderminster stuff,' and '*a haire waring*' for 'a hare-warren.' 'I wind send my boy a porpus to bring word how you dow,' writes Lady Shakerley; 'it would acacon a suet in the Cort of Egety.' With the same 'porpus' of avoiding an unnecessary over-elaboration never contemplated by the original writers, I have used the modern notation of the years and eschewed seventeenth-century abbreviations. The letters were originally written for ordinary people, and it is to ordinary folk, not specialists, that they are now presented.

I hope that the brief explanatory prefaces which precede each group of letters will not be found too tiresome; I have tried to confine myself to the bare minimum of information requisite. Those who require more may perhaps find it in my *England of Charles II*, to which in a sense this book is an appendix.

My thanks are due to that brilliant and generous scholar and friend of scholars, Mr. John Hayward, who has done me the service of reading my manuscript, to my friend and neighbour, Sir Harry Verney, for allowing me to include unpublished letters from the Verney MSS. at Claydon, as well as others already printed wholly or in part in the *Verney Memoirs*, etc.

ACKNOWLEDGMENTS

For permission to use copyright material I am indebted to the following :

Messrs. G. Bell & Sons Ltd. for permission to use an extract from *Lives of the Norths*, Vol. III, edited by Augustus Jessopp ; the Trustees of the British Museum for extracts from the B.M. Harleian MS., and *The Letter Book of Philip Stanhope, Earl of Chesterfield*, B.M. Add. MSS., 19,253, F. 24 ; His Grace the Duke of Buccleuch for extracts from *Christopher Monck Duke of Albemarle*, by E. F. Ward, published by Mr. John Murray ; the Controller of H.M. Stationery Office for publications of the Historical MSS. Commission ; Messrs. Faber & Faber Ltd. for extracts from Geoffrey Keynes' edition of *The Works of Sir Thomas Browne* ; The Friends Book Store for extracts from *The Life of William Penn, with Selections from his Autobiography*, by S. M. Janney ; Mr. R. G. Howarth and Messrs. J. M. Dent & Sons Ltd. for extracts from *The Letters and Second Diary of Samuel Pepys* ; Messrs. Kegan Paul, Trench, Trübner & Co. Ltd. for extracts from *Four Centuries of English Letters*, edited by W. Baptiste Scoones, and from *The Diaries and Letters of Philip Henry*, edited by M. H. Lee, and *La Belle Stuart*, by C. H. Hartman ; Messrs. Longmans Green & Co. Ltd. for extracts from *The Life and Letters of Sir George Savile, Bart., First Marquess of Halifax*, by H. C. Foxcroft, from *The Verney Memoirs*, and from *Cavalier: Letters of Wm. Blundell to his Friends, 1620-1698*, edited by Margaret Blundell ; the Most Honourable the Marquess of Lansdowne and Messrs. Constable & Co. Ltd. for extracts from *The Petty Southwell Correspondence*

1676-1687, edited from the Bowood Papers ; Messrs. John Lane the Bodley Head Ltd. for extracts from *The Chronicles of Erthig on the Dyke*, by A. L. Cust ; Lord Newton for extracts from *The Lyme Letters* and *The House of Lyme*, by Lady Newton, and published by Messrs. Wm. Heinemann Ltd. ; Mr. John Murray for extracts from *The Life of William Sancroft, Archbishop of Canterbury*, Vol. II, by George D'Oyly ; The Nonesuch Press Ltd. for extracts from *The Complete Works of Thomas Otway*, edited by Montague Summers, and from *Collected Works of John Wilmot, Earl of Rochester*, edited by John Hayward ; The Oxford Historical Society for extracts from *The Flemings in Oxford*, edited by J. R. Magrath ; The Oxford University Press for extracts from *The Letter Book of Sir George Etherege*, edited by Sybil Rosenfield ; Mrs. Pepys-Cockerell for extracts from *The Private Correspondence and Miscellaneous Papers of Samuel Pepys*, edited by J. R. Tanner ; Prof. V. de S. Pinto and Messrs. Constable & Co. Ltd. for extracts from *Sir Charles Sedley*, by V. de S. Pinto ; Sir Isaac Pitman & Sons Ltd. for the extract from *The Life of Thomas Ken, D.D.*, by E. H. Plumptre ; The Royal Historical Society for extracts from *The Letters of Humphrey Prideaux* (Camden Society), edited by E. M. Thompson, and *The Correspondence of the Family of Hatton* (Camden Society), also edited by E. M. Thompson, and from *The Lauderdale Papers* (Camden Society), edited by O. Airy ; Sir H. Verney for extracts from *Verney Letters of the Eighteenth Century*, edited by Margaret Maria, Lady Verney.

It has not always been possible to discover the present representatives of the copyright owners, and it is hoped that no copyright has been unwittingly infringed.

POSTMAN'S HORN

CHAPTER I

NURSERY AND SCHOOL

THE DAY OF BREECHING

The ideal of seventeenth century education was to fit a child for life in a dangerous and uncertain world as quickly as possible. It was in keeping with this ideal that, once infancy was over, children, instead of wearing the distinctive dress of childhood, should be put into tiny replicas of adult costume.

The first great step in a small boy's life was his ' breeching,' when, taken from the sole charge of mother or nurse lest he should be spoilt by too much ' dallying and fond cokkering,' he put on man's attire.

The writer of this letter was Anne, Lady North, of Tostock, Suffolk, the grandmother of the little Frank of its pages and the mother of its recipient, Sir Francis North, Chief Justice of the Common Pleas and later Lord Keeper of the Great Seal. Frank was his eldest son and after his death succeeded him as the 2nd Baron Guilford.

The missing muff, referred to in the postscript, was an article of male attire which became the vogue during the reign of Charles II. It was worn by men about town during the winter and hung round the neck by a riband.

TO LORD CHIEF JUSTICE NORTH AT HIS HOUSE IN CHANCERY LANE, FROM HIS MOTHER, LADY NORTH.
Tostock, 10 *October*, 1679.[1]

Dear Son,

. . . You cannot believe the great concern that was in the whole family here last Wednesday, it being the day that the tailor was to help to dress little Frank in his breeches in order to the making an everyday suit by it. Never had any bride that was to be dressed upon her wedding night more hands about her, some the legs and some the arms, the tailor buttoning and others putting on the sword, and so many lookers on that had I not had a finger amongst them I could not have seen him. When he was quite dressed he acted his part as well as any of them, for he desired he might go down to enquire for the little gentleman that was there the day before in a black coat, and speak to the men to tell the gentleman when he came from school that here was a gallant with very fine clothes and a sword to have waited upon him and would come again upon Sunday next. But this was not all, for there was great contrivings while he was dressing who should have the first salute, but he said if old Lane had been here she should, but he gave it me to quiet them all.

They are very fit, everything, and he looks taller and prettier than in his coats. Little Charles rejoiced as much as he did, for he jumped all the while about him and took notice of everything. I went to Bury and bought everything for another suit, which will be finished upon Saturday, so the coats are to be quite left off upon Sunday. I consider it is not yet term time and since you could not have the pleasure of the first sight I have resolved you should have a full relation from

Your most affectionate Mother, A. NORTH.

When he was dressed he asked Buckle whether muffs were out of fashion because they had not sent him one.

TOMMY GROWS A STOUT FELLOW

*Sir Thomas Browne was the scholar and physician who wrote
' Religio Medici.' He was knighted by Charles II on the
latter's visit to Norwich in 1671. His eldest son, Edward, was
a Fellow of the Royal College of Physicians and later became its
President. He lived in Salisbury Court, where a generation
earlier Pepys had been cut for the stone. His son Tommy,
referred to in this letter, was nine years old at the time.*

TO MRS. EDWARD BROWNE IN SALISBURY COURT
NEXT THE GOLDEN BALLS IN LONDON, FROM HER
FATHER-IN-LAW, SIR THOMAS BROWNE.
Norwich, 13 February, 1682.[2]

Dear Daughter,

. . . Your Tommy grows a stout fellow; I hope you
will come and see him this summer. He is in great
expectation of a tumbler you must send him for his
puppet show; a punch he has and his wife, and a straw
king and queen, and ladies of honour, and all things but
a tumbler, which this town cannot afford: it is a wooden
fellow that turns his heels over his head.

Your sister Frank presents her service to my daughter,
and begs that she would send somebody to Mr. Brown's,
at the Blue Bell and Key, in Little Queens Street, and buy
her a set of crayons which will cost a crown she is told:
perhaps cheaper.

THE WAY A CHILD SHOULD GO

*The next two letters have a rather melancholy interest.
Their writer, the notorious rake and poet, was already moving
fast towards the early and tragic close of his meteoric and dissolute life. His eldest son, Charles, had been born in 1670 and*

cannot have been less than seven or eight years old at the time that they were written. Rochester died at the age of thirty-three on July 26, 1680, and the boy a year later.

T O CHARLES WILMOT FROM HIS FATHER, THE EARL OF ROCHESTER.[3]

I hope, Charles, when you receive this and know that I have sent this gentleman to be your tutor, you will be very glad to see I take such care of you, and be very grateful, which is best shown in being obedient and diligent. You are now grown big enough to be a man, if you can be wise enough; and the way to be truly wise is to serve God, learn your book and observe the instructions of your parents first and next your tutor; according as you employ that time, you are to be happy or unhappy for ever. But I have so good an opinion of you that I am glad to think you will never deceive me. Dear child, learn your book, and be obedient, and you shall see what a father I will be to you. You shall want no pleasure while you are good, and that you may be so are my constant prayers. ROCHESTER.

T O CHARLES WILMOT FROM HIS FATHER, THE EARL OF ROCHESTER.[4]

Charles, I take it very kindly that you write to me (though seldom) and wish heartily you would behave yourself so as that I might show how much I love you without being ashamed. Obedience to your grandmother and those who instruct you in good things is the way to make you happy here, and for ever. Avoid idleness, scorn lying, and God will bless you; for which I pray. ROCHESTER.

A LITTLE PURITAN'S DREAM

The little Puritan who waked in the night in terror lest he had committed the sin against the Holy Ghost was a future first Minister of the Crown. Honest Robin Harley, like more than one great leader of the English Tories, came of ' rebel ' and ' nonconformist ' stock. His father, Sir Edwin Harley, of Brampton Bryan, Herefordshire, had fought in the Parliament's Army and was a staunch upholder of the dissenters. At the time of this letter Robin was not quite nine.

TO SIR EDWARD HARLEY, IN TOTHILL STREET, WESTMINSTER, FROM HIS WIFE, LADY HARLEY. 27 *October,* 1670.[5]

. . . Robin last night waked in the night and prayed and was troubled and it was a good while before he went to sleep again. I was asking him this evening what it was that troubled him, for Nan told me he prayed that God would rebuke the tempter. He said it was sin. He had heard of the sin against the Holy Ghost which was unpardonable but did not know what sin it was and was afraid to ask lest he had committed it or the devil should tempt him to commit it. The poor child with tears told me he was afraid if he died he should go to hell. . . .

MAKING VERY FINE YOUTHS

The eight letters that follow concern the educational needs of three small boys, Roger, Will and Harry Bradshaigh, who had been left, after the death of their father and the remarriage of their mother, to the care of their grandmother, Elizabeth, Lady Bradshaigh, and of their cousin and guardian, Peter Shakerley. In the first letter Lady Bradshaigh discusses the future of the youngest son, Harry (who was not to inherit an

*estate like his elder brother, Sir Roger) and the shortcomings of
the boys' tutor, the Rev. Mr. Francis, a subject to which she was
much addicted and which she resumed in her next letter.   In the
fourth letter she gives her views on the characters of the two eldest
boys whom Peter Shakerley has placed at Mr. Price's school at
Ruthin.   In the fifth a female relation at Ruthin reports on
their progress and linen to Peter Shakerley.   The next two letters
are written by little Sir Roger Bradshaigh himself and speak
for themselves.   The last introduces the great occasion of going
home for the holidays.*

*Old Lady Bradshaigh's spelling is nothing if not original.
A Protestant of the old school, brought up during the anarchy
of Civil War and Interregnum, she has her own individual way
of expressing herself on paper.   Nephew is ' neve,' prentice
' printas,' soldier ' solger,' liquor ' lecker,' and high simply
' hy.'   Indeed it is often exceedingly difficult to know what she
means: not one word in two is spelt in an easily recognisable
form.   Of Mr. Francis' iniquities she writes: ' he would have
tacken the shu off hes fott and have bett pore Roger about hes
hed with it and hath oft stroke both hem and his brothere Will
to the ground and pouncht them with hes fett.'   Again civil
is ' sevell,' rates ' rats,' ire ' ay,' because ' bacas,' and provoking language ' provockin langioge.'*

*Like grandmother, like grandson.   Roger renders waggoner
' wigginor,' scarce ' scirce,' and physic ' fisik.'*

T O PETER SHAKERLEY, GOVERNOR OF CHESTER CASTLE,
FROM HIS AUNT, ELIZABETH, LADY BRADSHAIGH.

                          Holker, 12 January, 1688.[6]

Nephew,
My son Preston as soon as he had your letter sent it
immediately to Mr. Abrahams, which will at the time
appointed meet you. Now, dear Nephew, as for Harry
I writ to you before that he loseth his time very much,

for since he came hither Mr. Francis doth not mind him nor will take any pains with him, that he might be taught to write and read and to cast a count so would be fit for a prentice. For there was a younger brother of the house of Haigh that was a woollen draper, and he lived as well as his elder brother, and a linen draper is a trade that many gentlemen's sons are put to and doth well.

But all these I shall leave to you to consider of. For a soldier's life is most ways a loose life and many ills comes upon it.

I would not have you to think that this is writ that either my son Preston or I am weary of him, for I am certain my son hath as great a love for him as if he were his own, and for my part it is my love to him that makes me write this. So pray consider of it for the good of the poor boy. If you had chosen a tutor that would have taken more pains with him, the poor boy might have done better, but Mr. Francis is very high and loves good liquor too well for a man of his coat. So I shall say no more but that I am

Your aunt to serve you,

ELIZABETH BRADSHAIGH.

TO PETER SHAKERLEY FROM EUBULE THELWALL, VICE-CHAMBERLAIN OF CHESTER.

Ruthin, 24 *June*, 1688.[7]

Honoured Sir,

I received yours this morning and in answer to the first part can only say that here is a good school governed by good and diligent schoolmasters and full of scholars, whereof very many are gentlemen of very good quality. The best place to board them will be at Widow Thelwall's. She keeps a private house and is a good careful woman,

and there your cousins will meet good and careful usage
and find Sir Roger Mostyn's grandson and heir and one
or two young gentlemen more schoolfellows and companions. The rate there will be £10 or £12 per annum
apiece. . . .

I shall be able to say more when I see you than I can
now write, for about five weeks hence I intend to see
Chester.

My humble service to your good lady. I am

Sir,

Your faithful humble servant,

EUBULE THELWALL.

TO PETER SHAKERLEY FROM ELIZABETH, LADY BRADS-
HAIGH. 'RECOMMENDED TO THE CARE OF THE
POSTMASTER OF STONE. POST 6*d*. PAID. CHESTER.'

Holker, 21 July, 1688.[8]

Dear Nephew,

I was very glad of your letter by this post and to know
you have found so good a place for my grandchildren as
I hear that place is, and that it is so good a school. And
the chief reason I so much desired to have them with
Mr. Masdin was your Mrs' care I know would have been
of them if with her. But I am confident and never had
other opinion of you but you would be very careful of
them and where you placed them. So I hope, it being
near to my brother Shakerley and not far from yourself,
they will want no friends to see that they be well looked
to. And pray, dear Nephew, speak to those that looks to
them that they have a care of Will's issue, for sometimes it
will be very sore and inflamed, so then we used to anoint
it with a little cream, and he must be kept from scratching
of it. I dare say it is a great preserver of his health.

Now, dear Nephew, I would gladly know whom hath told you that I did say anything of your wronging me of my jointure, for I do protest I never said it, nor was it my thoughts that you would do any such thing. For I always said that you would be just in all your accounts, and for my son Preston he doth protest he never did say anything that you should cheat me of my jointure, so they're very base that hath done this to my son Preston and me. But you had the fortune to send one of the basest and worst conditioned men with the children that ever came in any house, I mean Francis, their tutor, for he was a base lying fellow. I am sorry I should say so much of one of his coat, but it is truth, and those that tries him will find it. I do protest poor Roger told me he was very willing to go to any school you would send him to so that Francis might not teach him, for he would have taken the shoe off his foot and have beat poor Roger about his head with it and hath oft struck both him and his brother Will to the ground and punched them with his feet. So he was a hare-brained fellow and not fit to teach any child. This is truth I do assure you and he is a very dangerous fellow to have in a house, and this I writ that you may be careful what you say afore him.

I pray dear Nephew let me know how I may write to my dear Roger which I hope you will find will be careful to give you content and to be advised by you, for I shall always give him that advice. So with my service to your wife and the same to yourself, I am your aunt to love

and serve you,

ELIZABETH BRADSHAIGH.

To Peter Shakerley from Elizabeth, Lady Bradshaigh.

Holker, 6 August, 1688.[9]

Dear Nephew,

Your letter sent by James Bradshaigh I received, and I was very glad to hear you have placed my two grandchildren so well and the rates is not dear you give for their tables, and I am glad their landlady is so good a woman as I hear she is. And pray, good Nephew, give both Roger and Will a great charge to be civil in the house both to their landlady and to all the servants, and I have writ to Roger to be careful to carry himself so as not to give any occasion to think him proud or ill natured, for that in a gentleman is very ungrateful. And I must tell you that you must give Will a great charge not to give his brother provoking language, for when he was here he did it very oft. And really he hath the basest tongue that ever stood in any little boy's head, that I have many times wondered how the boy could invent such language to give his brother; and he will face an untruth and stand in it very strongly.

So if he should do any of these things now you must speak to the master to whip him for it, for his spirit is so high that it must be ire that must keep him under: fair words will do him no good. I write this to you because I would not have them disagree, for they are boys of high spirit both.

Harry is a very good child and presents his service to you, and his master tells me he hopes to make him fit for a calling, and that's what a younger brother must rely of. . . .

TO PETER SHAKERLEY FROM MRS. THELWALL.

Ruthin, 3 September, 1688.[10]

Honoured Sir,

In this you will find my layings out for Sir Roger and his brother which I wish I have not erred in or been too extravagant. I bought them the more shirts by reason those they have be very thin and not many of them. I think to mend them up to keep them with the four hollands which be for Sir Roger for to go abroad with, and the strong Doulas will serve for Ruthin and will hold out best for washing and winter wear. I hope they need not have more one year if not longer of that sort of linen. We shall fit up what fine linen you sent to serve both to save buying. And the better sleeves I tell Sir Roger he may well keep till he grow to them.

Pray God bless them: they be very fine youths and easily managed, as my aunt and cousin tells me that have the care of them. The only fault is they do not well agree. I receive the complaints of each sometimes. I question not but you will prevail with the one to submit and the other not to be usurping. We have been fain to acquaint Mr. Price and since they have been much quieter, I beg neither may know I mention it to you. And pardon if possible the rudeness of this and please to make my service acceptable to your good lady and Madam Hurleston. My husband is your most humble and thankful servant and begs what news you have with Sir Roger who does promise to be back on Friday. I wish them a fair day and well to you and am

Your most humble servant

MARY THELWALL.

What books they have had I have not yet paid for but must by Michaelmas Fair.

TO PETER SHAKERLEY FROM HIS WARD, SIR ROGER
BRADSHAIGH, BART.

Circa September, 1688.[11]

Dear Cousin,

I have writ to my grandmother by a waggoner, and as
soon as my clothes are made I desire you would send them
hither, for I stand in great need of them.   For the clothes
I have now on are a great deal too short, for they scarce
cover the half part of my breeches.   I want nothing at
present, but service to your lady with the same to yourself from him who will ever manifest to the world how
much I am

Your humble

servant to command

ROGER BRADSHAIGH.

TO PETER SHAKERLEY FROM HIS WARD, SIR ROGER
BRADSHAIGH, BART. (*aetat* 14).

Circa September, 1688.[12]

Honoured Sir,

I received your clothes you sent me.   They are a little
too long but that is no fault, and a little thing makes the
gold buttons being worn before to unravel.   And Madam
Thelwall thinks they are too good to spoil and advises
me to keep them till Christmas again . . . and to wear
the clothes with silver olive buttons, and says a frieze
would have been much better for every day.   For all
the boys that are gentlemen's sons wear them, for it so
cold and [they] are very cheaper.   I was not well but have
taken physic.   One day I was taken in the school with the
gripeing of the guts, which Mr. Price thinks to be the

worms. No more at present but my service to your lady from him who is

Your humble servant

ROGER BRADSHAIGH.

Mr. and Mrs. Thelwall gives their service to you and Mr. Price.

TO LADY SHAKERLEY AT GWERSILT FROM MARY THELWALL.

Ruthin, Monday morning, December, 1688.[13]

My honoured dear Lady,

. . . Sir Roger Bradshaigh is your most thankful servant and has engaged me to let you know they break school on Saturday morning and if possible glad he would be horses were to receive him out of school, his longing is such for Gwersilt.

I hope you will observe how 'twill be betwixt him and his brother. They do quarrel a little too much. I have a great respect for each and would not displease either by my goodwill, for I think them very fine youths both and much I shall miss their pretty company. But in my poor judgment Sir Roger ought not to be allowed to beat him till he be older and more schooled than now he can be. I grant the other has a tongue not to be borne, but then that is all as he says he has to defend himself. For the other occasions it: he will not by his good will let the poor little one come here and sit with us some nights but he shall have a banging for it, and he will not stay with us if he find his brother, that I pity the poor child mightily. But I hope in the time they be with you, the Governor may come and he may take notice of their quarrels and advise Sir Roger, he being more a man to bear with his little brother and correct him only with words and not blows. For those may do him a further prejudice about his head, coming daily upon him as they have done more than I could wish. My best service to dear Sir Geoffrey with many thanks to you both for Dolly and all other favours I rest

Your most affectionate aunt and ready servant,

MARY THELWALL.

We shall return your portmantel and all things safe when I send for Dolly. If you send Saturday for Sir Roger I shall be glad she come along, but then she must be dropped at Bodidrest for she must be there a night or two. But I believe you will not send till next week, for that will be a whole fortnight before the holidays. But, poor things, they long to be at so good a place. I will assure you Sir Roger makes a pretty lady: we have him to try the things. . . .

LOOKING FOR A SCHOOL

Sir Ralph Verney of Claydon, Buckinghamshire, was one of the great personages in the wings of the English seventeenth century scene. Son of Sir Edmund Verney, Charles I's standard-bearer, who fell at Edgehill out of loyalty to the master whose bread he had eaten, he had the distinction of being exiled by both parties to the Civil War—by the Royalists for having espoused the Parliamentary cause, and by the Parliamentarians for having refused to take the Presbyterian Covenant, the pill which the English Puritan conscience was constrained to swallow in return for Scottish help against the King. It was Sir Ralph who had taken down on his knees the shorthand notes which are our chief eye-witness account of Charles's attempt to arrest the five members. He plays the leading part in the most famous of all printed collections of seventeenth century correspondence, the

'Verney Memoirs,' guiding the affairs of a widespread territorial family until his death in 1696.

His eldest son, Edmund or 'Mun' Verney, whom we shall meet again in these pages, was living at the time when he wrote this letter in the house where these notes were also written two and a half centuries later. His own second son, also Edmund or Mun, was ten in 1678.

The choice in a quiet country district of five schools all within a dozen miles of each other shows that the system of private scholastic education in England was more advanced than is generally supposed. Little Mun was sent to join his elder brother, Ralph, at Mr. Blackwell's school at Bicester. It did not, however, prove altogether satisfactory, for a short while after Edmund Verney senior complained that whenever Mr. Blackwell was ill, which was often, ' the gentlemen boarders straggled at their pleasure.' He therefore wished he had the donation of the East Claydon vicarage ' to gratify some poor sober young scholar that would very carefully look to my sons and industriously instruct them in learning and virtue.'

TO SIR RALPH VERNEY, BART., FROM HIS SON, EDMUND VERNEY.

East Claydon, 18 February, 1678.[14]

. . . I went unto Water Stratford unto one Mr. Mason's house, the minister and schoolmaster there, to see what accommodation there was for my boy Mun in case I put him there to school. My man Wood's mother dwells there at present, and if I send him thither, he is to lie with her in a room good enough over the kitchen. All which I like very well, for she is a good discreet woman and says she will be mighty careful of him.

I like as well Mr. Mason himself who seems to be a very good conscientious man and scholar enough. His terms are but £12 per annum which is a 4th part less than

Mr. Blackwell's. But somewhere by the grace of God
I do firmly resolve to put out my boy Mun, and we have
good schoolmasters enough about us, viz. Mr. Blackwell
at Bicester, Mr. Rochford at Addington, Mr. Mason at
Water Stratford, and Mr. Almond at Thornton who writes
an admirable hand as I am told. All which I name unto
you desiring your opinion which of all these you like best
and I will put him there. . . .

TO EDMUND VERNEY AT MR. BLACKWELL'S SCHOOL
AT BICESTER FROM HIS FATHER, EDMUND VERNEY.
September, 1682.[15]

Child,
   I received a letter from your master Mr. Blackwell,
who complains of you in your business, and that you are
idly and evilly inclined, and particularly that you jointly
with some other, as bad as yourself, have lately mischiefed
a tablet or two of his, and that you rise in the nights which
was made to rest and sleep in. . . .
   You have much deceived me, your father, who blinded
with love to you, thought you no less than a young saint,
but now to my grief perceive that you are growing very
fast to be an old devil. . . .

THE HEADMASTER TAKES A NEW BOY

   *In this letter we see Dr. Cromleholme, the High Master of
St. Paul's from 1657 to 1672, receiving a new boy, a poor
protégé of Roger Kenyon, a Lancashire squire. He was a friend
of Pepys whom he had taught in his youth and who wrote of him
as ' a conceited pedagogue, . . . though a learned man, he
being so dogmatical in all he do and says.' This, however,
was probably no more than the usual impatience of a man of
the world with the scholastic manner. His wife, also alluded*

to in the letter, Pepys sets down as a ' pretty woman: ' ' never yet with child,' he adds, ' and methinks looks as if her mouth watered now and then upon some of her boys.' That was nine years before.

Dr. Cromleholme died in July, 1672, so that at the time of this pleasant scene, though he did not know it, his school-mastering days were almost over.

TO ROGER KENYON AT MANCHESTER OR PEEL FROM THOMAS GREENFIELD.

London, 20 February, 1672.[16]

According as you desired, I give you the account touching the Doctor's reception of Elisha Chew. Yesterday, Dr. Frankland went with myself and Mr. William Cayton along with the boy to Dr. Cromleholme, who readily gave the child, and us, a very free and welcome entertainment. And to be short, he gave us order to remember his love to the boy's mother, and to let her know from him that he received her boy as his own, and that he willed as carefully of him as if he was his own, and that he will (by God's blessing) give him learning and send him to Oxford, and that he doubted not of friends to get him preferment there.

He called up his wife, and said, ' Sweetheart, you must take this child as mine and yours,' which she denied not, but asked her husband who he was like. He would have her judgment first, whereupon she said the boy was very like a brother of hers, and he concurred with her in the matter.

He was very glad the boy was past the measles and small-pox. After we had drunk a glass or two of ale about, he laid his hand on the boy's head and blessed him saying, ' The Lord God Almighty bless thee, and not only give thee wisdom and learning, but his grace also.' Upon which, other company coming to him, we took our leave and departed; and to-morrow morning I am to go with the boy to him and carry with him his clothes. And this is all. . . .

' THE MEASLES BEING AMONGST MY CHILDREN '

In days when smallpox was as common as measles and families of ten or more the rule rather than the exception, the danger of infection was never long out of a parent's mind. ' I am ever disappointed in my intention to wait upon you,' wrote Sir George Savile to Sir Thomas Osborne in 1667,* ' which I would not omit if the coming to you now would not be a greater rudeness than staying away, the measles being amongst my children, which maketh me conclude I am an unwelcome guest and a dangerous one where there are so many little ones, besides the particular concern I am to have for my god-daughter's pretty face which I would not have spoiled though but for a week.'

The first of the three letters that follow is written by Lancashire Lady Bradshaigh about an epidemic of smallpox which had broken out among her grandchildren at a slightly earlier date than the period treated in her previous letters, and the second by an anxious mother to her ailing son at Westminster, and the third by a small invalid himself. The uncharitable references at the beginning of Lady Bradshaigh's letter are to her daughter-in-law, a fashionable young matron who, after her husband's death, had married again and betaken herself to London, where she was now engaging in a furious controversy with Peter Shakerley over the family heirlooms.

* Both to become famous, one as Lord Danby, chief minister to Charles II, and the other as the great Lord Halifax.

TO Peter Shakerley at chester from Elizabeth, Lady Bradshaigh.

Holker, 4 October, 1687.[17]

Dear Nephew,

I received your letter sent by Mr. Francis and by it I perceive you have taken a good course to price and sell the goods, for as long as they were in the house the London lady would have been nibbling and convening them away, for she hath neither good nature nor conscience in her but a false heart, or else she could not for shame have turned her back on those two pretty babes she left at Haigh. And since she knew how Sir Roger was of the smallpox she never writ letter to me but one, so I am confident she doth not concern herself what becomes of them all.

Poor Harry hath been so ill of the smallpox that I have had the doctor with him a whole week and upon Thursday last the doctor had but little hopes of his life, for they were very unkindly pocks and flat, but now I thank God he is very hearty, but in all my life I never saw any so full as he is so of the scar. They will mar a pretty face.

I am forced to keep the doctor still, for upon Saturday last poor Will began of the smallpox: they are come well forth so that I hope he will come well past them, for there shall neither be care nor charges wanting of mine to recover him. I do assure you their sore sickness hath been great charges to me, for since they began what with giving to the doctors and people to watch with them and the 'pothecary's bill, it hath cost me near twenty pounds. But to save the pretty boys' lives I am content to do anything. . . .

TO George Shakerley at westminster school from his mother, Lady Shakerley.

Gwersilt, [1697].[18]

My dear George,

If anything in this world could dry up my just sorrowful tears, hearing that you are better of your cold would and your promise to take to your study. It has very much revived my afflicted heart, and I am sure if you do your best God will assist you in his mercies. He never left his servants destitute, and your dear father's child will not want him if you call upon him. And be sure you observe your brother in obedience and mind what he says to you in all things, for he is a father to you. It is God's mercies to us that he is left to take care of us, and I do earnestly command you to be dutiful.

For prevention they advise me to have an issue made. It will be no pain to you, and if you be well it may be shut up at any time. I have written to your brother to beg of him to have it done to prevent this severe cough. You must have it made as soon as may be; therefore let me have no put-offs that am your disconsolate mother,

Jane Shakerley.

I hear Mr. Bruen of Stapleford is dead of a raging fever: God help his widow. Mrs. Anderton is dying, if not dead: happy, happy she. I thank you for your news, dear George.

TO Sir Ralph Verney at claydon from his son, John Verney.

Kensington, 22 *March,* 1658.[19]

Most dear Father,

I am sorry for to write unto you upon this account, but it is for to let you know that I have an ague every other day. Last Wednesday in the morning I had a fit, and on Friday another, and on the Sunday I had another, and how it may proceed I know not. However I hope that you are all in good health. So continually being

Your most humble and most obedient son

JOHN VERNEY.

'THE BEST NURSERY OF LEARNING FOR YOUNG CHILDREN IN THE WORLD'

In the next two letters we return to Edmund Verney of East Claydon and his two boys, Ralph and Mun. In the first, Edmund, who had ridden himself with Ralph to Winchester, writes sadly to the Headmaster of what he calls 'the best nursery of learning for young children in the world,' about his son's shortcomings during his first term: in the second he writes to Ralph himself.

TO THE HEADMASTER OF WINCHESTER FROM EDMUND VERNEY.

5 September, 1682.[20]

' Sir,

I received your civil letter for which I return you my very hearty thanks, as also for your pains about my son and care of him. I did fully intend to send him back to you or Mr. Usher, which of you I know not. But hearing you gave a very ill character of him here before a great deal of company at table openly at London since he left Winchester, I did not think it decent in me to trouble so accomplished a gentleman as you are nor your school with such a blockhead any more. For I know full well that *Ex quorvis Ligno non fit Mercurius,* and am sorry that my son should be composed of such substance that nothing can shape him for a scholar. But it is his fault and none but his, and the worst will be his own at long run, for William of Wykeham's foundation is I believe the best nursery of learning for young children in the world, and perhaps never was better provided with abler teachers than now at this present, yourself for a master, Mr. Home for an Usher and Mr. Terry for a tutor.

I have another son, whom I ever designed for Winchester also. I do not despair but that he may regain the lost reputation of his brother. But until the ill impression which my eldest hath left behind him in Winton be utterly erased and worn out, I am ashamed to send him lest the impression should prove a disadvantage to him in your school.

I understand that my worthy friend Dr. Sherrock hath paid all my son's scores within and without the College in Winchester. I pray deliver this enclosed letter from my son to Mr. Terry his tutor and you will oblige your humble servant Edmund Verney. . . . Things may (I hope) be so cleared that his brother may appear there with credit and honour hereafter, if I should send him. . . .

TO RALPH VERNEY AT WINCHESTER SCHOOL FROM HIS FATHER, EDMUND VERNEY.

London, 29 January, 1683.[21]

Child,

I received yours and have sent you a new hat as you desired. It is a black French *cordebec* with a hat-band on it, which sort of hats are most proper for you in your present circumstances. I hope it fits you.

I hear you long for oysters which I did not know from you but from others. I would send you some with all my heart if I knew how to send them to you good. However I will endeavour it. But then you must have a care that you eat not too much at one time lest they do you harm.

Rest assured that there is no reasonable thing that I can help you to but that you shall have provided you do your best endeavour to please me, as you are bound to in duty. And one main way is for you to incline your heart and mind briskly unto your studies and to take delight in them. And so God bless you and prosper you,

I am

Your most affectionate father

EDMUND VERNEY.

My service unto your master and mistress.

'IN EXCUSE OF MY SON'

The most famous school in England in the later seventeenth century was Westminster under the great Dr. Busby. This mighty squire of the rod was so great a man that he is said on one occasion to have kept on his hat in the King's presence lest his scholars should suppose that any man could be greater than he. Among his early pupils was the Poet Laureate, John Dryden, who remembered his floggings to the day of his death, but sent his two eldest sons to him for the same treatment.

The following letters, the first written by Lady Elizabeth Dryden and the second by ' Poet Squab ' himself, refer to the delinquencies of their eldest son, Charles, then fourteen. Despite the fears expressed in the correspondence, the boy was elected to Trinity College, Cambridge, in the course of the next year: after the Revolution he became Chamberlain to Pope Innocent XII.

Lady Elizabeth Dryden was a daughter of the Cavalier Earl of Berkshire and sister of the poet, Sir Edward Howard. Her name was not spared by scandal, and her relations with her husband were often strained. But they were both devoted to their children.

To the Rev. Dr. Busby, headmaster of Westminster school, from Lady Elizabeth Dryden.
Ascension Day (1682).[22]

Honoured Sir,

I hope I need use no other argument to you in excuse
of my son for not coming to church to Westminster
than this, that he now lies at home and therefore cannot
easily go so far backwards and forwards. His father and
I will take care that he shall duly go to church here, both
on holidays and Sundays, till he comes to be more nearly
under your care in the college. In the mean time, will
you please to give me leave to accuse you of forgetting
your promise concerning my eldest son, who, as you once
assured me, was to have one night in a week allowed him
to be at home in consideration both of his health and
cleanliness. You know, Sir, that promises made to
women, and especially mothers, will never fail to be
called upon; and therefore I will add no more, but that
I am at this time your remembrancer and always, honoured
Sir,

Your humble servant,

E. Dryden.

To the Rev. Dr. Busby from John Dryden.

[1682.][23]

Sir,

If I could have found in myself a fitting temper to have
waited upon you, I had done it the day you dismissed my
son from the college, for he did the message: and by
what I find from Mr. Meredith, as it was delivered by
you to him, namely, that you desired to see me and had
somewhat to say to me concerning him. I observed

likewise somewhat of kindness in it that you sent him away that you might not have occasion to correct him.

I examined the business and found it concerned his having been *custos* four or five days together. But if he was admonished and was not believed because other boys combined to discredit him with false witnessing and to save themselves, perhaps his crime is not so great. Another fault, it seems, he made, which was going into one Hawkes his house with some others; which you happening to see, sent your servant to know who they were, and he only returned you my son's name; so the rest escaped.

I have no fault to find with my son's punishment; for that is and ought to be reserved to any master, much more to you who have been his father's. But your man was certainly to blame to name him only; and 'tis only my respect to you, that I do not take notice of it to him. My first rash resolutions were to have brought things past any composure by immediately sending for my son's things out of college; but upon recollection I find I have a double tie upon me not to do it: one, my obligations to you for my education; another, my great tenderness of doing anything offensive to my Lord Bishop of Rochester, as chief governor of the college. It does not consist with the honour I bear him and you to go so precipitately to work; no, not so much as to have any difference with you, if it can possibly be avoided. Yet as my son stands now, I cannot see with what credit he can be elected; for, being but sixth, and (as you are pleased to judge) not deserving that neither, I know not whether he may not go immediately to Cambridge, as well as one of his own election went to Oxford this year by your consent. I will say nothing of my second son, but that, after you had been pleased to advise me to wait on my Lord Bishop for his favour, I found he might have had the first place if you had not opposed it; and I likewise found at the election that, by the pains you had taken with him, he in some sort deserved it.

I hope, Sir, when you have given yourself the trouble to read thus far, you, who are a prudent man, will consider that none complain but they desire to be reconciled at the same time: there is no mild expostulation, at least, which does not intimate a kindness and respect in him who makes it. Be pleased, if there be no merit on my side, to make it your own act of grace to be what you were formerly to my son. I have done something so far to conquer my own spirit as to ask it; and, indeed, I know not with what face to go to my Lord Bishop and to tell him I am taking away both my sons. For though I shall tell him no occasion, it will look like a disrespect to my old master of which I will not be guilty if it be possible. I shall add no more, but hope I shall be so satisfied with a favourable answer from you, which I promise to myself from your goodness and moderation, that I shall still have occasion to continue,

Sir,

Your most obliged humble servant,

JOHN DRYDEN.

HARD AND KNOTTY STUDIES

The education of a Catholic boy in an intolerant England presented difficulties unknown to Protestant parents. If there was not enough money to send him to one of the English Jesuit Colleges abroad, he had to depend on the resources of his own home. In this letter a poor Lancashire squire, constantly mulcted for his loyalty to his religion, tells his son-in-law, the penniless son of an Irish peer, Lord Mountgarret, of his educational progress with the grandchildren committed to his care.

The letter illustrates two important elements in seventeenth

century education—the purely classical nature of the studies and the democratic element provided by the association of the children of manor house and village in their play. Readers of 'Tom Brown's Schooldays' will recall how this last factor still operated even in the early nineteenth century.

TO THE HON. R. BUTLER AT KILKENNY FROM WILLIAM BLUNDELL.

Crosby, Lancs, 19 January, 1676.[24]

My very dear Sir,

Your kind acknowledgements of the very small service I have done you are thankfully accepted, and with a wish to serve you better. I do assure myself I have little cause to doubt but that both your sons which you are pleased to trust in my hands are like to be able scholars, if they want not means to learn, or (however the matter fall) right disposed men.

The younger in truth is lively, and hath a giddy airy way: yet do we now full well understand each other, and I find him exceeding tractable as any heart could wish. Edmund is much more staid, and, in things that please him, studious; yet in hard and knotty studies he is with some more difficulty persuaded to tug. I must call it indeed a tug for a child, before thirteen years old and a half twice to read over unto me and to render a laudable account (as Edmund your son hath done) of the Commentaries of Julius Caesar in Latin concerning his wars in Gaul.

Yet am I sorry so hopeful a youth should not spend his time much better and in a better place. He is almost a man's stature. And I would have him to dance and fence and speak Latin and French readily and see the world. We are here so far from speaking good Latin that our English is almost barbarous.

You may find us now and then up to the ears in Plutarch, in a hot dispute whether Alexander the Great or Cæsar was the braver man. And perhaps within an hour or two after, this gallant fair young disputant will be up to the knees in the brambles in the head of a whole regiment of pitiful tatterdemalions beating to start a hare. I blame not, but pity him for it. He hath seldom better company wherewith to divert himself.

And yet to my great admiration, he contracts as little rusticity as any I have ever met with in so hard a case. He is even too much delighted as well in reading of plays as in English history, wherein he is notably cunning. And whatever he hath learned of me, even from the first to the last (as I do religiously and faithfully assure you) hath been without the help of a rod. I have found other ways to excite him when I thought it was needful to do it.

Sir, he calls upon you now to change the scene. I wish you would soon provide him a better tutor and approve of these past and best endeavours of

Your affectionate friend and servant,

WILL. BLUNDELL.

ONE CONFOUNDING QUESTION AFTER ANOTHER

In this final letter on the early education of youth, Samuel Pepys, Secretary of the Admiralty, writing sixteen years after the close of his famous diary, tells his friend, Sir Robert Southwell, of the visits paid to him by the latter's fourteen-year-old son from Westminster School. Sir Robert Southwell, then living in scholarly retirement at King's Weston in Gloucestershire, had been a colleague of Pepys in the Government's employment, serving as a diplomat and as Clerk of the Privy Council. The two men had also been in Parliament together.

Pepys' allusion to the torturing questions of Sacheverell and

Lee refers to the persecution he had suffered eight or nine years
before at the hands of the Country Party, when as Secretary to
the Admiralty Commission he had to defend the naval administra-
tion in a factious House of Commons.

TO Sir Robert Southwell from Samuel Pepys.

10 *October,* 1685.[25]

Sir,

I can't but thank you for the acquaintance you have
recommended me to; and yet I am ready to wish sometimes you had let it alone. For I can't put a book or
paper into his hand out of a desire to entertain him but
he makes me sweat with one confounding question or
other before I can get it from him again; even to the
putting me sometimes to more torture to find the gentleman a safe answer than ever Sacheverell or Lee did.

Only to-day (I thank him) he has used me very gently,
upon occasion of two papers I got him to read to me, the
one an account I have lately received from Algiers of the
whole proceedings (by way of Journal) of the French
Fleets there, the other, the Statutes designed by Sir
William Boreman for the government of his new Mathe-
matical School at Greenwich, in imitation of that of the
King's at Christ-Hospital. Wherein asking our young
man his advice, as Sir W. Boreman does mine, he has
given it me with great satisfaction, without putting me to
any pain about it; only I have promised to carry him
down with me next week, when I shall be desired to meet
the founder upon the place. And indeed it is a deed of
the old man's very praise-worthy.

And for the young one, you may be sure I'll keep him
my friend (as you counsel me) for fear of his tales. For
o' my conscience the knave has discovered more of my

nakedness, than ever you did, or my Lord Shaftesbury either.   In a word, I do most heartily joy you in him, and (as evil as our days are) should not be sorry you could joy me in such another.   And so, God bless your whole fireside, and send you (for their sakes and the King's) a good occasion of removing your three parts a little nearer us.

I do most respectfully kiss your hands and am
Your most faithful, and most humble servant,

S. PEPYS.

CHAPTER II

UNDERGRADUATES AND DONS

CHOOSING A COLLEGE

In choosing a College at Oxford for her son, Mrs. Coffin could scarcely have consulted an authority of greater weight than Dr. Humphrey Prideaux, Prebendary and, later, Dean of Norwich. In his younger days he had been a reforming don at Christ Church, and several of his letters, written at that time, on the irregularities of University life are quoted later. At this period of his life he was much of a pessimist, for, like his contemporaries, Samuel Pepys and John Evelyn, he could see in the post-Revolutionary age of William and Mary nothing but wickedness. As he put it in another letter, ' The genius of the age is run into libertinism, and this is gone through all bodies and orders of men in the kingdom, and the Universities have drunk too deep of it.' Yet ten years later Blenheim had been fought, Gibraltar was captured, and the Augustan age in letters was fairly launched.

TO Mrs. Ann Coffin from Dr. Humphrey Prideaux.
                                    Norwich, 19 February, 1696.[1]

. . . In this place I am so far out of the way of hearing anything from Oxford that I am myself very much a stranger to that place, having no opportunity of being

informed of anything concerning it, all of these parts going
to Cambridge. I hope at Wadham College your son will
find all those advantages in his education which you can
wish. The greatest regard is to be had to the company
which he keeps, and in that College the Fellows being a
very good set of men, I hope he will have all manner of
advantage by his converse with them. . . .

My sister in her last mentioned Exeter College.
Whoever advised you there, was no friend: that is worse
than Christ Church, for at the latter there is something
of ingenuity and genteel carriage in the genius of the place,
but in the other, I never knew anything all the while I
was at Oxford but drinking and duncery. . . .

GENTLEMEN COMMONERS AND SERVITORS

*Modern minds are shocked by the former division of Oxford
and Cambridge undergraduates into special social grades—
Noblemen or Upper Commoners, Gentlemen Commoners, and poor
Servitors, Sizars or Taberdars. Such divisions were the expression of a universal belief in the importance of status in a
community still mainly feudal in thought and organisation.*

*In the seventeenth century the University, though fast ceasing
to be so, was still regarded as an intellectual microcosm of the
whole nation and not merely of its richest class. Consequently,
as these letters indicate, it seemed natural that the same social
status should attach to boys at the University as was theirs in
their home shires. In an age when dress was the outward and
visible mark of rank, a privileged undergraduate wore the
badges that denoted his quality—the laced silk gown of purple,
white, green or rose and the velvet cap with gold or silver
tassels. No one thought there was anything wrong or
unnatural in this.*

*It is easy to wax indignant over the lot of the poor servitors
who ministered to the needs of their more favoured fellow-*

students. Yet the servitor, unlike the hired college servant who fulfils the same menial tasks to-day, at least was not denied the privilege of a University education.

The two letters that follow also illustrate the territorial affiliations of the Colleges. Most of them were linked by their endowments to some particular part of the country: thus Brasenose drew its sons from Cheshire and Jesus from Wales.

The Queen's College, Oxford, was, and still is, the peculiar preserve of the north-west corner of England. It was natural, therefore, that the greatest of Westmorland magnates should send his son there.

Thomas Barlow, a former poor scholar of the College, was Provost of Queen's from 1658 till 1675, when he became Bishop of Lincoln. He was a Westmorland man himself, a considerable theological scholar, and one of the greatest time-servers of his age.

TO SIR JOHN LOWTHER, BART., AT LOWTHER, WESTMORLAND, FROM THOMAS BARLOW, PROVOST OF QUEEN'S COLLEGE, OXFORD.

Queen's College, Oxon, 5 April, 1670.[2]

Sir,

I received yours, and return my respects and hearty thanks for your kindness to the College and me, and for your good opinion of both, which appears in this, that you are pleased to trust us with the education of your grandchild, the heir and hopes of your ancient and worthy family. Sir, whenever you shall be pleased to send him hither he shall be very welcome, and you may be sure he shall have the best accommodation the College can give him.

For placing him in the College be pleased to know that we have two ranks of gentlemen in the College. 1. Those we call *Commoners*, which are gentlemen of inferior quality usually (though many times men of higher

D

birth and fortune will have their sons and heirs in that rank). 2. *Upper Commoners*, which usually are baronets' or knights' sons, or gentlemen of greater fortunes. These have some honorary privileges above ordinary *Commoners*, but are not (as in all other Houses generally) freed from any exercise the meanest gentlemen undergo. For we conceive, and (by experience find) and know it to be true, that to exempt them from any beneficial exercise is not a privilege, but indeed an injury and loss to them, seeing it is really a depriving them of the just means of attaining learning, which is the end they and we should aim at.

I do (with submission to your prudence) think it most convenient to make your grandchild *Upper Commoner*; it is some more honour and benefit to him, seeing he will be ranked amongst gentlemen of better birth and fortune, and so (in reason and probability) of more ingenuous breeding and civility.

For a tutor, in case you know any in our College to whom you would commend him, let me know it, and your commands shall be obeyed.   Otherwise if you shall be pleased to refer it to me, I shall commend him to such a one as shall carefully endeavour to direct and instruct him in the grounds of religion and good literature.   But whoever be his tutor, I shall (God willing) diligently oversee and take care of both, and assist them in attaining the end they aim at (piety and learning).   Though my employments here are neither few nor little; yet (if you give me leave) I shall at convenient times (privately) read over the grounds of divinity to him, that so he may have a better understanding and comprehension of the reason of that religion, which alone is, or can be a just foundation of true comfort here and of our hopes of a better life hereafter: this (next under God's blessing) being the likeliest antidote to preserve him from that impiety and atheism which prevail too much amongst us, and will (I fear) pull down some further calamity and judgments upon us.

Lastly, to send a servant to attend him will be some charge (though, to you, that be inconsiderable) and indeed (which is considerable) to no purpose. For he must have a boy (assigned by his tutor) to be his servitor, who must be a gown-man and a scholar, and will be able to do all his little businesses for him; and he may choose such a servitor as is a very good scholar and sober student, and so be helpful to him in his studies. Very few gentlemen, though heirs to very great fortunes, keep any men to attend them here; and those few which sometimes do, those servants having nothing to do themselves, commonly make their masters more idle. But I refer this (as all other things) to your prudence. I beg your pardon for this rude and I fear impertinent scribble. God Almighty bless you, all yours, and

Sir

Your very much obliged friend and servant

THO: BARLOW.

TO SIR JOHN LOWTHER, BART., FROM THOMAS BARLOW, PROVOST OF QUEEN'S COLLEGE, OXFORD. *Queen's College, Oxon, 26 May, 1670.*[3]

Sir,

I received yours; and 'tis true, I understood your meaning (where you mentioned sending a man to wait on your grandchild here) to be of a *Cloak-man*; and such persons (having usually little or no business with books) being commonly idle themselves, concur many times to make their masters so too.

But, it seems, I misunderstood your meaning, for you intended to send a young man, a scholar, who might wait

on him as his servitor: and (as to this) my cousin, Dr.
Smith, said truly that such a person will be very convenient to come with him.   For a servitor, who is a
Gown-man, he must have; and 'twill be much better
that he have one of whose fidelity and industry he is (by
experience) assured, than a stranger.   Besides, that boy,
if born in our Country will be capable of any preferment
in our College, and if by his civility and proficiency in
good literature he prove worthy, he shall not want it.

My respects remembered, I shall give you no further
trouble.   God Almighty bless you, all yours, and

Sir
Your very much obliged friend
and servant

THO: BARLOW.

' I DESIGN YOU FOR THE UNIVERSITY '

*Again we return to the Edmund Verneys, father and son.
Owing to the Civil Wars and his own father's temporary exile
and poverty, the elder Edmund had not himself had the advantage of a University education—a circumstance which may
possibly account for the fact that his spelling was rather worse
than that of most male contemporaries of his own class.
Having missed a valuable experience himself, he was determined
that his son should get the best of it and watched over his
University career with almost maternal anxiety.   In his first
letter he expresses his sense of the proper task of the seventeenth
century University—the training of younger sons and portionless
youths to earn a livelihood in one of the learned professions.*

To Edmund Verney from his father, Edmund Verney.

26 November, 1684.[4]

Child,

I received yours of the 23rd which tells me that Dorothy hath brewed broome ale for you. I hope to hear that you will find benefit by your drinking of it. And I am very glad to hear that the sores of your legs are almost healed, and that you will be more careful of yourself hereafter. For hurts upon hurts are of pernicious consequence and have to be cured, but must be endured when they happen. You begin now to be of an age that you must be a fool or a physician, at least for yourself.

I design you for the University, if you are fit for it, for I hope in God you will take to some honourable profession of your own accord. If not I am resolved you shall be of a mean one, for of some profession, high or low, I will make you, for I abhor you should go sauntering up and down like an idle lazy fellow. And so God bless you and send you well to do.

I am your loving father,
Edmund Verney.

To Mr. Edmund Verney at his chamber in Trinity College in Oxford, or at Mr. Thomas Sykes his tutor's chamber in the same college, from his father, Edmund Verney. (with a box and a trunk.)

London, 22 January, 1685.[5]

Child,

I shall be very joyful to hear of your safe arrival at Oxford, according to my kind wishes which attended you all the way for your prosperous journey.

I have this day sent you (by Thomas Moore the Oxon carrier) all your things mentioned in this enclosed note, except your old camelot coat, which I did not think you would need nor worth sending; your old hat I did not send neither, for it was so bad that I was ashamed of it. All your new things I bought you I put into a new box locked up and well corded up, and the key of this box I have also here-enclosed for you. But for the key of your trunk I could not find it, and it's no matter, for that lock is nothing worth, and Thom: made a shift to lock it with a key of mine, and it is well corded besides.

In your old breeches which are in your new box, you will find your five laced bands (the sixth you carried with you) and a new pair of laced cuffs, and your two guineas in your fob, and a new knife and fork in your great pocket. And so God bless you, and send you well to do.

I am your loving father

EDMUND VERNEY.

In your trunk I have put for you
    18 Sevile oranges
     6 Malaga lemons
     3 pounds of brown sugar
     1 pound of white powdered sugar made up in quarters
     1 lb of brown sugar candy
     $\frac{1}{4}$ of a lb of white sugar candy
     1 lb of picked raisins, good for a cough
     4 nutmegs.

TO MUN VERNEY AT TRINITY COLLEGE, OXFORD, FROM HIS FATHER, EDMUND VERNEY.

29 *January*, 1685.[6]

Child,

Mr. Palmer had a letter from his son at Oxford last Saturday morning very early, and my cousin Denton Nicholas wrote to his parents from Wycombe and again from Oxford since his last arrival. And when I take a journey I always write unto my father by every opportunity a perfect diurnal of my voyage and what else occurs worthy of remark. I writ to you a letter this day seven-night when I sent you your trunk and box, but never had any answer nor account from you since, which is such a piece of omission in you, to say no worse, that I believe neither Oxford nor Cambridge can parallel. For why I should be thus neglected by my son I cannot imagine: indeed I look upon it as an ill omen, that you should commit such a gross solecism at your first entrance into the University against your loving father

EDMUND VERNEY.

PARENTS AND COLLEGE TUTORS

Another great Westmorland family closely associated with Queen's College, Oxford, was that of the Flemings of Rydal. Daniel Fleming was born in 1633, educated at Queen's during the opening years of the Commonwealth, knighted by Charles II in 1681, and lived until 1701. Four of his eleven sons he sent to Oxford, three to Queen's and one to its allied foundation, Edmund Hall. His nephew, Henry Fletcher, son of Sir George Fletcher of Hutton and referred to in the first of these letters, was also at Queen's, which he entered as an Upper Commoner on April 25, 1678, at the age of sixteen.

The Rev. Thomas Dixon was a Windermere man who entered the Queen's College as batler in the year of the Great Plague of 1665 and became a Fellow in 1673. At the time of writing this letter he must have been about thirty. It was the usual practice for parents to make direct arrangements with the College tutors about the payment of their fees. Fleming of Rydal, like other landed magnates, implemented these with rustic gifts of ' venison pies and large tokens of ale '—marks of his goodwill towards his learned countrymen gathered round the board of his county's chosen college. ' If we had not been a great company of good fellows,' wrote the grateful dons after one such occasion, ' we should not have been able to get it spent, but we conquered it at last, and hope that His Majesty and yourself will be the happier for our remembrance.'

TO Daniel Fleming of rydal from the Rev. Thomas Dixon.

Oxon, 20 August, 1679.[7]

Worthy Sir,

Though you were pleased to own yourself my debtor in the beginning of your last: yet I found myself amply satisfied, contented and paid before I got to the end. I add, paid upon the account of the £5 in money mentioned therein which I received afterwards, as also the token, wherewith your nephew and I, your godson's tutor, Mr. Musgrave and some others drank your health with the ambassador, who passes for a servant or carrier amongst us, but is no less (as some say) than a Justice of Peace in his own country. . . .

Your nephew is in good health, and is like to keep himself so while he continues to rise at six of the clock in the morning, which he does not fail of as yet in term time. As to what you hint concerning his treating, 'tis wholly grounded, I fancy, upon his abundant kindness to his countrymen, to whom (if any of them happen to call upon him) he is very kind, and having the conveniency of a cellar (under the cloister belonging to Sir Joseph's building) is not stingy or niggardly of the liquor that's in it if they'll accept of it.   Yet he endeavours to shirk all he can himself, and I'll assure you he hates drinking as much as any man can do.   If he should be the least inclined that way, I should be very unworthy if I did not acquaint either you or his father with it.

I hope he gives his father a good account of the money he receives.   All I fear is that his expenses amount high, not so much upon the account of treats as curiosities (viz: pictures, clothes, pamphlets) and ornaments for his chamber, which will be of use afterwards.   I am sure his Battels are moderate and so are his other College Dues. . . .

I am

Sir, Your devoted servant

THO: DIXON.

To Daniel Fleming of rydal from his son, Henry Fleming.

Oxon, 3 August, 1680.[8]

Sir,

Yours of July the 10th with 15s. I have received, and am very glad to hear you are all well, and according to your order, I send here a note of all the books which I have bought since I came.   And for a Quintus Curtius, I had bought one before yours came to my hand, but however I shall keep them both.   I have done reading Logic and Ethics, and I now read a compendium of Physics.

These clothes which I have beginning to look a little old, makes me so bold as to desire you that you would be pleased to send me some cloth for a suit of any colour

with Rich. Burnyeats the next time he comes. So with
my duty to yourself and my love to all my brothers and
sisters I rest

Sir, your very dutiful son
HENRY FLEMING.

DISPUTATIONS AND LECTURES

*Private reading with College tutors, mainly in the classics,
was supplemented by formal and public Disputations in logic to
put ' briskness and metal ' into undergraduates. For those
shy and nervous these were somewhat of an ordeal, though
probably no more so than the written examinations of the present
day. A more formidable ordeal was the annual ' Act ' at the
beginning of July when Bachelors proceeding to higher degrees
engaged in solemn debates in the Sheldonian Theatre.*

*Lectures had been steadily declining in popularity as a form
of education since their great days in the medieval Universities.
Mun Verney's rebuke to his son for his neglect of them throws an
interesting light on the strong sense of noblesse oblige that
animated a seventeenth century squire.*

TO MUN VERNEY AT TRINITY COLLEGE, OXFORD,
FROM HIS FATHER, EDMUND VERNEY.

24 June, 1686.[9]

Child,

I pray when you speak in the Theatre do not speak like
a mouse in a cheese, for that will be a great shame instead
of an honour, but speak out your words boldly and
distinctly and with a grave confidence, and be sure to
articulate your words out of your mouth so that everybody may hear them plainly. . . .

TO MUN VERNEY AT TRINITY COLLEGE, OXFORD,
FROM HIS FATHER, EDMUND VERNEY.

London, 14 September, 1686.[10]

Child,

I received a letter lately from Mr. Sykes your tutor
unto whom you are very much obliged. Take my word
for it, albeit he makes a complaint of you for not fre-
quenting a certain afternoon lecture as you were wont
to do, yet otherwise he speaks very handsomely of you,
which rejoices my heart. For I take him to be a plain
dealer and an honest gentleman, and I hope you will
deserve those many good commendations he hath given
me of you.

It seems you tell him that you have particular reasons
that you cannot discover why you come not to those
lectures. This may possibly be, as to him and others,
but as to me who am your father there can be none.
Therefore, pray, let me know by the next post those
particular reasons. And if I like them, I will do what
I can with civility to get you excused. For look you
Child, anyone may pretend particular reasons which one
cannot discover for not doing what one ought to do or
for doing what one ought not to do. But that sham will
not pass among wise men: for such pretences to avoid
one's duty are always (with justice) interpreted in ill
sense, and I should be very sorry any such reflections
should fall upon you. You are under government, as all
subjects are in several kinds, and therefore are bound by
laws and rules and precepts divine to obey.

Besides it is a wrong to the Society not to come to
lectures, for if all others should forbear coming to them
as you do, the lectures must fall which are a support to
a College, and so by degrees Arts and Sciences and

Learned Societies must dwindle away and dissolve to nothing. But I hope none of my posterity will ever be the *primum mobile* of such a mischief to Learning. And so I shall close up my discourse about this business for this time and longing for your answer about it. . . .

A BRASENOSE UNDERGRADUATE

George Shakerley was fifteen and a half when in April 1698 he went up from Westminster to the Cheshire and Lancashire College of Brasenose at Oxford. His father, Sir Geoffrey Shakerley, being dead, he had been left to the care of his half-brother, Peter Shakerley, thirty years his senior and at that time M.P. for the great commercial constituency of Chester.

The correspondence tells its own story and, in doing so, throws a good deal of sidelight on the life of an undergraduate at the end of the seventeenth century. Peter's complaint about the amount of George's battels raises an amusing point, for in similar correspondences at all times one finds the older generation blaming the younger for its increased expenses, forgetting that the value of money had imperceptibly fallen during the intervening quarter century.

TO GEORGE SHAKERLEY AT BRASENOSE COLLEGE, OXFORD, FROM HIS HALF-BROTHER, PETER SHAKERLEY, M.P.

Dear George,   14 *April*, 1698.[11]

I had yours and sent the enclosed. I am very glad you have your health. Rise early, viz: out at 5 o'clock mornings, and go to bed at nine at night and it will continue. Be a good husband of your money and neither lend nor borrow any. Observe your tutor, Mr. Smith's directions, and follow his rules and orders.

> I pray God bless thee: so rests
> > Yours &c.
> > > P. SHAKERLEY.

My love to dear Leftwiche and be sure you love one another with a perfect and hearty affection.

TO GEORGE SHAKERLEY AT BRASENOSE COLLEGE, OXFORD, FROM PETER SHAKERLEY, M.P.

Westminster, 30 *June*, 1698.[12]

My dear George,

I am very sorry to find by the account your tutor hath sent me that you have been so excessively expensive this last quarter. He writes to me that you have had from him at several times £5. 9. 0. and that you are in your battels £10. 8. 5. Sir these two particulars are such as must not be allowed of for the future. I find also charged for shoemaker 18s. 6d. and £3. 6. 4. for bookseller, both which particulars are intolerable considering you had such stock as that you could not want in this short time. My father, had he lived, would have been extreme angry at this extravagance, for he said to Mother and others that £60 per an. should maintain you at Oxford. No more than £60 per an. was allowed to him, and he said it should serve you. I made £70 per an. serve me, but at the rate of your expenses this last quarter double that sum will not defray yours, which cannot be allowed. I have ordered your tutor not to allow you any money for the future but what he has an order under my hand for, and when you send me an account of your disbursements since the time I left you, with an account of what you had then, in your pocket, . . . and of what remains in your pocket,

I shall then and not before order you to receive what is fitting. Therefore since you had my directions to keep such accounts they may easily be transcribed and sent per next post, as I do expect them who am your

Very loving brother,

PETER SHAKERLEY.

Your battels I find are £10. 8. 5. which is double [word missing] quarter; for I was seldom more than 7s. per week, viz: 1s. per diem buttery and kitchen put together. I have desired Mr. Smith to look your name often and keep you to 8s. per week, which is enough in all reason. And when I was in the College the rule was that Gentlemen Commoners should not be allowed to battel more than 8s. per week, so I expect you to keep within that. . . .

TO GEORGE SHAKERLEY AT BRASENOSE COLLEGE FROM PETER SHAKERLEY, M.P.

9 November, 1698.[13]

Dear George,

I hope you receive mine with one enclosed to Mr. Smith. My mother has communicated to me yours of the 2nd instant wherein you desire to know when your allowance must commence, and whether you must have it in your own hands. In answer to the first, my mother and I intend to commence it at Christmas next, viz: the 25th of next month, and that to serve and be by way of advance to you for the quarter ending at Lady-day next. And for this quarter, I did return to Mr. Smith £10. He also received £5. 11. which my mother and I intend, expect and hope will defray all things whatsoever to the 25th of next month and to spare, because you will then have been in the College since I last paid Mr. Smith little more than half a quarter. If Mr. Smith pleases I would have you to be your own cash-keeper. I was so and hope you will be as frugal and careful of your money as I was; and remember that money is easy to fly away, but very difficult to get again, and as for those ridiculous treats in chambers or elsewhere your mother and I will not endure to allow 'em. An old friend of mine and the wisest of this age warned me from 'em with this experienced saying, viz: Great and many entertainments beget great and many acquaintance but no friends. I wish it may have the like effect upon you.

To conclude avoid tennis-court and all sorts of gaming— and mind your study, and pray to God to bless your endeavours therein. I intend to be at London the 26th instant—service to Mr. Smith &c.

Your loving brother,
P. SHAKERLEY.

TO GEORGE SHAKERLEY AT BRASENOSE COLLEGE, OXFORD, FROM PETER SHAKERLEY, M.P.

13 *June*, 1699.[14]

Dear George,

I have yours of the 11th instant, with the enclosed therein to William Dolben which shall send this post frank as you desire. I am sorry to find that you write in such haste that you do not spell your name as all of my family have done. We have always written it Shakerley, but you are in such haste to do something else that you write it Shakkerley. This sort of hasty slubbering over what you should take more time and leisure about will have an evil consequence at the last. I have seen the woeful experience of it in several youths already, and therefore I charge you as you expect either my favour or your own good that you be more sedate and

studiously considerate in everything you write and in
everything you speak or do. Nay your very thoughts ought
to be well scanned and reflected on by you. Do but
take more pains in employing yourself and your time in
your study, and this considerate disposition and temper
I plead for and is the first you should seek for, will
become habitual. . . .

TO GEORGE SHAKERLEY AT BRASENOSE COLLEGE,
OXFORD, FROM HIS MOTHER, LADY SHAKERLEY.
Gwersilt, Denbighshire, 22 July, 1699.[15]

Last night I received my dear child's letter by cousin
Wynne, which has given me some trouble that you should
be so imprudent as to ask leave, you knowing your
brother's temper and that it must come of himself. You
know last time he sent for you it came of himself.
Besides his anger is still for your great good. He says
you lose him if you do not mind your study, so you will
lose all your parts and learning, which is what I hope you
will stick to. For if you have that you need not fear losing
anybody's favour, for you will have it in your own fingers
that which will make you money, which will be able to
live without depending upon any brother. For Christ's
sake think of this and consider how little there is here for
you to live upon and pay taxes and wages and keep things
in repair. If you do not get some schooling we are
undone, and it will be impossible to live easy here upon
three score pounds a year. And that I do not clear
twenty betwixt repairs and taxes, and if I knew how to
spare more I would and care not what I suffered if I could
get it for you. As soon as I can meet with a safe hand I
will send you all I can get together, but as for your
coming home, I should be very glad to see you, provided
it did not hinder your study, but do not know when I

shall see your brother. I have not seen him yet; I now find the reason of it that he is angry, so it may be he may not come while he is in the country.

I must repeat my earnest request to you of minding your study, for God's sake and your dear father's sake who prayed for your well doing. . . . If you have but grace to follow your study we shall do well in spite of malice. I send you a catalogue of the books my uncle left you, which you are to have in case you will study the law: if not they are left to Nantclwyd House.

Pray let me hear from you as soon as this comes to your hands. I have writ three letters since I received any, notwithstanding your promise. I have nothing but sorrow and trouble here. Thursday last was interred my dear aunt White, of whom I have a great loss, and Ralph Lee was buried the same day. Cousin Thelwall is a very sad melancholy woman for her mother. God fit us. Dear George, I must end now with my paper, having but my poor prayers for you which I offer sincerely that am

Your disconsolated mother,
JANE SHAKERLEY.

Mrs. Hobson is here and gives you her service.

TO PETER SHAKERLEY, M.P., FROM GEORGE SHAKERLEY.
Brasenose College, Oxford, 11 *August,* 1699.[16]
Dear and honoured Sir,

I am much troubled that I should have the misfortune to send one of my letters unsealed. It was not out of any neglect nor slight in me, for the case was this. I had not time to write my letter betwixt disputation time and dinner, and so was forced to write it after dinner and had just done at twelve o'clock, the time of the post going out. I could not get a candle lighted anywhere soon enough, and so for fear of missing the post, I desired the man to seal it at the posthouse with a wafer. It being commonly done by others, I thought I might venture upon it once in such a case. I hope you won't impute it to me as a fault but rather a mischance. I am, honoured Sir,

Your very loving brother,

GEORGE SHAKERLEY.

Pray present my duty to my mother.

My battels the 4th week were 12s. 2d.

   the 5th week were 15s. 4d.

   the 6th week were 10s. 11½d.

This week is not yet cast up.

The reason of the 5th week's being so high was that our ale, being very good, some of my acquaintance came and put me on.

TO GEORGE SHAKERLEY AT BRASENOSE COLLEGE, OXFORD, FROM PETER SHAKERLEY, M.P.

Westminster, 6 April, 1700.[17]

George!

You will easily please me if you would but do three things for yourself, viz: In the first place fear and serve God sincerely, by being constant at the public prayers morning and evening and joining therein with a fervent devotion, and doing the like in your private retirements. And addicting yourself to a very virtuous, sober, honest, and a godly life.

In the next place by applying yourself closely to your study which you have hitherto been exceeding negligent of.

And in the third place by being a better husband of the money allowed you than you have hitherto been. If you lead a godly and a studious life, frugality and good husbandry will follow of consequence, so I shall judge of your devotions and study by the balance remaining in your hands each quarter for the future.

You may draw a bill on me for £25 payable at one day's sight.

And by doing as aforesaid you may retain me

Your loving brother,

P. SHAKERLEY.

TO GEORGE SHAKERLEY AT BRASENOSE COLLEGE, OXFORD, FROM PETER SHAKERLEY, M.P.

Westminster, 27 April, 1700.[18]

George!

The account I have of your neglect of study and expense of money, notwithstanding your repeated promises to the contrary, is what I thought I should not have been troubled with any more considering the holy vows and resolutions you made. Is this the method to resemble me? Is this the method to retain me your loving brother? No, I'll assure you, it is not, and that you shall soon find if you do not from the receipt hereof amend. You have in two of your letters told me you do not live sneakingly, and this you think is a modish way of excusing your expenses, but you must know I do resent it as an extravagance; and shall very considerably shorten your allowance for the future unless you forthwith reclaim and observe the wholesome rules I have in so many of my letters prescribed to you. Thus have I fairly cautioned you and so take you care at your peril.

Your brother Jack came hither last night, and shall come to you at Oxford, therefore do not you so much as think of coming hither, but rise early and fail not to come constantly both to morning and evening prayers before psalms begin, and keep close to your studies, and avoid all expenses whatsoever which are not absolutely necessary. This do if you expect any favour from

PETER SHAKERLEY.

TO PETER SHAKERLEY, M.P., FROM GEORGE SHAKERLEY.

Brasenose College, Oxford.[19]
(*Written on the back of the previous letter.*)

Last night in bed I received yours. Either part of it was sufficient to have kept me waking, though the cause might have risen from two different passions, joy and sorrow, sorrow for the first and joy for the latter part of it. The news of my brother's safe return was too sweet not to have some alloy of bitterness along with it, and if any set rules can be ascribed to Providence in her disposing of human affairs this may deservedly be esteemed one. I am sorry you should have such an account of me but must beg leave to think that they you have it from are neither your friends nor mine. I doubt not but there are these people in the worldly interest it is that I should not be in your favour. How far they are instrumental in insinuating a bad opinion of me into you, let God and their own consciences judge.

That I have not followed my studies as I ought to have done I confess with shame, but who is he that has? where is he to be found? *Numquis apud Parthes Armeniesve latet?*

I would not by this argue myself comparatively studious, for such a way is odious to all, but really Sir one of the greatest obstructions to my study has been your continual chiding of me. A man should sit to read a book as free from cares as from prejudice, for as the one biases the judgment, so the other distracts the thoughts. The concern I have always had upon me upon your account has made me sit in my study not a few hours every day without being able to set anything cheerfully, for the hopes of pleasing has always seemed to me a more generous engagement and a nobler motive to undertake a thing than the fear of the contrary. The worst of men has sometime or other deserved a good character, and I think my circumstances very bad when I have such overseers as only take notice of the worst of my actions.

I can boldly defy them all to charge me with any irregularity besides sometimes missing prayers and very rarely coming in at the gates, not once in a fortnight I am positive. The best of the society fall under the same faults and them, that I guess are so careful of others and ought to set a good example, the most of all.

My expenses I must confess are more than are absolute necessary, but if temperance as all other virtues lie betwixt two extremes, I think I have not been of late very faulty that way. I have done like him who by doubting found out a first truth, and by my own folly that way begin to grow wise, for according to the learned one step to knowledge is to know your own ignorance, and he that knows he knows nothing knows a great deal. I will retrench them for the future, but desire you not to judge of my studies by them, for a man cannot study as he ought to do all day without some refreshment in the evening: 'tis that which makes him return fresh to them which otherwise cloy him.

I humbly submit all this to your consideration, not any ways designing to follow my own counsels any more than you approve of them, and so wholly resigning myself to you, I rest

Your very loving brother

G. S.

I thank you heartily for the fishing rod, though I am sorry I can't be trusted with it. 'Tis not an edged tool though if it were I hope I am past cutting my fingers.

' MY LATE SICKNESS '

The frequency of epidemic disease and, in the low-lying, damp climate of Oxford and Cambridge, of agues and fevers, the primitive conditions of College life and the slowness of posts and travel, filled the correspondence of those whose sons were at the University with anxious enquiries about their health. These had to be answered by the College tutors, who were expected to watch over the undergraduates' health and take charge of them when forced to take to their beds in the dark and airless rooms of medieval buildings.

Edmund Verney's spelling in the first letter is worthy of note: ' kooleing tankord ' and ' stiaminghot ' (for steaming hot) being remarkable even in that age. As a matter of fact the spelling of the landed gentry was improving fast during the reigns of the last Stuarts, though that of their womenfolk still lagged behind.

TO MUN VERNEY AT TRINITY COLLEGE, OXFORD, FROM HIS FATHER, EDMUND VERNEY.

6 *July*, 1686.[20]

Child,

I heard that the players are gone down to Oxford, but I am unwilling that you should go to see them act for fear on your coming out of the hot playhouse into the cold air you should catch harm, for as I did once coming out of the Theatre at a public Act when it was very full and steaming hot, and walking abroad in the cold, and gave me such a cold that it had like to a' cost me my life. Your best way in such a cold is to go home to your own chamber directly from the playhouse and drink a glass of sack. Therefore, be sure you send your servant at your hand for a bottle of the best Canary and keep it in your chamber for that purpose. Be sure you drink no cooling tankard nor no cooling drinks whatsoever. . . . Harken thou unto the voice and advice of me thy father, loving thee better than himself. . . .

TO Daniel Fleming of rydal from the Rev. Thomas Dixon.

Oxon, 7 September, 1679.[21]

Honoured Sir,

In my last by Burnyeat I gave you to understand that we were all in good health. But we have not all continued so ever since, for your son has been indisposed and much out of order of late, especially about ten days ago: at which time he was taken with a pain in his belly which caused it to swell and produced an hard lump on the outside, and a gripeing within, both which together inclined him to a fever and disturbed his rest very much. Whereupon (for fear of the rest) I sent for a doctor after the apothecary had been with him a day or two. And they two together did so order the matter, that, through God's blessing and their care, he escaped the violence of the distemper and is in a manner perfectly recovered.

He has been abroad these two or three days and begins to pick up his crumbs again manly. I suspect that eating of green fruit was a great occasion of his malady. I have advised him to forbear it for the future. I shall satisfy the doctor and the apothecary and send you the particulars at the return of the carrier. I would have writ to you when he began to be amiss, but that he was not willing. I suppose he'll acquaint you with his condition this post.

Your nephew (who is in good health) went to see him very often; he desires to have his duty presented unto you. . . .

My respects to your son William. I am your servant

Thomas Dixon.

TO Daniel Fleming from his son, Henry Fleming.

Oxon, 11 September, 1679.[22]

Sir,

For fear you should hear of my late sickness, and not of my recovery, I made bold to write now to acquaint you, that I have been troubled lately with a fever and the gripeing of the guts very sore for two weeks, but I am now (God be praised) very well again. So hoping that you are all well with my duty to yourself, and my love to all my brothers and sisters I rest

Sir,
Your dutiful son
Henry Fleming.

VICIOUS LADS AND SILLY PREACHERS

Residence at the University was not always beneficial. Silly lads who are neglected by their tutors readily fall into the fashionable vices of their age.

Dr. Humphrey Prideaux was a young reforming tutor of Christ Church, where he had taken his degree in 1672. He was a Hebrew scholar of distinction and later became Archdeacon of Suffolk and Dean of Norwich. His correspondent, John Ellis, another Christ Church man, was serving as a clerk in the Paper Office in London. He was to rise, after a long subordinate career in the public service, to the offices of Under-Secretary of State and Comptroller of the Mint.

TO John Ellis from Dr. Humphrey Prideaux.

Oxford, 18 August, 1674.[23]

I am got again to Oxford, but had such miserable bad company in my journey here, that were it not that at London I had yours it would be sufficient to make me repent my journey thither. I had a whore on one side and a pitiful rogue on the other; and two scholars in the opposite seat violated my ears with such horrid, dissolute and profane discourse as I scarce should have thought the Devil himself dared either use or teach others, were it not that I was so unfortunate as to have this miserable experience thereof.

One of them was a dull rogue, and only sordidly affected debauchery to be thought brave, and by his discourse only seemed to arrive to the beastly part thereof. . . . His name is Fincher, son to one Major Fincher, who liveth not far from this place and pretendeth to a great deal of sanctified piety but hath given very bad demonstration thereof in the education of his son. The other seemed to be a lad of very ingenious parts, much younger than the other, and I believe his pupil. But having better abilities hath gone infinitely beyond him, and in his discourse expressed such a violent affection to vice that he seemed to me to be mad therewith and in a frenzy all the while I was with him. His name is Daniel, and son to one Colonel Daniel of Lancashire, a gentleman of good account and wealth in those parts, by whom he was sent to the University about last Christmas. But his designs being after another sort of education, he hath not yet put on a gown, that he may not be obstructed therein by the discipline of the University; and truly I think he hath employed his time so well as not to remain ignorant of anything that his own vile nature can incline him to or the devil teach him. It grieved me to think so dissolute a person was to be planted in a papist county, to give scandal to the religion by which he is named, and make the adversaries thereof rejoice; but, considering his course of life, I think I may without much uncertainty expect, and without uncharity hope, he may never live to it.

This ill company made me very melancholy all the way. Only once I could not but heartily laugh to see Fincher be sturdily belaboured by five or six carmen with whips and prong-staves for provoking them with some of his extravagant frolics.

I must beg your pardon for being so impertinently tedious in this relation. These two gentlemen being persons of quality and heirs to considerable estates, I thought fit to give you this account, that, if hereafter by chance you have anything to do with them, you may from hence learn what kind of men they are. . . .

On Sunday morning I went to hear one Bayley of Magdalen preach, who is esteemed the mightiest man amongst his own, but made a very sorry piece and was guilty therein of several absurd blunders. For he proved the frailty of man's nature in that by the weekly bills it appeared more always died than were born, as if all those that died were not born but dropped from the skies to be mortal here and afford him an argument that wanted better sense. . . . Several others I omit to tell you, because I will have room enough to write those your tutor Woodroffe was guilty of in a sermon, preached the same day at the funeral of Alderman Harris, whom he observed to have been buried in the sheet that was given him at his christening after having kept it eighty years; and thereon gave advice to everyone to give their godsons such gifts as might put them in mind of their mortality. He likewise observed that he catched a cold by lying on the ground thirty years ago in the King's service; that the last time he received the Sacrament was on his birthday; that being a tailor he got his estate by his honest employment, which is an epithet which I think doth not belong to that trade. He contradicted the Psalmist for saying that man's life is but threescore and ten, Alderman Harris living eighty years. Some of the choicest things I cannot tell you, not being his auditor; and those that were refuse to give as good an account as I would have, out of a consciousness perchance that they themselves cannot make better. This same sermon, as far as it was applicable, was formerly preached on the Duke's coachman. . . .

THE BATTLE OF THE DONS

The acerbity of learned men towards one another can seldom have been more divertingly illustrated, even at Oxford, than in the famous quarrel between Anthony Wood and Dick Peers. Anthony Wood, the antiquary, was at this time forty-two years of age. His 'History and Antiquities of the University of Oxford,' begun in 1663, was published in Latin in 1674 at the expense of Dr. John Fell, Dean of Christ Church, who gave much of his time to the supervision of the University Press. Fell, a man of benevolent but autocratic views, employed Richard Peers, a poor Student of Christ Church who had been a protégé of Dr. Busby's at Westminster, to translate Wood's work into Latin. In doing so Peers and the Dean frequently combined to alter the text to the fury of Wood, who afterwards wrote: ' Peers was a sullen, dogged, clownish, and perverse fellow, and, when he saw the author concerned at the altering of his copy, he would alter it the more, and study to put all things in that might vex him, and yet please his dean, Dr. Fell.'

The ludicrous story of the Master of Balliol and the Vice-Chancellor is in the true Oxford tradition. The former was a Shropshire man—according to Anthony Wood: ' in his younger years accounted a brisk disputant, and, when resident in his college, a frequent preacher, yet always esteemed an honest and harmless Puritan.'

The Vice-Chancellor and Master of Trinity was Dr. Ralph Bathurst, a Royalist and one of the founders of the Royal Society.

TO JOHN ELLIS FROM DR. HUMPHREY PRIDEAUX.
        Oxford, 23 August, 1674.[24]

. . . I must beg your pardon for being the cause of a
trouble which will be cast upon you by Dick Peers.   As
soon as I returned, I informed him of Busby's desire to
have his book and that I was employed to get one for
him which hath put him upon a design of presenting one
to him, as likewise to the Bishop of Rochester, out of a
conceit that his presents will be rewarded with very
considerable returns, the schoolmaster's place at least.
Little Penny being again upon his journey to Rome, he
was designed for the presenter of them, but . . . he
hath altered his resolution and pitched on you; and, I
suppose, accordingly about Tuesday or Wednesday the
books will be left with you, with direction how to dispose
of them.

    In the third page of the preface, towards the end of the
page, you will find two paragraphs, to which are prefixed
1° and 2°, which are omitted in all other copies.   In the
first of them there is given an account of the translator
and how much he translated, which Peers is very willing
everybody should know, that, as he saith, he may not be
accountable for the improprieties and other unexcusable
faults committed by Reeve who translated the rest.   In
the second Wood accuseth the Dean and Peers for altering
his copies, and calleth God to witness that whatsoever
harsh or derogating expression be found in any part of
his book he is not the author of it.   The latter being put
in without the Dean's consent, at his being at the Bath,
and the former without the author's by Peers himself,
made both angry, and was the cause of much contention
between Wood and the Dean, the Dean standing for the
former paragraph and the expunging of the second, and

Wood for the second and the expunging of the first. Neither could there be any end put to the contention till each party receded something from their pretensions. There was an agreement made at last by omitting both, and the preface printed o'er again without making any mention of Peers, which exceedingly grieveth him. But he, having got the former prefaces into his hands, taketh great care to disperse them about, and I doubt not but that this will be bound up with all the books he presenteth.

I suppose that you have heard of the continual feuds and often battles between the author and the translator; they had a skirmish at Soladin Harding's, another at the printing house, and several other places. But Peers always coming off with a bloody nose or a black eye, he was a long time afraid to go anywhere where he might chance to meet his too powerful adversary, for fear of another drubbing, till he was Pro-Proctor; and now Wood is as much afraid to meet him, lest he should exercise his authority upon him. And, although he be a good bowzing blade, yet it hath been observed that never since his adversary hath been in office hath he dared to be out after nine, lest he should meet him and exact the rigour of the statute upon him. However Dick hath not forgot his old fears, but, although armed with an office, yet, by reason of his former drubbing, fears his adversary as much as formerly, so that both parties being afraid of each other, each liveth in peace. But however each forgetteth not his enmity to each other, and [I] suppose it was only an effect of this that Wood would not let the translator's name be inserted in the preface, I not being able to imagine any other cause why he should be against it, than that he was unwilling thereby to gratify his adversary in that which he knew he did most vehemently desire.

Busby hath lately given £50 to Balliol College, on the account of his acquaintance with Dr. Good, the Head, who is a good honest old toast, and understands business well enough, but is very often guilty of absurdities, which rendereth him contemptible to the young men of the town. He hath lately, out of a desire to be a fool in print, set forth a dialogue between a Protestant and new converted Papist, whom he calleth Dubitantius and Firmianus. If you will be pleased to be acquainted with their talk, I doubt not but that they will make you good sport, for I assure you they dispute the case most sturdily.

Not long since he preached at St. Mary's, and in the midst of his sermon, in a queer tone, bawled out that about fifty years ago he remembered he read such a passage in a book *De Anima*, and then, after a long pause, recoll[ect]ing himself, cried out, ' Ah, 'tis to let, 'tis to let,' which made us then all laugh and ever since call him ' To let.'

There is another ridiculous story of him, which I do not well believe; but however you shall have it. There is over against Balliol College a dingy, horrid, scandalous alehouse, fit for none but draymen and tinkers and such as by going there have made themselves equally scandalous. Here the Balliol men continually lie, and by perpetual bubbing add art to their natural stupidity to make themselves perfect sots. The Head, being informed of this, called them together, and in a grave speech informed them of the mischiefs of that hellish liquor called ale, that it destroyed both body and soul, and advised them by no means to have anything more to do with it. But one of them, not willing so tamely to be preached out of his beloved liquor, made reply that the Vice-Chancellor's men drank ale at the *Split Crow*, and why should not they too? The old man, being nonplussed with this reply, immediately packeth away to the Vice-Chancellor, and informed him of the ill example his fellows gave the rest of the town by drinking ale, and desired him to prohibit them for the future. But Bathurst, not liking his proposal, being formerly an old lover of ale himself, answered him roughly that there was no hurt in ale and that as long as his fellows did no worse he would not disturb them, and so turned the old man going. Who, returning to his college, called his Fellows again and told them he had been with the Vice-Chancellor, and that he told him there was no hurt in ale; truly he thought there was, but now, being informed of the contrary, since the Vice-Chancellor gave his men leave to drink ale, he would give them leave too; so that now they may be sots by authority.

I must beg your pardon for troubling you with so ridiculous a tale, and desire not to think me an idle fellow in spending my time to insert it. When it was first told me it made me heartily laugh, and I hope it will you too. . . .

SOME LEARNED FOOLS

Dr. Benjamin Woodroffe, whose foolish funeral sermon on Alderman Harris has already been referred to in an earlier letter of Dr. Prideaux's, was a Student of Christ Church who later became chaplain to the Duke of York and Principal of Gloucester Hall.

The burning of Northampton occurred on September 20, 1675. It was notorious as a rebel or ' fanatic ' town, and the humanitarianism of the highbrows towards the unfortunate victims of the fire was probably stimulated by political considerations and is not without parallel instances in modern times.

TO JOHN ELLIS FROM DR. HUMPHREY PRIDEAUX.

Oxford, 27 September, 1674.[25]

. . . Our town affordeth nothing worth informing you; only Woodroffe daily exposeth himself to contempt by his ridiculous actions. Last night he had Madam

Warcup at his lodgings, and stood with her in a great window next the quadrangle, where he was seen by Mr. Dean himself and almost all the House toying with her most ridiculously, and fanning himself with her fan for almost all the afternoon.

A little before, he put the doctor's men out of commons for having the victuals on their table before he came in. It is a custom used by the servants, that if the Canons come not before an half hour past six to take their victuals and fall to. Woodroffe coming in at the third quarter and finding the meat on their table, raged most furiously, which not being touched by the servants was carried back again to the Canons' table for Woodroffe to eat thereof if he had pleased. But he, being exceeding offended at their insolence, as he called it, in bringing victuals to his table which had been defiled by having been on theirs, commanded his man to carry it to the prisoners, at which the rest of the Canons were exceedingly angry, and sufficiently rebuked him for it the next day, and commanded their men not to let their victuals go so patiently another time. By which they have been encouraged since to affront [him] to his face, and he forced to take it patiently. . . .

TO JOHN ELLIS FROM DR. HUMPHREY PRIDEAUX.
Oxford, 8 November, 1675.[26]

. . . Our town affords little news worth your knowledge. That which is most talked of at present is what each college contributeth towards the rebuilding of Northampton. Our scholars are ridiculously liberal to this fanatical town. If all others should equal them in their contributions, Northampton would get double what it lost by being burnt. Such ridiculous pride and emulation in giving much having so possessed all our scholars, that poor rogues that are scarce worth forty shillings think themselves undervalued if they give not twenty. Most of our fellows of Houses are in this humour; but I thought five shillings as great an alms as I could give or that roguey town deserve. We shall from our University alone, although now very thin, send above £500; and this we do to exceed Cambridge, which place we are informed hath given £300. . . .

CHAPTER III

'A FLAME THAT SO TORMENTS ME'

A PASSIONATE LADY

Barbara Villiers was a daughter of the most discussed family of the English seventeenth century, and a cousin of the two famous and ill-fated Villiers Dukes of Buckingham. Her father, William Villiers, second Viscount Grandison, had fallen for the King in 1643. Born in 1641, she grew up during the Civil Wars and Interregnum, that vexed and broken period—comparable perhaps to our own post-war years in Central Europe—of which Clarendon wrote that the young people thereof of either sex were educated in all the liberty of vice without reprehension or restraints :

> *Children asked not blessing of their parents; nor did they concern themselves in the education of their children, but were well content that they should take any course to maintain themselves, that they might be free from that expense. The young women conversed without any circumspection or modesty, and frequently met at taverns or common eating-houses; and they who were stricter and more severe in their comportment became the wives of the seditious preachers or of the officers of the Army. The daughters of noble and illustrious families bestowed themselves upon the divines of the time or other low and unequal matches. Parents had no manner of authority over their children, nor children any obedience or submission to their parents; but everyone did that which was good in his own eyes.*

About 1656, some four years before the Restoration and when she herself was fifteen, Barbara fell in love with Philip, second

66

Earl of Chesterfield, a young man of twenty-three educated in the same lax principles and notorious for ' exceeding wildness.' The affair continued for some years, and it seems that in the way of nature he tired of her sooner than she of him. In 1659 she was married, probably unwillingly, to Roger Palmer, son of Sir James Palmer of Hayes. A year later she became the mistress of Charles II on his restoration to his father's kingdom. As Countess of Castlemaine and later as Duchess of Cleveland in her own right she was for many years the most criticised figure in England.

In the last of these five letters, Lord Chesterfield, a man of many gallantries, appears to have been addressing some other lady.

To the Earl of Chesterfield from Lady Ann Hambleton and Mistress Barbara Villiers.
1657.[1]

My Lord,
My friend and I are just now a bed together a contriving how to have your company this afternoon. If you deserve this favour, you will come and seek us at Ludgate Hill about three o'clock at Butler's shop, where we will expect you. But lest we should give you too much satisfaction at once, we will say no more. Expect the rest when you see

Your &c.

To the Earl of Chesterfield from Mistress Barbara Villiers.
1657.[2]

My Lord,
I would fain have had the happiness to have seen you at church this day, but I was not suffered to go. I am never so well pleased as when I am with you, though I

find you are better when you are with other ladies. For
you were yesterday all the afternoon with the person I
am most jealous of, and I know I have so little merit that
I am suspicious you love all women better than myself.

I sent you yesterday a letter that I think might convince
you that I loved nothing besides yourself, nor will I ever,
though you should hate me. But if you should, I would
never give you the trouble of telling you how much I
loved you, but keep it to myself till it had broke my
heart. I will importune you no longer than to say that
I am, and will ever be, your constant and faithful humble
servant.

To the Earl of Chesterfield from Mistress
Barbara Villiers.

1657.[3]

My Lord,

The joy I had of being with you the last night has made
me do nothing but dream of you, and my life is never
pleasant to me but when I am with you or talking of you.
Yet the discourses of the world must make me a little
more circumspect. Therefore I desire you not to come
to-morrow, but to stay till the party be come to town.
I will not fail to meet you on Saturday morning, till when
I remain your humble servant.

To the Earl of Chesterfield from the Hon.
Mrs. Palmer (*when she was very ill of the smallpox*).

1659.[4]

My Dear Life,

I have been this day extremely ill, and the not hearing
from you hath made me much worse than otherwise I
should have been. The doctor doth believe me in a

desperate condition, and I must confess that the unwilling-ness I have to leave you makes me not entertain the thoughts of death so willingly as otherwise I should. For there is nothing besides yourself that could make me desire to live a day. And, if I am never so happy as to see you more, yet the last words I will say shall be a prayer for your happiness, and so I will live and die loving you above all other things who am,

My Lord,

Yours, &c.

TO THE LADY——FROM THE EARL OF CHESTERFIELD.

Bretby.[5]

Dearest Joy of my Life,

You have obliged me more by your letter than I could have expected, for I shall ever value the least mark of your kindness above all other things. I am now dismally alone, and you may easily believe the want I have of your company, for how often do I wish to have you again in my arms, how often do I please myself with the thoughts of the joys we have had, and how often do I resolve to love you as long as I live. And yet I need not resolve it, because it is impossible for me to love you less.

I am now going to Scarborough and soon after that to London, so that I am not like to see you neither this summer nor the next winter, and God knows how old your absence in that time will make me; but I would put off these journies, my business, or anything to have you here. Ah! if I had but hold of your —— how quickly would I pull you to me and kiss you a thousand times. But these fancies make me extravagant, and I am lost in love's labyrinth, whenever I come to mention the passion with which I am

Dearest Life,

Your &c.

'REMEMBER POOR OTWAY'

Thomas Otway, the poet and dramatist, was born at Trotton, Sussex, in 1652, the son of a poor clergyman. After leaving Oxford, where he failed to take his degree, he devoted himself to the theatre. Soon after he fell in love with a young actress, Elizabeth Barry, who made her reputation by acting in his plays but who had already given her heart to the dissolute Lord Rochester, who had trained her for the stage and whose mistress she became. Otway died in 1685, after a brief, chequered and tragic life, lit by a great achievement, the tragedy of ' Venice Preserved.'

TO Elizabeth Barry from Thomas Otway.[6]

In value of your quiet, though it would be the utter ruin of my own, I have endeavoured this day to persuade myself never more to trouble you with a passion that has tormented me sufficiently already, and is so much the more a torment to me in that I perceive it is become one to you who are much dearer to me than myself. I have laid all the reasons my distracted condition would let me have recourse to before me: I have consulted my pride whether, after a rival's possession, I ought to ruin all my peace for a woman that another has been more blest in, though no man ever loved as I did: but love, victorious love! o'erthrows all that, and tells me it is his nature never to remember. He still looks forward from the present hour, expecting still new dawns, new rising happiness; never looks back, never regards what is past and left behind him, but buries and forgets it quite in the hot fierce pursuit of joy before him.

I have consulted too my very self, and find how careless nature was in framing me; seasoned me hastily with all the most violent inclinations and desires, but omitted the ornaments that should make those qualities become me. I have consulted too my lot of fortune, and find how foolishly I wish possession of what is so precious; all the world's too cheap for it. Yet still I love, still I dote on, and cheat myself, very content because the folly pleases me. It is pleasure to think how fair you are, though, at the same time, worse than damnation to think how cruel.

Why should you tell me you have shut your heart up for ever? It is an argument unworthy of yourself, sounds like reserve, and not so much sincerity as sure I may claim even from a little of your friendship. Can your age, your face, your eyes and your spirit bid defiance to that sweet power? No, you know better to what end heaven made you; know better how to manage youth and pleasure than to let them die and pall upon your hands. 'Tis me, 'tis only me you have barred your heart against. My sufferings, my diligence, my sighs, complaints, and tears, are of no power with your haughty nature: yet sure you might at least vouchsafe to pity them, not shift me off with gross, thick, homespun friendship, the common coin that passes betwixt worldly interests. Must that be my lot?

Take it, ill-natured, take it; give it to him who would waste his fortune for you; give it the man would fill your lap with gold, court you with offers of vast rich possessions; give it the fool that hath nothing but his money to plead for him; love will have a much nearer relation, or none. I ask for glorious happiness; you bid me welcome to your friendship: it is like seating me at your side-table when I have the best pretence to your right-hand at the feast. I love, I dote, I am mad, and know no measure; nothing but extremes can give me ease, the kindest love or most provoking scorn.   Yet even your scorn would not perform the cure: it might indeed take off the edge of hope, but damned despair will gnaw my heart for ever. If then I am not odious to your eyes, if you have charity enough to value the well-being of a man that holds you dearer than you can the child your bowels are most fond of, by that sweet pledge of your first softest love, I charm and here conjure you to pity the distracting pangs of mine; pity my unquiet days and restless nights, pity the frenzy that has half possessed my brain already, and makes me write to you thus ravingly: the wretch in Bedlam is more at peace than I am!   And if I must never possess the heaven I wish for, my next desire is (and sooner the better) a clean-swept cell, a merciful keeper, and your compassion when you find me there.

Think and be generous.

TO ELIZABETH BARRY FROM THOMAS OTWAY.[7]

You were pleased to send me word you would meet me in the Mall this evening and give me further satisfaction in the matter you were so unkind to charge me with. I was there but found you not; and therefore beg of you, as you ever would wish yourself to be eased of the highest torment it were possible for your nature to be sensible of, to let me see you some time to-morrow.   And send me word by this bearer where and at what hour you will be so just as either to acquit or condemn me; that I may, hereafter, for your sake, either bless all your bewitching sex; or, as often as I henceforth think of you, curse womankind for ever.

To Elizabeth Barry from Thomas Otway.[8]

Could I see you without passion or be absent from you without pain, I need not beg your pardon for this renewing my vows that I love you more than health or any happiness here or hereafter. Every thing you do is a new charm to me; and though I have languished for seven long tedious years of desire, jealously despairing, yet every minute I see you, I still discover something new and more bewitching. Consider how I love you; what would not I renounce or enterprise for you! I must have you mine or I am miserable, and nothing but knowing which shall be the happy hour can make the rest of my life that is to come tolerable. Give me a word or two of comfort, or resolve never to look with common goodness on me more, for I cannot bear a kind look and after it a cruel denial. This minute my heart aches for you; and, if I cannot have a right in yours, I wish it would ache till I could complain to you no longer.

Remember poor Otway.

'MORE FOOL SHE'

Christopher Hatton was born in 1632, the eldest son of the first Lord Hatton of Kirby, whom he succeeded in 1670. The writer of this letter was a frequent and spirited correspondent: 'you need not make any of your compliments to me,' she once informed him, 'for I do not expect them.'

TO CHRISTOPHER HATTON FROM ELIZABETH BODVILE.

July, 1661.[9]

. . . Here is news that a young lady in Cambridgeshire has drowned herself for love, they say; but more
fool she, for that is but cold love, methinks. She threw
herself into a well and the water was not deep enough,
and they say she was starved to death. And now to
break your heart, my Lady Berkeley is like to die of a
fright, being with child. Pray do not you be desperate
and drown yourself in a well too, for you know as long
as there is life there's hopes. . . .

'WHEN ALL WERE ABED'

*The hero or villain of this episode, Harry Savile (whom we
shall happily meet again) was a son of Sir William Savile of
Thornhill, Yorks., and younger brother of the great Marquis of
Halifax. He was a fat, jovial fellow, one of the best letter-
writers of his age and much addicted to gallantry: he is said
even to have ventured on the Duchess of York. Though to the
young and witty his company was irresistible, his elders found
his light-hearted presumption intolerable, and he was per-
petually involving himself in scrapes. At the time of this one
he was twenty-nine. He was only saved from its consequences
by the personal intervention of the King, who, though he often
had cause to be angry with him, could not help liking him.
The affronted lady was the widow of the eleventh Earl of
Northumberland and a daughter of the loyal Cavalier Earl of
Southampton, who had been made Lord Treasurer at the Restoration. Her brother-in-law, Lord William Russell, who ordered
Savile to quit the house, afterwards became the Whig leader in the
Commons and suffered death on the scaffold for his treasonable*

designs at the time of the Rye House Plot. The host, Robert Spencer, Earl of Sunderland, was to earn the reputation of being the most cunning and treacherous politician of his age, while another member of the Althorp house party, Lord Ashley—better known as the first Earl of Shaftesbury—was in after years to direct with consummate skill and daring the most unscrupulous political campaign of our parliamentary annals. Under the circumstances Harry Savile may be said to have put his hand in a hornets' nest.

Sir Charles Lyttelton, the writer of this letter, was a son of Sir Thomas Lyttelton of Hagley, Worcestershire, to whose baronetcy and estates he ultimately succeeded.

TO CHRISTOPHER, FIRST VISCOUNT HATTON, FROM SIR CHARLES LYTTELTON.   26 *September,* 1671.[10]

. . . I know not too if you have heard of Harry Savile's adventure at Althorp. He being there with Will Russell, my Lady Northumberland, Lady Ashley and others, one night when all were abed he comes up to Lady Northumberland's chamber and, finding her door open, goes in and up to her bedside in his nightgown; and, when he is there, calls ' Madam! Madam! ' till he wakens her, and says that he came to acquaint her with a passion he had long had, in the dark, which he durst not own to her in the light. She, being mightily amazed to hear his voice, rung a bell by her bedside; upon which presently her women in the next room began to stir. He begged her not to discover him, and so went away. She immediately rises and goes to bed in another room to Lady Ashley and acquaints her. They send for Will Russell and tell him. He goes to Harry Savile, advises him to quit the house presently or he would be affronted; which he does too. Lord Sunderland and Will Russell follow

him to London to fight him. The King has notice and
prevents it. H. S. since has withdrawn himself,
ashamed for so ill a conduct, nobody know whither;
some say beyond sea. . . .

THE GIRLS THEY LEFT BEHIND THEM

*The author of this charming letter is unknown; its recipient
our old friend, the second Earl of Chesterfield. Its occasion was
the news of the battle of Sole Bay, fought on May 28, 1672, at
the beginning of the Third Dutch War, when Lord Sandwich's
flagship, the ' Royal James,' blew up with all hands after a
desperate resistance. Francis Digby, her captain and son of
the Earl of Bristol, went down with the ship. Captain
Fretcheville Hollis was killed on board the ' Cambridge,'
which he was commanding in the action. Lord Maidstone,
Mr. Roger Vaughan and Richard Nicholls were young gentlemen
of the Court serving in the Fleet as volunteers.*

TO THE EARL OF CHESTERFIELD FROM THE LADY R.
IN THE TIME OF THE DUTCH WAR.

1672.[11]

My Lord,
    There is so little difference between the tenderness of
my friendship and love that only those who know them
both can make the distinction. Would not anybody else
believe I were in love that knew how oft and with how
much kindness I think of you, what pleasure your letter
brought me, and that though it was so welcome and I so
joyed to find you remembered me yet I wished that I had
began first. For I long to show all the esteem I have for
you, and if I could express it and that you have no
aversion for me, 'twould not be a very disagreeable
entertainment, now you are alone and without a passion.

But I wonder what you do all day, for though indifference be easy, yet 'tis strangely dull, and that dead calm one finds oneself in where there is no transport nor no pain is not a life (in my opinion) that can please a soul so full of fire as yours.

I know not whether you are satisfied with your condition, but I am sure the ladies in Town that are unconcerned have reason to rejoice, for we hear nothing but dismal news of death from the Fleet. Love has no employment but weeping and everybody's business is to enquire after the volunteers. Am not I happy that amidst all these glooms can sit in my closet and write to you. But not to pretend to more force than I have, I confess that I am really in some pain, for there are people there I cannot wish ill, and we fear that my poor cousin Ned is lost, for we can hear no news of him since the Lord Sandwich's ship was burnt. You know I love the Lady Kinnoul and she is in the greatest trouble in the world for her brother; he really was a brave youth.

I imagine you have an account of the war from your friends of the other sex, and that they have told you how handsomely Mr. Digby died and also of Mr. Vaughan's fate. If you have not better intelligence than mine I will constantly inform you of all we know here in every kind. At this time the sea is our theme, and we discourse of what is done there in all places. Here is a lady just now come to see me who tells me that Sir Fretcheville Hollis, the Lord Maidstone, and Dick Nicholls are killed. Do we not pass our time very ill? Pray imagine if I should not have reason to be better pleased if I were walking by a river side or in a grove with you, and that neither of us thought of anything in the world besides. But then we might chance to fall in love again and that would be more disquiet to

Your ever faithful humble servant.

HE FOLLOWED HIS DEAR

This charming story explains itself.

TO THOMAS COKE FROM FRANCIS HOPEGOOD.

Astead, 24 August, 1696.[12]

. . . At a pretty house in this parish has for six months past lodged a gentlemanlike sort of man with a pretty young woman, and without any other servant than one maid. Nobody knows who they were nor from whence they came, more than from London: nor what their names were, for they went by none, real or sham. What was the fancy, I can't tell.

My spark and his dear Phillis, who they say is young and pretty, were without the least interruption. But fortune at last playing the jade, yesterday morning came down one of the King's messengers with a warrant to apprehend her for a plotter in woman's clothes. And accordingly he took her away with him, but told the gentleman he had his liberty to go where he pleased. The happy man could not forbear smiling when he followed his dear. . . . He left word with the landlady to keep the lodgings for him, for that he and she would soon be back again. Some envious devil or other that envied both their happiness contrived this information surely to disturb them. . . .

CHAPTER IV

COURTSHIP AND WEDDINGS

CHOOSING A WIFE

The object of seventeenth century courtship (of the more honourable kind) was to find, as Sir John Moore's correspondent put it, ' a most truly modest, virtuous, maiden gentlewoman,' or, what was perhaps even better, a well-dowered widow, who could bring a substantial property with her and help make a home and support a family. The correspondence of the time abounds with allusions to suitable ladies. In such courtship there was little romance: the ideal was ' a fit wife for him, and one that needs not much wooing, and yet she might be young, beautiful and rich.' But only one of these requirements was really essential. ' Ten thousand pound ladies never stick on hand,' wrote one correspondent, and another recorded the triumph of a well-portioned lady, ' about forty years of age, not handsome and hath long been known by the name of Duck-legs.' The person who therefore necessarily did most of the wooing was the family solicitor.

The first three letters written to Joshua Edisbury of Erthig explain themselves. In the third letter, John Verney, younger brother to Edmund of East Claydon, tells his father of his efforts to secure a wife. He had just returned from the Levant, where he had been learning his trade as a Turkey merchant and had resolved to strike while the iron was hot:

' the first proffers,' he wrote, ' are best and at a man's first coming from Turkey, for then estates are least known and rumours run high.'   His aim was a well-dowered housewife, ' never bred to plays nor parks, but a sober, discreet and godly young woman.'   But though he was quite frank about the business nature of his matrimonial aims, he was fastidious enough to insist that his prospective bride should be paraded up and down Drapers' Garden by her father to see if there were nothing ' disgustful ' about her.

The match with Miss Edwards came to nothing, and the story of John Verney's first marriage must be left to the next chapter.

Sir John Moore, a man of seventy at the time of Ursula Hull's letter to him, had been Lord Mayor of London in the latter part of Charles II's reign.   His first wife had died a few months before.   It does not appear, however, that he adventured on that triumph of hope over experience, a second marriage.

TO JOSHUA EDISBURY FROM RICHARD EDISBURY.

Plymouth, 25 March, 1694.[1]

Honoured Sir,

I acquainted my father last post of an affair I thought long ago to intimate; but thought convenient all this time to disclose it till now considering the danger of delaying so long lest another break his mind before me. Which is my having had a real affection for a young lady in this town three or four years by which, continuing still more and more towards her, so that would willingly break my mind either to her or her father betimes, lest by delaying another make known his love before me, for she is beloved by many.   But first would be advised from my father and yourself herein and whether it be more proper in discovering my mind to them in the state I am or to let it alone till I foresee how my affair of the rope yard will go. The lady is of a very good family and her father a very fine gentleman and hath several employs and a great merchant here, but, the number of children which he hath being nine, suppose he cannot give her upwards of five or six hundred, but in process of time (he being still as it were a young man) may add much to this fortune. To which I desire to hear from you at your leisure in this my present condition before you leave the town.

Your most affectionate kinsman and

humble servant,

RICHARD EDISBURY.

To JOSHUA EDISBURY, FROM HIS NEPHEW, THOMAS DELVES.

Dodington, 19 May, 1694.[2]

. . . Sir, as to your enquiry after a lady, that may be suitable to my liking, I must own and acknowledge your great favour in it; yet I think £6000 is not so much as I should wish in my circumstances. I have heard of a young lady near Nottingham, worth ten thousand pound, who (if all I have heard of her be true) is most likely. She is Sir Thomas Willoughby's sister, and lives at Wollerton. It is said that she hath kept her brother's house several years and hath altogether been used to a country life. If you please to enquire what you can about this lady, I shall esteem as a great kindness, and to add to your former favours conferred upon, Sir, your most obliged nephew and servant,

THOMAS DELVES.

G

TO JOSHUA EDISBURY FROM SIR JOHN WYNN.

22 *November*, 1695.[3]

Honoured Sir,

I received your last intimating the information you have of the lady's having a cancer which I shall endeavour to inform myself of, though an infirmity of that nature is commonly kept very secret.   As to the other matter you are pleased to honour me with, I have often seen the lady and know her father . . . and she lives at St. James' with her brother Mr. Harrison that married her sister.   I have been told they were co-heiresses and the estate £400 a year apiece.   At other times I have known her represented as having £600.

She had the character of a pious lady and to be well tempered as most ladies are before they are married, tho' her face in my opinion doth not much promise it. . . .

TO SIR RALPH VERNEY AT CLAYDON FROM HIS SON, JOHN VERNEY.

London, 20 *August,* 1674.[4]

Honoured Sir,

I purposed by this conveyance to send down my necessaries to Claydon and to follow them Saturday next myself.   But my mind is now altered.   And to let you know the true cause on't, 'tis thus.

If you please to remember I once spoke to you about one Edwards who hath a son and two daughters to settle in the world.   And ever since your departure hence a friend of mine and this Edwards have once in two or three days had some discourse about me tending to a match with his eldest daughter (aged about 19).   But Edwards being a hard man always insisted that I should come to his house and he would discourse with me about settlements and desired to know my estate. Which propositions I sent him word made me smile, when I think of coming to his house, and tell him I had a great respect for his daughter never by me seen. And for to let him know my estate, 'twas as unlikely I should do that as this. So I desired my friend neither to give himself or me any more trouble about this.

Thus three or four days passing, and Edwards, perceiving my friend to be silent, did sundry times strike into his company and at last spoke himself, and agreed to walk his daughter the next morning in Drapers' Garden, where with my master I met them and continued walking together near two hours. This was done that I might have a sight of her to see if I found nothing disgustful. But we interchanged not one word with her, only my master asked her three or four questions, for 'twas agreed on that all should be as by accident and he said he would not acquaint her with the reason of his walking there—but we are at liberty to believe him.

Now it remains on my part to give her a visit, which I intend to do in two or three days, to let them see her eyes have not quite dazzled my reason. And truly though her beauty is not like to prefer her to the title of a Duchess, yet she is a very passable woman and well shaped, and showed herself without any artificial gracings, save that her gown and petticoats were all new. But her head was not in the least adorned for a surprise, which I liked ne'er the worse. For in Turkey we say, If you want a horse buy a lean one, and then you'll see what fatness (that creature's ornament) would have hid from you. But to leave this airy way of writing, which I hope (since I beg it) you'll pardon—the gentlewoman is a passable handsome woman, and her father able if he be but willing to give her money enough. As things proceed hereafter you shall have more from me on this subject.

. . . The last time I saw my Lady Hobart, which was
three days since (before I saw my mistress) she said if I
went not to Claydon this year she would conclude 'twas
courting some woman hindered me, and put her little
engines in the fire to see if she could discover any such
thing. But now I always stand on my guard against her
female politics. . . .

Begging your prayers and blessing, I rest,

Sir, Your obedient son,

JOHN VERNEY.

TO SIR JOHN MOORE FROM URSULA HULL.

21 *November*, 1690.[5]

Right Worshipful and Worthy Sir,

I presume upon your goodness to make a favourable
construction of my not coming to wait on you so long, I
being in no capacity to bring money to answer your
expectation, do most humbly beg your pardon herein to
a poor widow that truly honours your Worship, and wishing I could show that honest mind I bear to all the world.

I hear you have buried your good lady long since.
May it please you, worthy Sir, to pardon my boldness
herein. If it should please your Worship to have thoughts
of another and have as yet not disposed your thoughts to
any, be pleased without offence to let me tell your
Worship of a lady, a most truly virtuous, modest, maiden
gentlewoman who hath neither father nor mother nor
brother or sister. She hath £400 a year besides much
money. Her £400 a year is free land of inheritance to
give to whom she please; a more pious, modest and good
woman is not to be found.

A gentleman of your knowledge can satisfy you of the
truth of all. But no one under the sun knows of this

my writing but myself only. Though I am a mean woman she is most worthy. I beseech you, Sir, to pardon this boldness in your Worship's most faithful and very humble servant,

URSULA HULL.

INTERRUPTIONS TO THE MARRIAGE SETTLEMENT

The complications and bulk of a seventeenth century marriage settlement and its preliminary correspondence have to be seen to be believed. Like all legal correspondence concerned with the devolution and limitation of property it is necessarily very dull to anyone not financially interested.

The letter from Richard Cholmley to Ralph Thoresby is an example of one of the more human items to be discovered in such bundles of pre-matrimonial correspondence. The portion which a particular jointure merited, and vice versa, could be exactly measured by skilled hands: a daughter or a son was worth precisely so much, and parents, with their children's welfare to consider (not to mention the strengthening of their own estates), could not afford to make concessions for purely sentimental reasons.

The second letter, written just after the end of the century, is an example of the only kind of pre-nuptial correspondence allowed to the principals to a marriage. The young lady, who was the ultimate heiress to her great-grandfather, the last Baron of Kinderton, did not even venture to write to her suitor but approached him indirectly, and then only during the indisposition of her parents, through his half-brother and guardian, Peter Shakerley. Incidentally, she never married George, owing to the intransigent attitude of Peter over the proposed settlement, and in the end gave her hand (or rather had it bestowed for her) on Henry Vernon of Sudbury, ancestor of the present Lord Vernon.

*The third letter refers to Peter Shakerley's own wooing of
his bride, Elizabeth Mainwaring, a quarter of a century before.
In this case the marriage negotiations were so prolonged that
the young people fell in love with each other before the settlement
was completed by the family lawyers. The bride's father, who
had already secured most of the points he was seeking, took advantage of the fact to expedite the wedding, which took place at
his own home. The fatal impetuosity of the bridegroom per-
sisted even before the altar, as his triumphant father-in-law
reported to the outwitted and indignant Sir Geoffrey.*

TO RALPH THORESBY FROM RICHARD CHOLMLEY,
ESQ.
                              Sprustie, 25 *October,* 1684.[6]

Sir,

    After you went from hence, I did read over the par-
ticulars you gave me of your estate; and the truth is,
I cannot but admire at your singularity in setting down
old debts and the furniture of your house and £50 in a
chapel, laid out by your pious father, which is possible
may be employed for the end it was builded for; but,
if not, I suppose the house will be of far less worth than
it cost. I could comment upon every one of these particulars, and lay before you how gray-headed the furniture
of the house may be before you have a wife to inherit it.
I might tell you how long the debts you reckon of,
according to what you told me, hath been owing, and you
showed me no bond or bill for; but possibly I might find
a wrong interpretation made of such reflections.

    Therefore, Sir, in soberness, I am much dissatisfied
with the particulars you gave me in an account of, as
falling far short of that you valued your estate to amount
unto, and am truly sorry that there should be any mistake
betwixt us. For, except I should go against all friends'

advice and expose my daughter to a life of temptation, I cannot obtain what I truly longed after, viz. to have so pious a son-in-law as I esteem you to be. But your estate falling so far below expectation upon a due value, I must entreat you to give me time to consult with some of my friends and yours, that I may act as becometh a wise parent. And when I have come to a consultation with my friends, and a conclusion within myself, I shall impart myself more fully to you in a line or two, being not willing that you should have any more needless chargeable journeys to this place till at least we have advised with our friends. The bearer being to come early on Monday to your town, I beg your pardon that my lines are so hasty from so bad a pen; and however things fall out, that yet I may be accounted one of your well-wishers is the earnest request of, Sir,

Your humble servant,

RICHARD CHOLMLEY.

TO PETER SHAKERLEY, M.P., AT WESTMINSTER FROM MISTRESS ANN PIGOT. (*London postmark*, 27 *February*.)

Brockton, 25 *February*, 1702.[7]

Sir,

The great indisposition that my father and mother are under occasioned by severe colds, makes them altogether unfit to think of writing themselves, and fearing you should be uneasy that you do not hear from them, therefore command me, tho' a very indifferent scribe, to let you know this. I must confess I am much out of countenance to think of discovering my defects in this sort to you, but my father and mother's commands, and their persuading me you're so good a friend that will excuse all faults, is the only thing that could have prevailed with

me to have done this. My father and mother present
humble service to you, and I subscribe myself,

Sir,

Your humble servant,

ANN PIGOT.

My father and mother join in service to my cousin
George Shakerley. They beg his pardon they cannot
now write to him.

TO SIR GEOFFREY SHAKERLEY, M.P., AT HULME,
CHESHIRE, FROM SIR THOMAS MAINWARING.

Baddiley, Cheshire, 12 *February,* 1678.[8]

Sir,

Our children are now fast tied, and I hope God will bless
us, them and theirs.   I will assure you there shall be no
ambuscadoes laid, and to satisfy you that the groom is
father's own son, we had much ado to keep him from
kissing his bride before matrimony was all read.   We are
very much troubled to want your company and my Lady
Shakerley's here at this time, and the more because it is
occasioned by your distemper.   But I should be glad to
see you here before you go up, if your occasions will give
you leave; and if you do not come, I hope my Lady will
let us see her here after you are gone.   For I suppose it
will not be convenient for us to come to Hulme till you
return from London.   All here present their service to
you and my Lady Shakerley, and so particularly doth

Sir,

Your most affectionate brother

and servant

THO: MAINWARING.

Your daughter presents her duty to you and my Lady
and desires your blessings.   I will speak to my son
Shakerley (who also presents his duty to you both) to

wait on you on Friday or Saturday unless you send to
have him come sooner, which he will send his man
to-morrow to know.

THE GIRL WHO TRIED TO CHOOSE ON HER OWN

*The next two letters introduce the kind of exceptions that
prove the rule. Nancy Denton was a daughter of Dr. William
Denton, a fashionable London physician who flourished in the
reigns of Charles I and Charles II and under the Commonwealth.
Her maidenly essay to choose a mate on her own was abandoned
almost with panic on the first sign of paternal displeasure.*

*Elizabeth Verney, youngest daughter of Sir Edmund Verney
of Claydon, the Royal Standard-bearer who had fallen at Edgehill, was of sterner stuff. Rendered desperate by long waiting—
the result of the portionless period of the Interregnum when the
Verneys, like most county families, were living from hand to
mouth—at the age of twenty-nine she took the law into her own
hands and married Charles Adams, a poor clergyman. In this
letter she beseeches the forgiveness of her indignant brother,
Sir Ralph Verney, the head of her family. As a matter of fact
the marriage, so inopportunely begun, was quite successful.*

T<small>O</small> M<small>R</small>. F<small>ORD</small> <small>FROM</small> M<small>ISS</small> N<small>ANCY</small> D<small>ENTON</small>.

19 *May*, 1662.[9]

Sir,

As I have been obliged to you for your value, and kindness to me, so I must beg this farther obligation from you,
as to lay aside all thoughts of farther kindness or addresses
to me. For that upon the presumption of my father's
great love for me, I made it known to him, not doubting
but that I should have had his consent upon reasonable
propositions. But the truth is, instead of procuring his
consent I find him so implacably enraged and so absolutely

peremptory in the denial, that there is no possibility or
hopes, either by my own or any other friend's mediation
ever so much as to think of it or treat about it (though you
had the whole estate of your father in present). I am
very well assured that if I should be so unhappy so to
marry, he would never give me anything of his estate
living or dying, or ever see my face again. And therefore
being obliged by the Law of God and nature to him, and
my own happiness to comply with him in this his resolution, I do earnestly desire you to think no more of it,
for I shall not on any account whatsoever. And so I
rest,

Your servant,
ANNIE DENTON.

'TO MY EVER HONOURED BROTHER, SIR RALPH
VERNEY, KNIGHT AND BARONET, AT HIS HOUSE IN
MIDDLE CLAYDON,' FROM MRS. ELIZABETH ADAMS.
London, 19 November, 1662.
(Endorsed Sister Betty's letter declaring her mar-
riage.) ¹⁰

Dear Brother,

I should have written to you the last week for to have
begged your pardon for the great fault I must acknowledge myself to be in, in the marrying without your consent. But I was so full of grief to think what a piece of
folly I had committed that it made me not fit to write. . . .
I confess this piece of indiscretion in me is enough to
put me in despair of your pardon. But I hope you will
show me more mercy than I do deserve.
I trust in God I am not so much lost as some think I am,
because I have married one as has the repute of an honest
man and one as in time I may live comfortably with.
Therefore, dear Brother, let me humbly beg your free
pardon for this great fault of mine, which I should be

willing to acknowledge upon my knees were I in your presence to do it. The thoughts that I have done anything without your advice does so trouble me that I am able to say no more at the present than that I am

Your most affectionate sister

and servant

ELIZ: ADAMS.

THE CORROSIVE OF A DENIAL

The next eight letters, taken from the Verney MSS. at Claydon House and partly printed in the ' Verney Memoirs,' tell the story of the first and unsuccessful wooing of Edmund Verney, who in an earlier chapter we met in a later stage of his life as 'an anxious and stern father. At the age of twenty-two he fell in love with his cousin, Mall Eure, a co-heiress of Lord Eure, her grandfather. To carry his suit he importuned the girl's mother, Mrs. Sherard, his own father, his friend Dr. Thomas Hyde (a cousin of the future Lord Chancellor), his cousin, Dr. William Denton, and the parson at Claydon, the Rev. Edward Butterfield. The latter was something of an authority in such matters, for a year before, on his presentation to the living of Middle Claydon, he had only been able to obtain admittance to the rectory by wooing and winning the immovable widow of his predecessor.

The first letter is an interesting example of conversational English. One has the feeling that Mrs. Sherard really spoke as she wrote.

TO SIR RALPH VERNEY AT CLAYDON FROM THE HON. MRS. SHERARD.

17 *March,* 1658.[11]

Sweet Nephew,

I cannot write to you concerning any other business at this time but that which is a trouble to me. . . . God lend me life and health; you cannot imagine the trouble I am in that I cannot answer your son's inclinations as to my dear Mall. For she hath other thoughts than to marry, and I cannot but cherish her in them, for I should do myself and her an injury.

I doubt not but in the way of reason to satisfy your son that he may think of some other, for that I hope he will do. For she assureth me she will never marry, and I have engaged myself to her I will neither force her nor persuade her. I must ever own her obligations to him for his affections and yours to be no less by reason you have expressed so much of the conditions you were pleased to yield to in this that you would not have done elsewhere. And I hope you will believe me that I dislike neither him nor yourself nor your estate, for that my own heart can clear me of. I hope this will give you full satisfaction. As to her answer to her cousin, I have left to her, and what she writes is her own not mine. So with my best wishes to you both I rest

Your most affectionate aunt

MARG: SHERARD.

TO THE HON. MRS. SHERARD FROM SIR RALPH VERNEY.

March, 1658.[12]

' Copy of a letter for Sir Ralph Verney to send to Aunt Margaret penned by Dr. Hyde about Mall Eure.'

' Never sent.'

Madam,

Yours of the 17th of March hath cast me into some perplexity, only because I cannot but sympathise with you in any matter which affects you so nearly, especially when I consider that the occasion thereof flows from myself and my son, who do both as earnestly desire and study your content as the nearest relations you have in the world can do. But when I consider the whole matter in itself, and the result of your letter thereupon, methinks a little consultation with our friends and a fair debate between ourselves may out of this subject produce our mutual content.

Your daughter's resolution of single life upon serious consideration may be judged even by herself not fit to be adhered unto, when the end of her nativity and the means of her health are thoroughly weighed. And upon the same grounds I believe you may be induced to persuade her to the contrary. For that can hardly be firmly resolved against which God and Nature dictate, and may prove the best restorer and preserver of health. Towards the bringing of all which about I am glad to read that you dislike not either person, relation nor estate propounded. . . . I hope this expression of yours will be a means to facilitate the business, which I am the more desirous should take effect because I see Mun is so far gone in his affection that I think it bootless to make further trial of taking him from it. Truly upon the best considerations I have, my hope is that with God's blessing and with our concurrence it will prove a happy match on all hands.

TO Mun Verney from his cousin, Mall Eure.

Circa 20 March, 1658.[13]

Good Cousin,

Your last letter was the first that ever I received from you with regret. For the very great expressions of affection I give you humble thanks for, and it is not the least of my trouble I cannot nor never shall make any return in that nature. This is the greatest truth in the world, which pray, oblige me to believe and urge me not further to give such unpleasing denials. I must confess under my own hand what you and most of my acquaintance have heard me say that 'tis my resolution, not my vow, never to marry. In this I am so firmly fixed that nothing but my mother's positive commands shall have power to alter. And so much hath she obliged me to as to give me her word three years since never to force me to alter my condition upon that score.

I have taken the liberty to answer your letter myself without consulting my mother or any other person. Sir, let this satisfy you. If reality may plead a cause, my letter will not miss its errand. Therefore I shall content myself with the belief you will not persist any further and in so doing you will oblige

Your humble servant,

MARY EURE.

TO DR. DENTON FROM HIS NEPHEW, EDMUND VERNEY.

Claydon, circa 4 April, 1658.[14]

Dear Uncle,

I received yours of the 1st of April, 1658, but I do not mind your rebukes for my thoughts are never quiet nor content but when they are fixed upon my mistress. . . . My mistress insisting upon not marrying at all is but what modesty prompts all virgins to say, and Nature teaches to break in my judgment. Marry, the confirmation of it grounded upon fear raised by her French physician and strengthened by her personal weakness might signify something, if I knew not that one month's perfect health backed with our Doctor's opinion here that matrimony will perfect the cure and is in truth a sovereign if not the only complete medicine for all feminine infirmities, will easily and fully answer these objections, nay quite turn the tables.

Besides methinks there is a loophole in her letter to me, through which I fancy that I see some glimmering of hope, which is this: she will never change that resolution unless her mother command her, and her mother hath promised her never to do it. Sir, I do most earnestly beg of you that you will be pleased to stand my good friend during this critical time of suspense in this grand affair of my life, which is that you will endeavour by all means possible to persuade the mother that she instruct the daughter of her duty . . . and that having no exceptions here either to person, relations or fortune, she may safely adventure upon me, being that I love her so entirely, whereas in any other conjunction, she must run much hazard. And you may tell her moreover that I vow myself so gone that it is impossible for me ever to place an affection anywhere else, and that the more I strive against it the more I am hampered in it, so that if she give not an answer of comfort I must perish and thus ends, her and

Your most humble and faithful servant
EDMUND VERNEY.

TO THE HON. MRS. SHERARD FROM THE REV. EDWARD BUTTERFIELD.

19 April, 1658.[15]

Madam,

I humbly thank you for my courteous usage at your house. In obedience to your will I have cast all the cold water of yours and your daughter's reasons and denials upon the flames of that passionate young gentleman in whose noble heart the fire had taken such fast hold before, and is grown to such a strength that it converts all things into fuel, and will I fear in time destroy the whole fabric, if you can do no more to quench it than for aught I see others can.

'Tis infinite pity such generous love in a person so wise, so sober, provident and hopeful, the only expectation of a family so well deserving, should be ruined by so sad a fate. Methinks I would not have you guilty of his blood: how will you answer it another day to those his and your deceased dear relations? And truly 'tis unkindly done of that young and so virtuous lady to be so good, so amiable, and to appear so to this wretched world as a destructive meteor only to the miserable beholders.

If you will not help, yet pity him at least. I know you have sometimes felt yourself the power, the tyranny of love, and let him go at least and take the doom of his rash and wrong affection from those lips that gave him this fatal wound; who can tell but that may be his cure. In my conscience he would be as good, as kind, as provident, as happy a husband for her as the world affords. I desire not to trouble you with a reply to these my saucy lines. Only your pardon for my freeness; I cannot plead the cause of a friend and lover with that coolness and discretion that many can. You will find the story no romance. I am, Madam,

> Your most humble servant,
> EDWARD BUTTERFIELD.

TO MISTRESS MARY EURE FROM EDMUND VERNEY.

12 *April*, 1658.[16]

Madam,

You are so perfect empress of my heart that in obedience to yours by Mr. Butterfield, I have used more violence upon myself these three weeks than a Russe who takes it for an honour to destroy himself at his Prince's command. For my affection is so pure that it carries with it an absolute resignation of myself to you though with my own destruction, and in conformity to your order, I believed that you were then best enjoyed by me when I wrought your greatest content. Believe me (Madam) this zeal hath forced me out of myself, as far as any saint ever was, in a rapture; yet after all my art and diligence to put this candle under a bushel, it burnt the more furiously, because I tried so much to extinguish it. For I protest before the majesty of God, I find by strong experience that I can no more obtain of my will to abate of your love than I can of my memory that there is no such person as you are, or my understanding that you are not adorned with all those perfections, the idea whereof doth so possess and ravish my soul.

I vow by your supremacy and my allegiance that I can ascribe the growth of my love to this vast height to no other cause but your huge merit, and my great care not to sin against it through unadvisedness or indiscretion. This made me study how to compose my father's displeasure, and answer your lady mother's scruples and your desire of single life, before I totally submitted to the sweet conquest your goodness hath over me. To which I am now so complete a captive that all the neglect you can fasten on your slave, or the diversion friends can prompt me to, are able to beget no other thought in me than of living and dying your *devotee*. Wherefore I beseech you to consider how it can become your nature, so full of grace and goodness, to call me not Naomi but Marah, for the Lord hath dealt bitterly with me and the waters of Marah are bitter to your supplicant by giving bitterness of spirit to that heart which begs your compassion and comfort. Your own knowledge of the integrity thereof cannot but tell you this deserves not the corrosive of a denial, and my faith and knowledge of your candour and sweetness assure me that no word so harsh can fall from your tongue or pen.

I beseech you to give me leave to add one grain of reason to all this weight of affection, which is that your resolution is contrary to that end whereto God and nature ordained you: not regardful to your dearest relations dead and living, but above all injurious to yourself. . . . If you put my affection in one scale and your resolution in the other, and if only judgment held the balance (which I reasonably hope kindness may somewhat bias) I shall not be condemned for prizing this so great and well-grounded truth that it is impossible for me to live or die other than, Madam, sweetest lady,

Your most passionately devoted vassal,
EDMUND VERNEY.

TO THE HON. MRS. SHERARD FROM HER DAUGHTER, MARY EURE.

8 May, 1658.[17]

Madam,

Be pleased to accept my humblest duty and to know that since you left Whitsuntide I have received a wandering letter from my cousin Edmund Verney. How it came to Melton I know not, but there Joseph found it. Really I was never more surprised in my life, for I thought my last to his might have prevented his farther troubling himself. For since you have always been pleased to leave me to myself I could wish he knew that if he write or speak a thousand times it will not prevail with me at all. I am sorry he forceth me to say, if I would marry it should not be him. Not that I have anything against my cousin, but esteem him as he is my near relation. But never whilst I breathe will I be wrought to have the least thought of giving him any encouragement in his pretensions. He would much oblige me to leave persisting in it.

Madam, I shall not answer his letter without your command, which I hope I shall not receive because I should unwillingly obey it.   All the acknowledgment in the world I render you for your long past promise of never persuading me to marry.   Sweet Madam, that is my resolution; when I change it, your Ladyship shall know, but I believe I shall never trouble you with that message.   Be pleased to pardon this long impertinency and grant me your blessing.   Thus I remain, Dear Madam,
your obedient daughter,
MARY EURE.

TO MARY EURE FROM EDMUND VERNEY.

Covent Garden, 24 May, 1658.[18]

Madam,

My last made you my confessor; and this humbly begs leave to tell you that a penitent cannot esteem himself forgiven till he find himself restored to grace.   Therefore I beseech you to use your power.   Enjoin me penance whereby I may learn and expiate the depth of my guilt and your displeasure.   I have ransacked every corner of my heart, and called every thought thereof concerning my mistress and her mother to a strict account and can find nothing but height of affection for the one and of respect and duty for the other.   Yet good natures are solicitous when a misapprehension befalls them, as much as if they were really guilty; this makes me profess that I am more angry with myself that your Ladyship should imagine any hardness of disposition in me than it is possible for me to be were I really so.   And I shall commit but a slender brag if I declare myself not capable thereof.

Your Ladyship will be daily convinced of this truth if you please to admit me to a nearer relation, for I am among those objects which are seen and please best at a closer view.   Madam, a devout lover is in a sad case, for nothing more than that he cannot plead his own cause without playing the fool in commending himself, and I detest the one as much as I am none of the other.   Therefore I beseech your Ladyship that this may find grace in your sight, and return with some message of countenance and comfort to

Your most devoted and dutiful servant
EDMUND VERNEY.

'ADMITTANCE TO TREAT'

In the five letters that follow, Edmund Verney, now a few years older, is seen prosecuting his suit to the heiress of a parish adjoining his father's Buckinghamshire estates. Mary Abel, of the White House, East Claydon, was the only child of William Abel, Sheriff of Buckinghamshire in the year of Charles II's Coronation (1661), who died suddenly while attending to his official duties at Aylesbury.

The complications of the marriage settlement, which was to ' join the two Claydons together,' and whose delays caused the chivalrous and romantic-minded Parson Butterfield such anxiety, were finally resolved, and the young people were married in the summer of 1662.

TO SIR RALPH VERNEY, BART., FROM THE REV. EDWARD BUTTERFIELD.

Claydon, 15 August, 1660.[19]

Sir,

Though the business be not of that maturity as that you should necessarily be acquainted with it, yet perhaps you may be willing to know how things stand, and I could not well satisfy myself without giving this short account of my transactions. I went on Monday and found the gentlewoman under such a cloud of sorrow and reservedness, that I could not without some difficulty fasten any discourse upon her, being never alone yet always as it were alone and silent. When I took my leave I gave her a brief touch of what I desired to have spoken more at large, if my modesty and her reservedness could have contrived it. Yet what I said I heard from one of her confidants (for from herself I received so low and still an answer that I could not tell what to judge of it) she took very kindly. I have been twice there since and by means I used I gave her fully to understand what I had to say. . . .

She professes much respect to you, and saith after she hath advised with her friends and the young woman's she will make a more satisfactory return, but would not by any means the young woman should be spoken to till she had first broken it to her. She wants not suitors and those of good quality, yet I think you shall have the first admittance to treat, she being as yet free from any engagement. The young woman wants not wit, though she may breeding, and for aught I can learn is resolved to marry where she thinks she may live happy. And if there be a liking between the young folk it may be a match. But you must step in and negotiate it, or else 'twill hardly be. . . .

Sir, by this you can best judge what is fit to be done; and I think your presence will be necessary to set things right. . . . I have not nor shall neglect anything that I thought might with discretion conduce to promote the business.

Your most obedient servant,
ED: BUTTERFIELD.

TO Sir Ralph Verney from the Rev. Edward Butterfield.

16 *November,* 1661.[20]

Sir,

I have been all this day from eleven of the clock to four this afternoon, at East Claydon, where I found them wondrous kind and free both in their discourse and entertainment. Greatly pleased they are with Squire Duncombe's wooing, and the passages of it with Joseph Busby's daughter who was the day before and Thursday also with him at his house and he with them all the week and always drunk. And if he could have had a priest they say he would needs have been married at midnight in spite of all his friends, and away he is gone home with her again.

They do so openly and with so much affection own the match with Mr. Verney, that except it were really done, I do not see how they could do more. Stephen Choke says Mr. Verney will have as good a dispositioned gentlewoman as can be. Mrs. Goffe says they want Mr. Verney extremely, especially one of them. Mrs. Wiseman says she is resolved to marry him. I told them you had been like to have been robbed going up. The young woman coloured at it and seemed to be much concerned for it, and expressed a great deal of satisfaction for your escape. I told it on purpose, how true I know not, but had the relation from Will Lea. She wears the ring Mr. Verney gave her openly, and both speaks of him with much pleasingness, and seems to delight to hear of him.

Truly, Sir, me thought there appeared in all they did and said such innocent and hearty intentions as to the business desired, that I could not in discretion press anything more than what easily dropped from them for discovery of what you writ about. Mrs. Wiseman told me she was offered divers good matches and a Lord, but was resolved against all such motions and thought she might be as happy in this as she desired. I never saw her so pleasant before. . . .

TO Edmund Verney at mr. gape's house in covent garden from the Rev. Edward Butter-field. *Middle Claydon, 24 February, 1662.*[21]

Sir,

I went immediately with your letter to East Claydon where it was very kindly received. I found Mrs. Mary in her morning dress, a white and black petticoat and waistcoat, and all clean and fine linen, so lovely, proper and brisk, I protest I knew her not at first sight.

I perceived she was somewhat concerned those two deeds could not be found. . . . She saith she will write about it to Sir Robert Wiseman and her Uncle Gale and do what she can to find them out, but at present and without further help she knows not what to say. I found she had a letter from Mr. Gale who sent her word you had had no meeting about a treaty as yet, which she wondered at but conceives now the reason might be because those deeds are missing. . . .

They made themselves merry at Valentine's day in drawing Valentines, and very unwilling she was to be brought to draw (6 or 7 papers being put together rolled up) for fear she should not draw you. But being persuaded to it at last she ventured, and they say very fairly happened on you to her great satisfaction. I dare say you have her heart, and if with her you can carry her estate, sure you may be very happy in her. Which is and shall be the prayer and hearty wishes of your affectionate friend and servant,

Ed: Butterfield.

I cannot but add, had I gained her as you have done,
I would marry her, if she would have me, though I
begged; and think to see more happy days in such a
choice than in another with thousands per ann.

TO Edmund Verney at mr. gape's house in covent
garden from the Rev. Edward Butterfield.

Sir,   *Middle Claydon, 26 May, 1662.*[22]

I cannot forbear to salute you and wish you joy any
longer. My humble respects to your right virtuous lady.
You cannot think how much I long to hear you are
married. No news will please me without it, and therefore till it be done or very suddenly to be done, do not
write to me, for I cannot abide to read any letter that
speaks not so. For I have a great desire to see you happy,
and cannot fancy that any saint but the Virgin Mary can
make you so.

Sure you take more state upon you than Majesty itself.
I know you would be loth to be suspected to want the
masculine heat that renders others impatient of such
delays. Else what malignant star is it that retards your
bliss, and renders you the wonder of men? Sir, though
I hear nothing of it, I will believe you are or shall suddenly
be as honourable as you are really wished to be by, Sir,

Your most affectionate friend and servant
ED: BUTTERFIELD.

TO Edmund Verney from the Rev. Ed: Butterfield. (*'Leave this at Mr. Heron's, a cutler near the
Red Lion in Fleet Street.'*)   *Middle Claydon* [1662].[23]

Sir,

I thank you for your very civil return to my last letter.
But you left me very much unsatisfied as to the main

enquiry I sought after. Yet Mr. Henry Verney did somewhat resolve my doubt by assuring me that all would suddenly be finished. Heaven send a good end! But I fancy not these tedious delays; wheresoever the fault is, the blame and mischief too if any happen will certainly fall to you. I cannot but be concerned for you, though I know nothing of your matters. 'Tis the main concern of your life this; manage it prudently or you ruin both credit and fortune too for ever.

But to waive this sad discourse. Had you seen or heard directly how Mr. H. V. and Mr. Jo. Risley cheated one the other in the exchange of two admirable jades, with what craft and confidence it was carried, 'twould make you intermit a little of your serious thoughts to take a laugh. Make haste down into the country that now is very sweet and pleasant and you shall hear more of it. But be sure before you come, join the two Claydons together or 'twill never be half so pleasant to you.

My humble respects to your dear Lady, the maker or marrer of your wealth, in whom that you may be happy is the incessant prayer of, Sir,

Your affectionate friend and servant,

E. BUTTERFIELD.

A LONDON WEDDING

The first letter in this chapter described an unsuccessful attempt of Mun's younger brother, the merchant John Verney, to find himself a suitable wife. Now six years later, a London citizen of credit and renown, he has found one—Elizabeth Palmer of Little Chelsea, the ' dear heart ' and ' dearest dear ' of his subsequent correspondence.

Accompanying the announcement of his happiness John sends down to his father and brother, Mun, at Claydon, a paper box containing his wedding favours: ' a paper box directed to you though most in it is for my brother's family: it contains as followeth—In a paper sealed a pair of white gloves and a pair of coloured gloves laced with black Flanders lace, which I desire your acceptance of, and if the fingers be too long for you, Thom. Hobart saith he will alter them for you when in town. All Genoa gloves are long fingered. A pair of green fringed gloves for my brother; white and coloured lace gloves for my sister; pink-coloured trimmed gloves for Master Ralph; sky-coloured trimmed gloves for Master Munsey; white gloves trimmed with green, etc., for my little niece, and one of my wife's wedding garters for Master Ralph as one of her bridemen. These tokens of a wedding I desire them to wear for my sake.'

Dr. Adam Littleton, who performed the ceremony, was rector of Chelsea and a prebend of Westminster. He was famous in his age as a lexicographer. He was a friend of Pepys, for whom a few weeks before he had done a notable service. (See ' Samuel Pepys: The Years of Peril,' 321.)

TO SIR RALPH VERNEY, BART., AT MIDDLE CLAYDON FROM JOHN VERNEY.

London, 27 May, 1680.[24]

Sir,

. . . I am now to acquaint you (as I do my brother) that I am this morning going down to Westminster Abbey to meet Mrs. Eliz. Palmer, where after prayers we design to be married in Henry VII's Chapel by Dr. Adam Littleton (where he's a prebend) very privately in our old clothes. None will be at it but her father, mother, brother and Aunt J. White. From thence we go to the Rummer in Soper Lane in the City, whither I invite them . . . to dinner, and after dinner they go to Lady Gardiner's whence I shall accompany them home to their house at Chelsea. But we design it shall be past nine before we get home, and to keep the news of it within their own house till Sunday, when we shall publicly own it in Chelsea Church. I shall take care to send down gloves to my brother and you next week, for truly they are not yet trimmed. . . .

I return you most hearty thanks for your good wishes and prayers in this great concern of mine, and I make no doubt but I shall receive benefit thereby from the most high God, to whose protection I commit you and rest

Your most obedient son,
JOHN VERNEY.

A COUNTRY WEDDING

Here, again taken from the Verney MSS., possibly the finest single collection of seventeenth century domestic manuscripts in the world, is a description of a country wedding of 1675 at Stowe, now a public school and then the home of the Temple family.

The wedding ceremonies recall those of two years later when the Princess Mary was married to William of Orange, and merry King Charles himself drew the curtains of the nuptial bed with a shout of ' St. George for England ! '

It is ten miles from Stowe to East Claydon, so Mun's homeward journey probably began at about midnight.

TO SIR RALPH VERNEY FROM EDMUND VERNEY.

East Claydon, 26 August, 1675.[25]

Sir,

. . . Being invited to Stowe I dined there yesterday. Nelly Denton and Jack Stewkeley went with me. We met Sir Harry Andrews, and his Lady and daughter, his only child there, as also Cosen Risley and his lady and Jack Dodington, and three sisters of Lady Temple, and Mr. Stanion, husband to one of them, and Ned Andrews and Grosve: his father-in-law, and Thom. Temple and another old Temple with three or four very drunken parsons, which made up our company. Lady Baltinglas was invited and promised to be there but failed.

We saw Sir Richard and his fine lady wedded, and flung the stocking, and then left them to themselves. And so in this manner was ended the celebration of his marriage *à la mode*. After that, we had music, feasting, drinking, revelling, dancing and kissing. It was two of the clock this morning before we got home, which made me lie abed longer this morning than usually, therefore must make haste to end . . .

Sir, Your most humble and obedient son,

EDMUND VERNEY.

CHAPTER V

MARRIAGE

' I KNOW NOT HOW TO GIVE OVER '

On the whole the matrimonial letters of the seventeenth century make pleasant reading. To a deeply religious people marriage, a sacred rather than a secular matter, was not lightly to be set aside; it was founded in the common interest of a well-secured settlement, spent commonly amid the serene influences of a full and quiet country life, and cemented by a large nursery. Children were the great end of marriage: ' to begin my letter to a new married lady,' wrote Mary of Orange to her friend, Lady Bathurst, on her wedding, ' it must be with wishing you much joy, and nine months hence two boys, for one is too common a wish.' Such wishes, being universal, the cradle was quickly filled with ' sweet brave babes.'

To these considerations making for successful marriage must be added the comparative insecurity and discomfort of seventeenth century life, even for the richest. Life was uncertain and no man could take the safety of any member of his family for granted: it was often exceedingly uncomfortable, and few could recall or look forward to any state of life more desirable than that afforded by a fond and constant wife.

Richard and Elizabeth Legh of Lyme, Cheshire, who correspond in the first four letters, were married in 1661, and continued to address one another as lovers throughout the quarter of a *century of their married life, which was only brought to a close by his death. The bent of their correspondence and of many another is indicated in a letter of Richard's in 1670 in which he writes, ' Dearest, I want nothing this night to complete the joy I am in but thy dear company and the brats.'*

TO Mrs. Legh at lyme, cheshire, from Richard Legh, m.p.

London, 8 January, 1666.[1]

Dearest,

I perceive by thy last of the 3rd December thou hast not received mine, this being the third I have writ to thee since I came to Town. I dare not as yet affix my name to the back-side, lest they should (not knowing my hand) neglect the sending of them. But, dear Soul, do not trouble thyself if a post should slip, for assure thyself I shall not.

The weather is now breaking here. If God send it holds on and the Parliament sits, I shall take orders for sending for thee or come down to thee as speedily as possible. I weigh every minute double without thee. . .

Dear Heart, I am never so pleased as when I am writing to thee. Now I am quit from company, it is 2 o'clock i' th' night and I am not sleepy and I cannot leave off. No news is pleasant to me but what I have from thee that thou and thine are well. The God of all mercies continue it so amongst us, and if it be His blessed will enlarge his blessings to us which is the continued prayers of, Dear Soul,

Thy unfeigned loving husband

R. Legh.

TO Mrs. Elizabeth Legh at lyme, cheshire, from
her husband, Richard Legh, m.p.

London, 11 *May*, 1675.[2]

. . . This day I dined with cousin Cholmondley. . . .
He drunk thy health and said he wondered thou durst
adventure of me. The last time he saw thee was when
thou wast very young. I told him if he saw thee now, his
wonder would cease. Now I am at the Committee of
Privileges and have stole up to the Speaker's Chamber to
scribble these, and am never so happy as when I talk of,
write to, or think of thee, my dear Soul, who am thine

Whilst I am

R. Legh.

TO Richard Legh, m.p., from his wife, Mrs.
Elizabeth Legh.

May, 1675.[3]

My dearest Soul,

Methinks I am sorry thou shouldst not have the
pleasure of seeing a play sometimes, for though in thy
absence it is the greatest comfort in the world to me to
hear from thee, yet I desire thou may have thy satisfaction
as well as I mine. My dear dear, farewell to thee. All
thy dear children are well. Poor Peter says he dreams
of thee, and if he don't, I am sure I do. Thou seest I
know not how to give over, though I have but little to
write.

Adieu, Thine whilst

E. L.

TO Richard Legh from his wife, Mrs. Elizabeth Legh.

1684.[4]

My dear, dear Soul,

I met thy very kind letter. I shall treasure it up amongst those things I love best, for I am sure it pleases me better than any jewel in my cabinet.

When I received thy letter I knew not whether to turn to Hadock or Norton, but I hoped thou would come hither to me, and therefore I turned hither. Really I have not been warm in bed since thou left me; therefore have what pity thou canst upon her that is entirely thine whilst

E. L.

TO Thomas Coke, m.p., at his house in st. james's place from Lady Mary Coke.

Melbourne Hall, Derbyshire, 13 *January,* 1702.[5]

Since my dear encourages me to the only pleasure I have or ever can think of in your absence, which is by expressing my kindness by all opportunities, you need not fear but I'll trouble you every post, though at the same time I am sorry I have nothing to repeat but still constant assurances of my being ever yours. And that sound is so extreme pleasing to me from you, that I will not doubt but it has the same effect from me to you.

My sisters and I being now alone, we sit working all day long in their room and sup there sometimes, musing in the fire till our eyes are burnt out of our heads, and then that moves my spleen to laugh to think if any of our town acquaintances could see us. I believe if I were dying I could not help a jocose now and then.

But 'tis now a fortnight since my dear went, and I flatter myself that in one month more perhaps my happi-

ness may appear here in you. . . . Adieu, my dear;
make me happy as soon as you can, for with you I can
have no doubts nor fears: and without you there never
was, nor never can be, any real satisfaction to her who is
most faithfully, my dearest, ever yours.

'MAKE MUCH OF YOUR DEAR SELF'

*In the last chapter squire Mun and merchant John, the two
sons of Sir Ralph Verney, wooed and at last won their wives.
Here we see the sequel. In Mun's case it was a tragic one, for
a few months after his marriage his bride developed the first
symptoms of the insanity which, with a few lucid intervals,
endured for the remainder of her life. Poor Mun, as the correspondence of which this letter is a part shows, had need of that
' courageous and cheerful spirit ' to which he exhorts his wife, for
without it his life at East Claydon was likely to be a sad enough
one. But he bore his cross with exemplary patience and good
humour. We have already seen him, in an earlier chapter,
mothering his children.*

*Happier than ' Nobill Soul '—the name that his nearest
friends and relations gave to Mun—John Verney was ideally
happy in the fifteen-year-old girl he took for his first bride. The
letters written between them during their rare separations are
among the most charming in the whole of the great Verney
collection. But their happiness was short-lived, for after
bearing her husband four children, Elizabeth Verney died at the
age of twenty-one.*

TO Mrs. Mary Verney in London from her
husband, Mun Verney.

Claydon, 29 March, 1664.[6]

My dear Wife,

It was no small joy to me the reading your lines, and
the hearing of your riding forth, whereby I take it for

I

granted that you are not so ill as you would seem to be. This good news came to me by my man after my return from Northampton Fair, where I have bought you three gallant bay coach-horses, for to carry you abroad a airing after your tedious sickness. Therefore pray thee to be of a courageous and cheerful spirit and chase away all those timorous and melancholy thoughts which make thee conceit thyself in more danger than really thou art.

My dear soul, if thou hast any kindness for me be ruled by me and the rest of thy friends, who are with thee, and do not think thyself more knowing than all of us. But think thy husband adviseth thee best, when he desireth thee to banish all despairing fancies, and to submit unto our great Maker's pleasure, be it in life or death or any affliction whatsoever, and that not only without repining but also with cheerfulness. And as touching my particular part, thou mayest assure thyself it hath and shall be acted with all the demonstrations of a pure and sincere love towards thee, and I do send my servant as my forerunner to know at this time how thou dost. Hoping to hear yet of thy growing better and better before I see thee, which shall be as soon as possibly my business will permit, yea and sooner too if thou requirest it . . .

TO MRS. VERNEY AT CLAYDON FROM HER HUSBAND, JOHN VERNEY.

24 September, 1681.[7]

Dearest Dear,

I wrote you this morning by the coach since which I have received your pretty lines under the 22nd. And for your tender expressions there is nothing but a reciprocal love can make you returns, and that be confident you have.

Pretty Precious is grown much, and her nurse to that degree of bigness that you can't imagine. I have this morning been blooded in two veins under the tongue, and find myself much better than any day yet, so that I am going to Chelsea with Aunt Jinny, Thomas coming with the coach for me. I have put up in a paper box directed to you, your black crape manto, your embroidered sleeves and your purple manto, to dress you in when the mornings are cold, so pray make enquiry for the paper box and let me know whether you received it. Make much of your dear self and 'twill do comfort to me then to hear of your welfare and pleasure.

My Mother hath bought the child a Morelly coat striped yellow and black and some lace for caps, that which you left being, as she thought, too narrow. She hath put that on under it I think. I hope you were made much of at Hillesden, Radcliffe and Stowe, otherwise the ladies there lose their reputation with me.

Pray send one of your shoes to Aylesbury or Buckingham to have a pair of clogs fitted to it, that you may walk about without taking in wet at your feet. And what letters you receive from me either burn 'em or lock 'em up in the little cabinet. I thank you for your ten thousand kisses and wish I had one half dozen from you in the mean time; but for this vacancy we'll have the more when I return to you whom God preserve. I rest your truly loving and most affectionate Dear

JOHN VERNEY.

I have had my hair cut.

AN ANXIOUS WIFE

Christopher, second Duke of Albemarle and son of General Monck, was Lord-Lieutenant of Devonshire at the time

of Monmouth's Rebellion. Monmouth had landed at Lyme Regis on June 11, and Albemarle, who, apart from his loyalty to the King, had the scores of an old Court quarrel to settle with him, was advancing against him at the head of the Devonshire Militia.

Albemarle had been married fifteen years to Elizabeth, daughter of Henry Cavendish, Duke of Newcastle, whom he had wedded at sixteen. Though both a Duchess and a Duke's daughter, news to her pen is ' nuses ' and rash ' rach.'

TO THE DUKE OF ALBEMARLE FROM HIS WIFE, ELIZABETH.

4 June, 1685.[8]

My dear Lord,

 The confusion I am in you will easily imagine by daily ill news. I have not slept all the last night, my fears have increased so fast and with such great reason. Dearest creature, you will wonder at this letter following the other so fast ; excuse the trouble I give you and when you consider the danger that is round you, you will pardon me easier for being so tender; did you know my thoughts your love to me would motion you to grieve for my present torment. I am too ignorant to advice, and my dear has too large share of judgment in war matters to fear anything can go amiss for want of conduct, neither do I think you will be a rash actor. God spare your life, you will be as great as you're good, I being for ever your affectionate dutiful wife,

E. ALBEMARLE.

MARRIAGE IN ECLIPSE

The next batch of letters shows marriage in eclipse—a wife who pretended to piety but deceived her husband and was not so devout as she seemed, a husband who told his wife that he

*would not rest till he had washed his hands in her blood—
Mrs. Denton was a sister of Sir Edmund Verney, the Royal
Standard-bearer—and a bold Cheshire lady who refused to be
browbeaten. When her lawyer-husband tried to intimidate the
last into divesting herself of her property in order to settle it on
his children, good Mrs. Dobson told him that it was not ' the
custom in Cheshire for wives to be throttled into kindnesses.'
I have printed both Mr. Dobson's reply and his wife's vigorous
commentary on it.*

*The fifth letter is from the Countess of Rochester to the
brilliant poet on whom she had bestowed her hand, when
all fashionable London had been courting the heiress Elizabeth Malet. Poor creature, she had made a sad match, but
had done it with her eyes open, for his mad ways had been
the talk of all the town long before she married him. Perhaps
the letters from him that follow—including the charming one
with its reference to his little son's sketches—may help to explain
the fascination he had for this unhappy lady, ' my most neglected
wife,' as he called her.*

TO CHRISTOPHER, VISCOUNT HATTON, FROM CHARLES
HATTON.

30 December, 1699.[9]

. . . Yesterday an acquaintance of mine came to see
me and did much divert me with some stories he told of
Sir Francis Compton, your old acquaintance, his fondness
of his new virtuous and pious lady. The day before,
Sir Francis came into company where my friend was; he
told them his lady was so very devout she was every day
several hours in her closet at her prayers. And he having
then seen her take up her Bible and prayer book and go
into her closet, he was assured she would be there shut
up for several hours. In the meantime he came abroad
to divert himself with taking a glass of wine. Presently
after which, my friend going to the playhouse, he was

fully convinced my Lady Compton did not make so long prayers as Sir Francis reported, for he found her in a vizard and mask in the 18d. gallery. . . .

TO SIR RALPH VERNEY, BART., AT CLAYDON FROM HIS SISTER, MRS. PENELOPE DENTON.

London, 21 August, 1662.[10]

Dear Brother,

God make me thankful I have not cried out my eyes for my brother Harry's absence, but before I conclude you will say that I have just cause to wish that he might never go from me. . . . If weeping in my lodgings and in the street by day and by night would break my heart, in earnest it were happy for me. . . .

Brother, if you did but know how much I suffer by Mr. Denton's outrageous carriage towards me, it would make your bowels yearn towards me. Several times since my brother Harry left the town he has been so outrageous with me that he has run after me with his knife in his hand and vowed to stab me; God make me thankful I clapped a door upon me, and my maid turned the key, so there I remained in the room till his great fury was over. . . . He did tell me that he should never be at rest till he had washed his hands in my blood. . . .

TO MRS. ELIZABETH DOBSON AT BIRCHES, CHESHIRE, FROM HER HUSBAND, EDWARD DOBSON.

Gray's Inn, 25 Feb., 1682.[11]

Betty,

If it be true, that you are obstinately in love only with yourself, I shall leave you to it. And notwithstanding your words, lines and actions, 'tis more than possible I may live (and that without the spirit of contradiction) with some satisfaction and contentment whilst my stay is on this side Heaven, where I hope my joys will be replete. May you live and enjoy the like, though you relax all affection and neglect all duty to

Your loving husband

E. D.

TO EDWARD DOBSON OF GRAY'S INN FROM HIS WIFE, ELIZABETH DOBSON. *In reply to his letter of* 25 *February*, 1682.[12]

My Dear,

'Tis true I love myself above all and 'tis as true that I love you. I am sure I gave a large testimony of it when I gave myself to you, and ever since my duty and care of you in sickness and in health has not been wanting. But whether you love me or not I may very well question in regard nothing will give you a content but to strip me of that which God and my friends have given me and to give it to your children. Few parents will undress themselves before they be ready to go to bed, though to their own children, and certainly it would not be prudent in me to do it for those that are not my own. You very well know it never was my desire to wrong yours in the least. If you have done them any 'tis unknown to me and I am sure perfectly undesired.

I wish we may both of us whilst we are on this side Heaven do nothing here to deprive us of those joys we expect to meet with there, which is most heartily the daily prayer of your poor afflicted E. D.

In my last to you I desired to know whether you would deposit good and sufficient securities for the fifteen hundred pounds into such persons' hands and keeping as I should appoint, to which you have given me no answer. If you will do this it were convenient either Mr. Borley or I should know that counsel may have time to make ready what is to be done against Chester Assizes. . . .

TO THE EARL OF ROCHESTER FROM HIS WIFE.[13]

If I could have been troubled at anything when I had the happiness of receiving a letter from you, I should be so because you did not name a time when I might hope to see you. The uncertainty of which very much afflicts me. Whether this odd kind of proceeding be to try my patience or obedience I cannot guess, but I will never fail of either where my duty to you require them.

I do not think you design staying at Bath now that it is like to be so full, and God knows when you will find in your heart to leave the place you are in. Pray consider with yourself whether this be a reasonable way of proceeding and be pleased to let me know what I am to expect for there being so short a time betwixt this and the sitting of the Parliament. I am confident you will find so much business as will not allow you to come into the country, therefore pray lay your commands upon me what I am to do. And though it be to forget my children and the long hopes I have lived in of seeing you, yet I will endeavour to obey you, or in the memory only torment myself without giving you the trouble of putting you in the mind there lives such a creature as your faithful humble . . .

TO THE COUNTESS OF ROCHESTER FROM THE EARL OF ROCHESTER.[14]

To my Wife,

Run away like a rascal without taking leave, dear wife—it is an unpolished way of proceeding which a modest man ought to be ashamed of. I have left you a prey to your

own imaginations amongst my relations—the worst of
damnations; but there will come an hour of deliverance,
till when may my mother be merciful unto you. So I
commit you to what shall ensue, woman to woman, wife
to mother, in hopes of a future appearance in glory.
The small share I can spare you out of my packet I have
sent as a debt to Mrs. Rouse. Within a week or ten days
I will return you more. Pray write as often as you have
leisure to

Your

ROCHESTER.

Remember me to Nan and my Lord Wilmot.
   You must present my service to my cousins. I intend
to be at the deflowering of my niece Ellen if I hear of it.
Excuse my ill paper and my ill manners to my mother;
they are both the best the place and age will afford. . . .

TO THE COUNTESS OF ROCHESTER FROM THE EARL
OF ROCHESTER.[15]

   I kiss my dear wife a thousand times, as much as imagination and wish will give me leave. Think upon me
as long as it is pleasant and convenient to you to do so
and afterwards forget me; for though I would fain make
you the author and foundation of my happiness yet would
I not be the cause of your constraint and disturbance, for
I love not myself as much as I do you; neither do I value
my own satisfaction equally as I do yours.

Farewell,

ROCHESTER.

TO THE COUNTESS OF ROCHESTER FROM THE EARL OF ROCHESTER.[16]

Madam,

I received three pictures and am in a great fright lest they should be like you. By the bigness of the head, I should apprehend you far gone in the rickets: by the severity of the countenance, somewhat inclined to prayer and prophecy. Yet there is an alacrity in your plump cheeks that seems to signify sack and sugar, and your sharp-sighted nose has borrowed quickness from the sweet swelling eye. I never saw a chin smile before, a mouth frown, or a forehead mump. Truly the artist has done his part (God keep him humble) and a fine man he is if his excellences don't puff him up like his pictures.

The next impertinence I have to tell you is that I am coming into the country. I have got horses, but want a coach: when that defect is supplied you shall quickly have the trouble of

Your humble servant

ROCHESTER.

Present my duty to my Lady and my humble service to my sister, my brother, and all the babies, not forgetting Madam Jane.

A FATHER-IN-LAW'S ADVICE

In this letter the Marquis of Halifax counsels patience to the young man—son of the 2nd Earl of Chesterfield—who a year before had married his favourite daughter Elizabeth, the only child of his second marriage.

To Lord Stanhope from his father-in-law, the Marquis of Halifax.

London, 4 November, 1693.[17]

Nothing ever came to me, my Lord, more unexpected than what you tell me in your letter. And it was the more so after I had conjured you, before you went, to tell me if you had any cause of dissatisfaction, which if you had done, you should have seen that, as I love you equally with my own children, I should not have been partial to your wife in any dispute where she was in the wrong.

If there is nothing more than that which you mention that giveth you offence, it will not, I hope, upon your second thoughts produce such a resolution as you seem to express. If a young woman, my dear Lord, sayeth a foolish thing in heat and, as she allegeth, in jest too, a husband is not to leave her for it, especially when she is ready, as it becometh her, to live wherever you think it necessary for yourself to be in relation to your health. For as to your wanting money to live in town, it is an argument that loseth its force by the means you may have of being supplied, which you might make use of without any scruple.

I will promise myself that upon a further consideration you will suspend at least the putting a thing in practice against which there are too many objections for one of your justice and good nature to answer. I am convinced your wife loveth you, and if she should not, I promise you I will not love her. For myself and my wife I will only say we will not yield to the nearest of your relations in our real kindness to you, and how we must be afflicted to be so disappointed in our hopes to see you live happily and kindly with your wife you may easily imagine.

Therefore let me earnestly engage you to make no

resolution till we see you, and let that be as soon as the consideration of your health will allow you. You shall find you can propose nothing, which you in your deliberate thoughts shall think reasonable, that shall not have our concurrence as well as our endeavour to promote it, and in the meantime, believe it as a truth that in the relation you have to me no man ever had,

A more affectionate humble servant,
HALIFAX.

I desire you will give my humble service to my Lord of Chesterfield. I need not tell you how much I desire to hear from you.

TRIUMPHANT IN ADVERSITY

The last four letters reveal the triumph of seventeenth century marriage in the hour of adversity : ' as for this little groaning wife of mine,' wrote William Blundell, the persecuted Catholic squire of Crosby, ' I think she will never fail me.' I have apportioned the adversity between the two great parties which for more than half a century fought one another and, whenever in the ascendant, trampled on one another for the mastery of England. In December, 1682, the Whigs were at almost the lowest ebb of their fortunes. Robert Ferguson, the stormy petrel of republican politics and the ' Judas ' of Dryden's ' Absalom and Achitophel,' was a fugitive in Holland and in daily danger of arrest at the hands of the agents of the English Crown which he had tried to destroy.

A quarter of a century before the Royalists had been suffering as dark or even a darker night. In the spring of 1655 a Wiltshire squire had raised the exiled King's standard in a forlorn hope at Salisbury. Surrounded and outnumbered he was captured a few days later by the armed forces of the Protectorate and sentenced to death for his treason.

TO Mrs. FERGUSON AT LONDON FROM HER HUSBAND, ROBERT FERGUSON.

Amsterdam, 12 December, 1682.[18]

Dearest Heart,

It is no small affliction to me that I have heard but once from thee since my arrival in Holland. And were I not in hope that thy letters are gone to Rotterdam, and that I may expect some from thence, I should be inexpressibly dejected. Nor should I take much pleasure either in my own health or safety, if I once understood that thou art either ill or in trouble. When I reflect upon my own escape, considering what warrants were out against me, how some thirsted for my blood, and how near I was once being apprehended, I cannot but hope that God doth preserve me for some further service, and that He will make us again happy in the enjoyment of one another.

I find correspondence difficult, seeing all letters are broken up which they suspect enclosures to us, and therefore I have given thee a direction underneath how thou mayest send to me with the best security. There hath been a messenger here already to enquire after us, and what may be there resolved upon as to the desiring this State to drive us home I cannot tell, nor am solicitous. We had a report before the last post came, and which had its rise among the Papists in this town, that the King was seized. I wish it be not like many other things, which they have foretold when they knew they were ready to be executed.

My dear, thou and my children sleep and awake with me, all the comfort I have in this world being bound up in you; and, next to an opportunity of serving God and my generation, I desire nothing so much as to be able to [approve] myself one that entirely honours thee.

R. FF.

Give my service and respects to all my friends.

To Mrs. Ferguson in London from Robert Ferguson.

Amsterdam, 25 December, 1682.[19]

My dear,

Thine of the 19th is come safe to hand, but with a renewal of my grief, in that thou still continuest weak. I cannot be with thee to assist and comfort thee in thy afflicted condition. Nor dost thou tell me whether we have any friends left to concern themselves in thee, either in the way of care or sympathy. However, the God that hath been our stay all our days will not forsake us in the time of our distress. My thoughts are concerning thee sleeping and waking, and I am sometimes resolving to venture over to see thee, whatsoever the hazard and jeopardy of it may be. And were it not more for reserving myself to thine and my children's benefit than any solicitude about my own safety, many days should not elapse before I were in London. . . .

For God's sake, and as thou lovest me and poor little Hannah, use all means towards thy recovery, and especially be cheerful, without which nothing else will have any effect. And while there is either any money, or goods that will sell, spare no cost for thy relief. Give my love to the children, and assure thyself that I will ever remain, my dear, entirely thine,

R. Ff.

To John Penruddock in prison from his wife, Arundel Penruddock.

3 May, 1655.[20]

My dear Heart,

My sad parting was so far from making me forget you that I scarce thought upon myself since but wholly upon you. Those dear embraces which I yet feel and shall never lose, being the faithful testimonies of an indulgent husband, have charmed my soul to such a reverence of your remembrance that were it possible I would with my own blood cement your dead limbs to live again, and (with reverence) think it no sin to rob Heaven a little longer of a martyr.

Oh! my dear, you must now pardon my passion, this being my last (oh fatal word!) that ever you will receive from me, and know, that until the last minute that I can imagine you shall live, I shall sacrifice the prayers of a Christian and the groans of an afflicted wife. And when you are not (which sure by sympathy I shall know), I shall wish my own dissolution with you that so we may go hand in hand to Heaven. 'Tis too late to tell you what I have, or rather have not done for you; how being turned out of doors because I came to beg mercy. The Lord lay not your blood to their charge.

I would fain discourse longer with you, but dare not; passion begins to drown my reason, and will rob me of my devoirs, which is all I have left to serve you. Adieu, therefore, ten thousand times, my dearest dear; and since I must never see you more, take this prayer: May your faith be so strengthened that your constancy may continue; and then I know Heaven will receive you, whither grief and love will in a short time, I hope, translate,

> My dear,
>> Your sad, but constant wife, even to
>> love your ashes when dead,
>>> ARUNDEL PENRUDDOCK.

May the 3rd, 1655, eleven o'clock at night. Your children beg your blessing, and present their duties to you.

TO Mrs. Penruddock from her husband, John Penruddock, on the day of his execution.

4 *May*, 1655.[21]

Dearest Best of Creatures! I had taken leave of the world when I received yours; it did at once recall my fondness to life, and enable me to resign it. As I am sure I shall leave none behind me like you, which weakens my resolution to part from you, so when I reflect I am going to a place where there are none but such as you, I recover my courage. But fondness breaks in upon me; and as I would not have my tears flow to-morrow, when your husband and the father of our dear babes is a public spectacle, do not think meanly of me that I give way to grief now in private when I see my sand run so fast and within a few hours I am to leave you helpless and exposed to the merciless and insolent that have wrongfully put me to a shameful death, and will object the shame to my poor children. I thank you for all your goodness to me, and will endeavour so to die as to do nothing unworthy that virtue in which we have mutually supported each other, and for which I desire you not to repine that I am first to be rewarded, since you ever preferred me to yourself in all other things. Afford me, with cheerfulness, the precedence of this. I desire your prayers in the article of death; for my own will then be offered for you and yours.

J. Penruddock.

CHAPTER VI

WOMAN'S BUSINESS

THE MAKING OF A NOTABLE HOUSEWIFE

The seventeenth century ideal of womanhood was ' a notable housewife.' The task of running even a small house, when labour-saving devices were almost unknown and public utility services negligible in the town and non-existent in the country, was enough to occupy any woman's time and energies. It was held to be much to her advantage. Thus, when poor Mary Verney showed signs—unhappily, only temporary—of recovery from the insanity that blighted her own and her husband's life, her father-in-law, the meticulous Sir Ralph, suggested that a vigorous attention to household matters would prevent any relapse.

In the second letter Mary Verney, attempting to follow this counsel, writes to her husband's aunt in London to buy household stuff for her for the White House at East Claydon. The young chatelaine's spelling suggests her manner of speech—fashion is ' fashing,' and height ' haith.'

The third letter shows a great lady, Frances Stuart, Duchess of Richmond, supervising her husband's building operations at Cobham Hall, Kent. A few months before she had eloped with her · husband, to the astonishment of the Court and the mortification of the King, who had long laid siege to her heart.

To Edmund Verney at east claydon from his father, Sir Ralph Verney.

Preshaw, 24 August, 1664.[1]

Mun, I very much desire to hear how your wife is now, and whether she begins to mind her household business, and ordering her family. In earnest you must persuade her to it by all the ways you can and commend her doing of it at all times. And though she do not do it well, yet you must commend her for it and keep her to it still. For as her condition is I had rather she should do it, though she do it ill, than anybody else though they do it well. Believe me though you lose by her doing of it, yet you will gain ten times as much by it another way; for if she would be brought to employ her mind about it, I am confident it would do her more good than all her physic. Let her govern the whole family, and let her give orders for everything in it, and not trust to others doing of it, but do it herself.

And I think 'tis best to get her to keep a house book, and set down all that's bought, and cast it up once a week (every Friday night). She herself may cast it up as often as she pleaseth, but you need do it but once a week. Be sure you put this on with all your endeavours, for if anything under heaven do her good, 'tis employment, a full and constant employment. God bless you both together.

Your loving father,

R. V.

To Mrs. Elmes at mr. gape's house, an apothecary in covent garden, from Mrs. Edmund Verney.

East Claydon, November, 1664.[2]

Dear Aunt,

You have very much obliged me, and I hope I shall not be behindhand with you in your kindness. But I can only wish it were in my power to serve you, and you should find me most obedient unto whom I owe more than I can express.

Sir Ralph and my cousin Leake both tells me, as you did before, that gimp is out of fashion. Therefore I shall quit myself of the trouble by taking your advice to work a dimity bed in green crewels. Cousin Leake thinks Mrs. Machel's a good pattern, and if you please that or my Lady Farmer's, Mrs. Dorothy Hervey can show you a breadth of it. I desire you would get it done as soon as you can. . . . For a drawing-room I should have two squabs, and six turned wooden chairs of the height of the long seats. Be pleased to buy a table and stands of the same colour; and for the same room a pair of andirons, dogs, fire shovel, tongs and three brass flowers with irons to fasten my glass. . . .

I beg your pardon for this trouble and remain,
Your most humble servant,
M. V.

To the Duke of Richmond from the Duchess of Richmond.
                                    Cobham, 11 July [1667].[3]

My dearest Lord,

Yesterday I received a letter from you; it is the second since you arrived at Dorchester, and for which I give you many thanks, because it has eased me of a great deal of care and trouble that I had, fearing you were not well. Oh, my dearest, if you love me, have a care of yourself, for longer than you are in health I cannot be in rest. . . .

I hope before this comes to your hands you will have leave to come home again, for I long extremely to see my dear Lord in whom consists all my happiness. I wonder you have not received your powder, for I sent it by Dick Rogers: the snuffers and pan I have again, for I suspected you had given them to have the arms changed, and I sent to Mr. Tilson for them.

I writ you word long since that Miller was returned, but he being wanting six days I thought he was run away: upon which I hired the other painter you mention to paint the bed-chamber. It is now almost done and likewise all that apartment, but the alcove cannot possibly be done in two months, which made me advise you not to let them go about it this summer. If you did but know how hard it is to get workmen at this time, and how lazy those are which are here, I am sure you would be of my opinion.

I have told Temple that you have ordered him money, but if he does not make more haste than he has done yet I will not pay it him so soon, for in earnest he is a very idle fellow. The next week Flexney shall buy some deal boards, for then Thayer will want some. Mr. Payne is at his own house, but will be here again in two or three days; then I am confident he will tell you, as I do, that 'tis the hardest thing in nature now to get workmen. I have given order to have the court enclosed with all speed imaginable—and there are a great many pales already cut. But now we cannot have sawyers to do the rest. I hope we shall ere long. Pray excuse this tedious letter and continue your kindness to her that is

Your most affectionate
wife and servant

F. RICHMOND & LENNOX.

. . . Since I writ this I received one from you in which I find I am still the happiest woman that ever was born in having the heart of my dearest Lord and the only joy of my life; which I will rather choose to die than lose. . . .

WANTED—A GOOD, MODEST MAID

Domestic service was comparatively a more important calling in the seventeenth century than it is to-day. On it depended the basic economy of the manor house, which was not a mere place of genteel residence but the economic and political centre of the village life, a unit that supplied almost all its own wants and in doing so provided employment for a vast host of servants of both sexes, indoor and outdoor. The households of some of the great noblemen numbered several hundreds of domestics, living together in a carefully graded hierarchy. Even quite a small manor house would provide work, food and shelter—of a congested sort—for three or four times the number that it does to-day.

Lady Shakerley was the wife of Sir Geoffrey Shakerley, Governor of Chester Castle, and consequently responsible not only for the household at her husband's home, Hulme Hall, but for an additional staff at the Governor's residence at Chester. Her correspondent was a country neighbour, Mrs. Starkey of Morthwaite, whom we have already met at a later period of her life as Mrs. Dobson, the Cheshire wife who would not be 'throttled into kindnesses.' In another letter Lady Shakerley writes to the same correspondent, ' I am glad you have heard of two good servants for me, and for the hiring of them I leave that to you, for I know you can do it better than I. For the work I have for them is the chambers to look to, and pewter to rub, and the washing of my finer linen, . . . and brewing and baking, and some few swine and poultry, and the scouring of all my pewter once a week, and when I have winnowing the two to winnow it up, which will not be much, for you know I have not much corn to winnow. I hope if you agree with them they will not think much to do what I set them to, for I have never been unreasonable yet to any servant I ever kept.' One would have liked to have heard the servants' point of view.

In the second letter Samuel Pepys, in the days before he began his diary, tells his patron, Sir Edward Mountagu, whose White-hall apartments he was employed to supervise, of the difficulties he was having in engaging a new servant to take the place of one who had eloped. The Mrs. Ann Crewe referred to in the letter was Mountagu's sister-in-law.

The third letter is written by our old friend Sir John Verney— now master of Claydon House—to his Steward in the country about the members of his London household. Perry was the footboy.

TO Mrs. STARKEY AT MORTHWAITE, CHESHIRE, FROM LADY SHAKERLEY.

Chester, 27 July, 1669.[4]

My dear Betty,

I thought to have written to you this day se'nnight but was prevented by some company that I had. Your letter I received sent by the upholsterer, and I assure you I have not stirred anyway out of town all this summer. But I should have gone to the Baroness of Kinderton's but was prevented first by the bad news. And it was well, for just then my two daughters fell into the measles, which I thank God they got very well past. And just now my footboy is in them and I am frightful for him, for I can get him to take nothing that will do him good. I pray God mend him, for he is one of the best boys that ever I had, and you know I have had enough bad ones, and so have I had women.

I have one of my women give me warning this last week, so I pray if you know or hear of a good modest maid and one that will work her work well. It is she that looks to my chambers and robes the rooms, and washes my linen. You know I have two below stairs, that one is to help the other what there is to do, which is easy enough for two

to do; but they have such fine lives that it spoils them.
Therefore I will have them when they come to spin
that they may be kept employed. If you hear of any I
pray let me hear from you before you agree them. My
wages are thirty shillings, besides the vails. So with my
dear love to you and your husband, I rest,

Yours till death,

KA: SHAKERLEY.

TO SIR EDWARD MOUNTAGU FROM SAMUEL PEPYS.

London, 26 December, 1657.[5]

My Lord,

. . . On Thursday night there came a woman from
Mrs. Ann Crewe, whom I received. But before I said
anything to her concerning the house, she began and asked
me if I knew what her work must be. I told her I
supposed Mrs. Crewe had acquainted her with that; she
told me, no. Whereupon I told her what had been the
office of them that had been before her. She answered
she never had been used to make fires, wash rooms or
cloths, scour or do anything like that, and that she expected only to take charge of the goods and oversee other
maids as a housekeeper. I answered I knew nothing to
the contrary but that her work was to be as theirs that
had been in her place before, but that if your intentions
were otherwise, Mrs. Crewe could best advertise her.
So she lodged here that night, and desired to be excused
from undertaking anything, till she had advised again with
Mrs. Crewe. Whereupon the next morn she went away
and since I have not heard of her. . . .

TO WILLIAM COLEMAN FROM SIR JOHN VERNEY.

18 *March*, 1699.[6]

. . . Yesterday Perry staying all the morning out on a small errand only to fetch three or four quarts of milk, as soon as he came in, seeing me angry (tho' I have not strength to beat him), out of doors he went and ran away, being then half drunk. For of late he keeps some very ill company and sits with shabby fellows at the alehouse, but never would to anybody confess who his comrades be. He hath served me thus many times of late and I have often threatened to have him beat but never yet hath it been done. I hear he was yesterday in the afternoon with two fellows at the *Blue Lattice* near Holborn Bridge and drinking brandy, and that he lay last night at the *Mitre* alehouse in Hatton Garden but left it early in the morning: I think it's a house of no good repute. Where he is rogueing to-day I know not, I fear he will be trepanned on shipboard, and so sent away to the West Indies, where the rogue will fetch above twenty pound. . . . Pray see if you know of any pretty sightly boy about us that would be a footboy, in case Perry doth not return.

Ralph and all my girls live now with me. Ralph came last night; this being his birthday I keep him till Monday. The blackbird whistled the next day he came to town, and continues to do so.

Judith desires to go live at home, her mother being old and crazy. But many people think she is in love and loath to be far from him. However she goes off very civilly, and offers to stay till we are provided. I am sorry for it because she is both a creditable and good natured maid.

Lady Gardiner hath a sore foot, Carey Stewkeley the

yellow jaundice, Carolina the toothache, Kitty a cold, and Peg Gardiner weaker than when at Claydon. So that there's a sickly family! I rest yours,

JOHN VERNEY.

THE RECIPE BOOK

Food—its fetching from market, garden or dairy, its preparation in the great kitchen or still-room and its storage in order to supply an ever-changing and unknown quantity of guests and casual passers-by—was the perpetual concern of the lady of a country house. The next four letters illustrate this concern: the first is written by the housekeeper of Wimpole, Cambridgeshire, a poor relation of the Chicheley family, to a married daughter of the house about her methods of making puddings and bottling gooseberries; the second by one Lancashire chatelaine to another about bad oysters and good cider; the third about a game pie which Denbighshire Lady Shakerley had sent to her stepson, Peter Shakerley, the member for Chester; and the fourth about some bubbly wine which threatened to fly into the face of the former Lady Shakerley—the first and Lancashire wife of Sir Geoffrey—whose domestic anxieties we have already recorded.

TO MRS. LEGH AT LYME, CHESHIRE, FROM MRS. ELIZABETH BEAUMONT.

1674.[7]

. . . I have no receipt for puddings nor ever had. I make them always by guess. Indeed I did teach Mrs. Fountain, but it was with letting her see me mingling them, and I wish I was as near your Ladyship that I might do the same for you. But I'll tell you everything I use to put in them, and give you the best directions I can, and then you must put them together to your own taste.

My last white puddings I put all these things in: grated
bread and milk and cream and eggs, mace and cloves and
salt, citron and candy orange and lemon peel, rose water
and sugar, and a little sack if you please, and a great deal
of marrow, and always very well beaten, and musk and
amber. And you may put a little saffron in through a
tiffany into your milk. Mangle your grated bread and
your cream, and eight or ten eggs with half the whites
together as for a boiled pudding, but pretty stiff and put
almond in. A matter of half a pound I think will serve;
if you find there is not enough, you may put in more next
time. There must be a pretty deal of the citron and
oranges and lemons cut small, for I never put any currants
in these puddings; and so put in all the ingredients
according to your taste and the marrow in little lumps.

I have here sent your ladyship the receipt for drying
gooseberry. 'Tis I am sure a very good way, for nobody
in England, I am sure, doth sweetmeats better than this
gentlewoman that gave me this. And 'tis the true way
she used to do them I dare say. The way is something
tedious, but you have so many pair of hands that will be
ready at peeling them that you will rid a great many in a
little time.

I would gladly know how your gooseberries proved that
you put up for tarts. Mine proved very good and looked
as fresh as when they was fresh pulled off the trees and
baked, and I have made very good gooseberry fool with
some of them. A bottle will make a good handsome
cream glass full; only you must put the yolk or two of an
egg more in, because they do not afford so much pulp
as when they are green, but it lasts as well every jot.
And you must set them on the fire with a little water and
boil them till they are so tender that the pulp will rub
through a hair sieve. . . .

To Mary, Lady Bradshaigh, at haigh, lancashire, from her sister-in-law, Mrs. Elizabeth
Preston.   *Holker, 3 March* [1683].[8]

Honoured Sister,

This is to return my humble thanks to you for your
good present you intended me, and indeed am as thankful
as if they had proved as good as could be, but I could not
pick one oyster out of all the barrel that was good. I
would have sent you cockles from hence but now the
best lies on the other side of the water, so John Wright
promised me to get some and bring for you.

I return my dear brother very many thanks for the fine
grafts which I hope if God bless us all with good health
you may eat of its fruit. The cider I pray tell him cost
£5 5. o. the two hogsheads and three shillings carrying to
Lancaster and from thence to Preston eighteen shillings,
so his part comes to £3 3. o. which if he please to pay to
my mother, for I have desired her to return some money
for me to Powis.

I suppose the time now draws near for the cider to
begin to work. So I would advise my brother when it
comes to put in a pound of good white powder sugar and
let it work with that for one week and then put in another.
I think it clears the cider and makes it brisk, but you must
put in loaf sugar when you bottle it.

I shall not give you any longer trouble now but to pray
to God for your safe and happy deliverance which will
be most joyful news to her that really is, in all sincerity,
honoured sister,

Your most affectionate sister and most humble servant,
Elizabeth Preston.

Mr. Preston gives his humble service to you and my
brother. He is now taking physic for he hath not been

very well all winter.   Dr. Baynard was with him last week
and says it is the foulness of his stomach that makes him
so pained in his head.

T O GEORGE SHAKERLEY AT WESTMINSTER SCHOOL
    FROM HIS MOTHER, LADY SHAKERLEY.

Gwersilt, 9 September, 1697.[9]
My dear George,
   I am as much ashamed as troubled that such a pie should
come within your brother's doors.   I have fretted sorely
about it but too late to help.   I am sure it must be sweet
for they were just killed when put in the pie.   There
were two very fat geese, eight wild ducks and eight wood-
cocks, and in the box a pair of stockings for you.   I hope
the fowl may be eaten by you and the servants, but be
you sure it comes not to your brother's sight lest he
should be offended.   I never had such a chance to
anything.
   Matthew Oulton, Mr. Oulton the beer brewer's son, a'
Friday last was playing with pistols with Mr. Smith's son,
his next neighbour, but off the pistols went and shot Smith
who died soon after, which chance has terrified me
extremely.   God comfort his parents.   I charge you
upon my blessing to have a care how you meddle with guns
or any firearms.   Serve God and obey your brother as you
tender the displeasure of a careful, sorrowful mother.

JANE SHAKERLEY.

T O MRS. STARKEY AT MORTHWAITE FROM LADY
    SHAKERLEY.

Chester, 12 *July,* 1668.[10]
My dear Betty,
   Many hearty thanks to you for all things and this cheese
which you here have sent me.   I am so much in your

debt that I know not how to requite the last, but must pay it with acknowledgement. And that is all the recompense I am able at this time to return, which is a poor requital. But I wholly rely upon your goodness to pass by all my failings.

I am just now packing all up for my removal to the Castle which we must do this next week. I pray God send it good for us, but I am very fearful of it by reason of so much company which I know comes there, and the company that is there. I have bought you a dozen pounds of loaf-sugar and three ounces which comes to nine shillings and threepence. You need not send me money for we shall call on you as we come back. I would gladly if I could come to your house as we go, if we could get from hence upon Friday next, but if I get Mr. Shakerley in a mind to do it, I will send you word.

I am confident your wine is extraordinary good for I would have opened one of your bottles, but it would have flown in my face, so I have let it alone till it be quiet. I will be careful of your bottles and return you them with safety and ten thousand thanks. So in . . . with my dear love to you and your good husband,

Your truly loving till death,
KATHERINE SHAKERLEY.

FETCHING COALS

Bringing home the coals was a summer anxiety which only concerned those who lived reasonably near a colliery district. Except for the sea coals which travelled in vast fleets of tiny colliers from the Tyne to the Thames to feed London's chimneys, coal had necessarily to be carried on the heavy unmetalled roads of seventeenth century England. The cost of moving it any distance by land was prohibitive, and even where it was possible the roads were usually only dry enough for the operation for a few weeks in the middle of the summer.

The Dobsons, living in north Cheshire, close to the south Lancashire coalfield, were exceptionally fortunate in this respect.

TO MRS. ELIZABETH DOBSON AT MORTHWAITE FROM HER HUSBAND, EDWARD DOBSON.

Gray's Inn, 2 June, 1677.[11]

My Dear,

. . . I intend on Tuesday to go to Enfield to keep Court there on Wednesday and to receive the rents. The weather here is very good and seasonable. By the next carrier I send you two gross of corks, a scarf and hoods and some gloves and some linen and ribbon for the children and some new-fashioned ribbon for arm-strings for yourself.

Let me know the next if you would come up that I may order a place for you in the Lichfield Coach and send Anthony to meet you at Lichfield.

I like the design very well to have coals brought so near as that we may fetch them every day. They may continue in the carts that brings them which our men may take and the other take back our empty carts, or else they may lay them on a bank. It will not be much labour to load them again. . . .

As for tobacco and small beer, you may tell the brick-maker I am unprovided being no house-keeper at Birches, but they may buy malt and Nan shall brew it for them. And when I give them to drink shall be when I find their work is well done. When the bricks are in making care must be taken to keep out the swine, geese and poultry from treading upon them. I suppose they will not use much block wood to burn the bricks, for they are used to burn with coals only and small wood.

When John and Thomas go first for coals they may make an agreement for their quantity and also for one team to go twice a day to bring the coals so near Birches as we may fetch them every day, or hire a waggon which will carry near two cartloads at once to help one of our teams, and let the other team stay near the place where the coals are got and to bring the coals every day and lay them on a bank. . . . The brick men must be paid at every week's end 2s. 6d. a thousand and then to be counted as they lie. . . . I suppose the plasterers have done for I would have no other workmen but the joiners whilst the brickmakers are there, that they may be supplied with beds.

My Betty, I heartily wish myself with thee, for I have nothing to do in this town but business which confines me much to my chamber. Thine,

E. Dobson.

The next five letters illustrate the friendly interest in one another's concerns of two housewives, one a country woman, Mrs. Dobson, and the other a townswoman, living in King's Street, Westminster, during her husband's service in Parliament. Hulme, referred to in one of the letters, was Peter Shakerley's Cheshire home.

TO Mrs. Shakerley at westminster from Mrs. Dobson.

Morthwaite, Cheshire, November, 1690.[12]

Dear Madam,

I am very sorry to hear by yours you are still troubled with that tormenting pain of toothache, and that you are so subject to great colds. If your little house be green and have been long without fires it may very well be the occasion. I hope by this time you are well again, which I shall truly rejoice to hear of.

The reason I do not sooner return my answers to your kind letters is by reason the postman that brings them hither from Warrington comes either late at night or so early in a morning that I cannot write to send my letter back by him, and being four miles from Warrington cannot well send but on a Wednesday when some of my own family goes to the market; therefore beg you will not take it ill from me.

Pray make my most affectionate service acceptable to your good husband and accept of the same yourself from your ever obliged, truly loving friend and servant,

E. D.

True love to pretty Mrs. Aperd.

I design the next week to send you a small pot of cocks and some fat tame fowl, but will give you notes of the carrier's name and the day he will be in London and where he lives, before he comes to town.

TO MRS. DOBSON AT MORTHWAITE FROM MRS. SHAKERLEY.

Westminster, 29 November, 1690.[13]

Dear Mrs. Dobson,

Your obliging letter I had and shall always rejoice to hear of your welfare but by no means take anything remiss from so good a friend. If you do not write so often I shall conclude 'tis business or want of an opportunity is the reason.

I thank God I am better of my pain.

We have at present a very warm season, but when the cold weather returns I fear I shall be further troubled with it. Our house is warm enough; though 'tis new finished for us yet the walls are not new. I impute my colds to keeping at home much which makes me so tender I cannot 'scape them when I do stir abroad.

Mr. Shakerley, I thank God, has yet been pretty well, and so has Nanny. They are both your faithful servants.

I am out of countenance to hear you speak of a present when you have already laid greater obligations upon us than ever we shall be able to acknowledge, but I can assure you a grateful sense of your true and hearty kindness shall ever remain with, dear Madam,

Your affectionate, faithful friend and servant,

ELIZABETH SHAKERLEY.

TO MRS. DOBSON AT MORTHWAITE FROM MRS. SHAKERLEY.

Westminster, 13 *December*, 1690.[14]

We have received dear Mrs. Dobson's noble present, and delicate fowls they be as ever I saw. You had before obliged us by all sorts of kindness beyond expression so I can say no more but assure you of our hearty thanks for them all and all your favours. Mr. Shakerley will have one of them baked in quarter pies to carry into the fields with him that he may every day drink his good old friend and benefactor's health. I wish it were in my power to serve you in anything wherein I might appear in any measure grateful: none living will be more ready.

I am glad to hear you are so well this winter. I thank God Mr. Shakerley and I are both pretty well and are both our dear friend's most entirely affectionate servants,

E. SHAKERLEY.

I am sorry there is so ill a fever about you. I hear nothing of it here. Nanny is your servant: she has a violent cold which is very rife.

The fowls are very fresh and good.

L

MRS. DOBSON'S REPLY TO MRS. SHAKERLEY (*on reverse*).[15]

Both yours, dear Madam, I received and am truly glad to hear that you and Mr. Shakerley are better in health and sorry pretty Miss has got so severe a cold, but hope she will get quit of it in a small time.

We have had very little of cold weather here as yet but for most part warm and moist, which in many places brings distempers, tho' none hereabouts in this neighbourhood, and I thank God I and my little family have been and are very well. But my servants, all but Robin, leave me this Christmas, so that I shall have a little trouble till I have settled my new servants.

I am very glad my small token came well to you. I wish I did not over-salt the geese and turkey, for the Welsh weather we had here when they went up made me, I fear, give them too much salt.

No more but humble service to Mr. Shakerley and beg you will accept of the same from her that is both his and your humble servant and ever obliged friend.

TO MRS. DOBSON AT MORTHWAITE FROM MRS. SHAKERLEY.

Westminster, 3 January, 1691.[16]

This comes to report to dear Mrs. Dobson how glad I am of the continuance of your health. Mr. Shakerley and I have both bad colds, but I thank God neither of us are confined by it. I wonder to hear the weather is so wet and warm with you: we have had the sharpest season of frost and snow that has been known here. It squeezes my pocket to keep fires to preserve life, coals are so dear.

Mr. Shakerley is your true lover and servant. So soon as the Parliament will give him leave he designs to take his pleasure in fowling, but they sit very close this Christmas and 'tis not certainly known when the King goes for Holland. But 'tis said very soon.

I have nothing of news so will detain you no longer than to wish you a good new year and assure you I am in the height of sincerity

Your affectionate friend and servant

E: SHAKERLEY.

THEY SAY IT IS THE FASHION

There is only space for four letters to illustrate two other 'women's matters,' both of them perennial—the fashions and the vagaries of their husbands. In both cases the first Lady Shakerley serves: in one she goes shopping for her friend Mrs. Starkey, afterwards Mrs. Dobson, in the great provincial centre of Chester, and in the other is deprived of the power to go a'visiting through her husband taking the coach to pieces. The two other letters about women's clothes are both from Mrs. Dobson's pen, written at a later period of her life, and addressed to the wife of her old friend's son, Peter Shakerley. A manto was a cloak of a Spanish or Italian type.

TO MRS. STARKEY AT MORTHWAITE FROM LADY SHAKERLEY.

Chester, 4 *May,* 1667.[17]

My dear Betty,

I have got you here a suit of lace much as you wrote for. I wish it fits you and that you like it. They say it is the fashion and I see those that go into strict mourning as for father or mother wear them, so that I hope it

makes up as you would have them. Now in summer,
when hot weather, you may wear plain holland as your
linens are made, and holland cuffs.

My dear Betty, I pray let me know how you do for I
am as heartily concerned for you as you are at all times
for me. And I pray God bless my most dear Betty with
her health is and ever shall be the prayers of her that is
and ever will be

Yours till death,

KATHERINE SHAKERLEY.

My dear love to your good husband. I have sent you
a pair of chamois gloves which cost two shillings. But if
the gloves do not fit you send them back again, and I can
have them changed, but your blacks I cannot for they
were made purposely for you. I hope these will fit you
if the handkerchiefs be not something too wide. And I
wish you do not think too dear, but I cannot help you for
this town is a dear town for all things.

TO MRS. STARKEY AT MORTHWAITE FROM LADY
SHAKERLEY.

Chester Castle, 1669.[18]

My dear Heart,

If I were with you I am sure I should be a great deal
better than I am. But I know not how to come, for
Mr. Shakerley pulled the coach asunder to make it up
new and it is not set together yet all out, and it is about
a quarter of a year since it has been a'doing. When it
will be done I know not, for I trudge on foot so far as I
go. If you had been as nigh me as we lived at Hulme,
I had been happy for I should have been often with you.

This week I should have been all week with you, for
I cannot write you word how troublesome a week I

have had.　But I have comforted myself to be in an Inn.
But I have not got so much as the innkeeper's wife too,
which would have given some comfort to my troubles if
I could have had a good purse by my side to have received
money.

I will say no more but I heartily wish myself with you,
and then I am sure I should be very much refreshed, but
it joys me to hear that you are well.　The Lord continue
it and ever shall be the prayers of her that is

your faithful and ever dearest

KATHERINE SHAKERLEY.

My dear love to your good husband, and my two
daughters.

TO MRS. ELIZABETH SHAKERLEY AT WESTMINSTER
FROM MRS. ELIZABETH DOBSON.

Morthwaite, Cheshire, October, 1690.[19]

Dear Madam,

I hope you have received my last letter with the enclosed note of account of your bedding at Hulme, and
in this I enclose my measure to entreat you will do me
the kindness to get me a pair of stays, and my manto made
up.　I would have the stays to suit my black satin petticoat which you know is trimmed with gold fringe. . . .
I have a pair made me of coloured stays which suits my
coloured petticoat.　If they still wear mantos lined I
desire mine may be lined, but I leave both stays and that
to yourself, whom I am sure will manage better than I
can direct.　Pray put me up a fan in the box with the
stays and manto and a bill of what is let forth, and I will
either return or send the money by the carrier that brings
them. . . .

To Mrs. Shakerley at Westminster from Mrs. Dobson.

Morthwaite, circa 29 January, 1691.[20]

I have received, dear Madam, your noble and very kind token which I return my most humble and hearty thanks for. The box came but from Warrington this evening and I writ this by the same messenger, so that I have not time to try my manto but like it very well and desire you will send me a pair of stays to suit it and my petticoat as I writ in my last, and if they wear ribbons a suit ready made up as they wear them and a pair of ruffles suitable to the head. . . .

A FAST GIRL

The common round, the trivial task of domestic life did not suit all women. In this letter Lady Gardiner complains to her brother, Sir Ralph Verney, of the restless goings-on of her step-daughter, Ursula, the child of her second husband, John Stewkeley of Preshaw, Hants. In doing so she sums up in epic phrase an eternal plaint of womanhood—'your sex will follow your Enclynations which is not for women's convenincys.'

To Sir Ralph Verney, bart., at Claydon from Lady Gardiner.

Preshaw, 4 May, 1674.[21]

Dear Brother,

I am glad you and your family is well. And I am much as I used to be. My husband, though he hath his cough, will not willingly defer his journey to London, so I say nothing but wish he had stayed at home, acknowledging my folly that I am never at heart's ease when he is at so great a distance. But your sex will follow your inclinations which is not for women's conveniences.

I should be more contented if his daughter Ursula
were not here, who after eight months pleasure came
home unsatisfied, declaring Preshaw was never so irksome
to her, and now hath been at all the Salisbury races,
dancing like wild with Mr. Clarke, whom Jack can give
you a character of, and came home of a Saturday night
just before our Winton races, at near twelve o'clock when
my family was abed, with Mr. Charles Turner (a man I
know not, Judge Turner's son, who was tried for his life
last November for killing a man, one of the number that
styles themselves Tyburn Club), and Mr. Clarke's brother,
who sat up two nights till near three o'clock, and said
she had never been in bed since she went away till four
in the morning, and danced some nights till seven in the
morning.   Then she borrowed a coach and went to our
races, and would have got dancers if she could, then
brought home this crew with her again, and sat up the
same time.   All this has sufficiently vexed me.

Her father was six days of this time from home, and
lay out three nights of it, and Friday she was brought
home and brought with her Mr. Turner's linen to be
mended and washed here and sent after him to London,
where he went on Saturday, to see how his brother Mun
is come of his trial for killing a man just before the last
circuit.   And since these were gone, I reflecting on these
actions, and she declaring she could not be pleased without dancing twelve hours in the twenty-four, and taking it
ill, I denied in my husband's absence to have seven ranting
fellows come to Preshaw and bring music, was very angry
and had ordered where they should all lie.   She designed me
to lie with Peg G., and I scaring her and contradicting her,
we had a great quarrel, which made her father very angry
with her.   But if he would he had better judgment to
make her stay at home, who is, I think, mad.   Page says
he is confident she is crack-brained.   And now she

condemns her father for not laying up money to marry her. . . .

I fear she will never be quiet at home, and we have not to give her to live abroad. . . . Pray excuse this trouble, since I wrote it to you as my secret misfortune that am in all conditions

Your affectionate sister and servant

CARY G.

CHAPTER VII

SPORT

HORSE, HAWK AND HOUND

' In all your letters,' wrote one Englishman to another in a time of political stress, ' I find not one word of horse, hawk and hound.' It required a time of exceptional crisis to cause such an omission. Magistrates, legislators and agriculturists, the country gentry of England were also ardent lovers of field sports, and the people of England shared their tastes.

The country was still largely unenclosed and game was plentiful. Shooting, which for a long time past had been slowly taking the place of the older sports of fowling and hawking, was growing into a science, and most squires kept and trained their pointers, setters and retrievers. As for horse dealing, it provided a means of sport, travel and profit, and entertainment for the entire nation: ' had you seen or heard how Mr. H. V. and Mr. Jo. Risley cheated one another in the exchange of two admirable jades,' wrote one countryman to another; ' with what craft and confidence it was carried, 'twould make you intermit a little of your serious thoughts.'

Hunting was universally practised, but was still rather a miscellaneous sport, where every hedge squire kept his own hounds and went after anything that ran. Foxes were the exception. The main pursuit was hare-hunting.

TO THOMAS COKE, M.P., FROM WALTER BURDETT.
Formark, 19 December, 1698.[1]

. . . 'Tis so long since you left us that perhaps our
country fare may be a variety to you. Therefore I made
bold to send you this week from Knowle hills half a dozen
little birds. I call my ducks swans, so that you'll guess
I'm fain to magnify whatever I have. These fowl will
come to you by the name of turkeys, and I wish you,
your Lady and sisters a merry Christmas with them.

My horse which you write of in yours (a grey stone
horse) you may guess according to the character I shall
give that I am not willing to sell him out of our country.
Though really I am willing to part with him to do such an
honour to my breed as your letter mentions. His age
is five, his height is fourteen hands and three-quarters of
an inch without his shoe.

'Tis pity he should ever be bitted, he has so fine a
mouth, and carries himself so well in a snaffle. But at the
beginning of hunting he was somewhat wilful, and to
recover him of that I clammed him till I stirred his grease.
How quiet he may be when he comes to be used again, I
cannot yet answer: he is in good heart, but low in flesh.

If any come to see him upon the account you mention,
let him bring an assurance he comes from you. Otherwise I shall not set a price of him to go out of the country,
for I can have as much as a reasonable body could ask
here, if I only sold him for money. . . .

TO THOMAS COKE, M.P., AT THE HOUSE OF COMMONS,
WESTMINSTER, FROM SIR ROBERT BURDET, BART.
Bramcoate, 20 December, 1698.[2]

. . . If you had regarded our sport of hunting I might
have told you stories of chases in Staffordshire, and of

my misfortunes. The two servants that used to hunt with me are both disabled. At the latter end of a fine chase, I broke the small bones of my grey mare's leg. But the runaway horse carrieth me bravely with a mere snaffle. I always see the sport though to the hazard of my neck, having bruised my shoulder by tumbling over a slough, and ventured drowning the same day, but have many proverbs on my side. These things only prove tricks of youth. If you hear of a runaway horse, recommend me to him: I love them mightily. . . .

TO CHRISTOPHER, VISCOUNT HATTON, FROM CHARLES HATTON.

21 *October*, 1693.[3]

. . . We are in a house from whence we have so great a prospect into the country that out of our parlour window, whilst I am now writing, we can plainly and distinctly see the hounds as they are hunting in the adjacent fields, and hear the sound of the horns and cry of the dogs. My wife is much pleased, but it will occasion me many a long walk, and the stones are much harder than they were twenty years ago and every day grow harder and harder, and the last yard of the way home seems much longer than the first furlong going out. . . .

HORSE-RACING

During the seventeenth century horse-racing first became established as the sport of English Kings. James I kept an establishment at Newmarket and Charles II built himself a house in the town which he visited regularly every spring and autumn. It was here that in 1671 Evelyn saw ' the jockies breathing their fine barbs and races and giving them their heats.'

' The King [is] highly pleased with all his Newmarket

recreations,' wrote a member of the Court, ' by candle light
yesterday morning, and this morning a' hunting the hare; the
afternoon he hawks, and courses with greyhounds; to Norwich
to-morrow, on Monday here again.   The Cup rid for here next
week before the Queen.   As thou prizes earthly paradises, bring
a maid of honour behind thee next week.'*   King Charles's
enthusiasm was communicated to his subjects.   All over the
country the gentry who established local race meetings of their
own met together to establish rules for them.   In the first letter
three of the most famous of English racing families are represented—by the ninth Earl of Derby, by Caryl, Lord Molyneux,
and by Sir Thomas Grosvenor, the third baronet of Eaton,
whose marriage to Mary Davies, heiress of the manor of
Ebury, founded the fortunes of the ducal house of Westminster.
The last recurs in Joshua Edisbury's entertaining account of the
race at Farndon.   As for Mun Verney's letter about the meeting
in Quainton meadow, it was the last he ever wrote, for next
morning when his servant entered his room at East Claydon he
found the letter unfinished and his master dead.

TO Sir Geoffrey Shakerley at gwersilt from
his son, Peter Shakerley.
Haigh, Lancs., 6 July, 1681.[4]

Honoured Sir!

I have matched Sir Thomas Grosvenor's horse to run
against the Lord Brandon's at Wallasey the four mile
course upon Tuesday the second day of August next for
£200 a horse upon £100 forfeiture; 10 stone weight.
The Lord Derby has articled with me.

I expect my horse here this week from Holker; if you
please you shall have him for what he will lie me in when
he comes.   And if you are pleased so to take him I
desire you will send me a line or two to the Forest upon

* State Papers Dom., Charles II, 247, No. 86.

Friday how you will have him disposed of; and if you
are not pleased so to have him I desire you will please to
signify so much to me then, that I may make use of the
first opportunity of selling him, which I think I can do
to good advantage.

My master Molyneux wants a horse to ride against
Brandon's for the Plate at Wallasey, and I am told that
his thoughts are upon mine. So humbly begging to
know your pleasure upon Friday at the Forest race whether
you will please to have the horse or not, with mine and
my wife's humble duties to yourself and my Mother and
service to Madam Dolben and Madam Owen, craving your
blessing I rest

Honoured Sir!

Your most obedient son

PETER SHAKERLEY.

TO JOHN VERNEY AT LONDON FROM EDMUND
VERNEY.

East Claydon, 3 September, 1688.[5]

Dear Brother,

I received yours of the 29th last past, and understanding
from my cousin Nat Hobart and my son what good sport
there was at Quainton Race the first day where Chesney,
the horse courser, made thousands of men run after him
with their swords drawn; he shot his pistol at Sir
Thomas Lee's man, Mr. Cull, and overthrew him and his
horse together, and swore like any lover that he would
have the other pluck at Mrs. Horton's £5,000 still. So
the next day I went myself to the race, and carried my
cousin Cary and my daughter in hopes to meet with the
like diversion, but he was not so obliging to the company
as to give them the same pastime. So my cousin Denton's
man, Valentine Budd, rid for the plate and won it. It was

a silver server. His horse that won it was a grey. There was a child rid over and almost killed, and old Claver of Weedon fell off from his horse being very drunk. I saw my cousin Charles Stafford there, and several ladies and gentlemen, but not T. S., nor Sir R. T. nor Sir J. B. who is gone away nobody knows where, nor anybody knows when he will return. Sir W. D. never came to the race, which troubles his granddam extremely. I have a story to tell in the next sheet, that will fill it up and so I shall conclude this who am your most loving brother and servant

EDMUND VERNEY.

TO JOSHUA EDISBURY FROM KENRICK EDISBURY.

13 *March*, 1694.[6]

Dear Cousin,

Mrs. Leigh tells me you expected from me an account of the races at Farndon, therefore I now send it you. On Monday only ran a horse of Mr. Massey's which he calls Bubble and rode him himself against a mare of Mr. Egerton's which he also rode himself. Mr. Massey got the plate. The next day there were four horses run, one of Sir Thomas Grosvenor's, two of my Lord Cholmondley's whereof Mr. Egerton rode one, and Mr. Massey rode the same horse which got the plate the day before, which seems a poor sorry little bit; the odds was two to one on Sir Thomas Grosvenor's horse against all the rest. The first heat he got, then Mr. Massey desired his rider he would not shame them but (being secure of the plate) that he would only save his distance the second heat and let them struggle for it, but he swore he would get them all if he could. The second heat (a little before the turning towards the Warehook bridge) Mr. Massey being foremost and Sir Thomas his man offering to put by him,

Mr. Massey rode him quite out of the way, by which means
Mr. Egerton got above 100 yards before them and held
before turning the pole, and back again to the turning
beyond the Warehook bridge.   Then Sir Thomas his man
having waited, Mr. Massey put up with Mr. Egerton, but
he crossing rid him out of the way again.   In the meantime,
Mr. Massey making the best of his way, got so far before
that he got the heat, though Sir Thomas his horse was not
above a length behind him at the end.   The third heat
Mr. Massey took the leading at first, ran it through and
got the plate, though Sir Thomas his horse ran it very
close up with him from first to last. . . .

KENRICK EDISBURY.

THE HAMPTON COURT OLYMPIC

*At the time this letter was written England was torn by one of
the bitterest political conflicts of her history.   Charles II's
third Parliament, recently summoned and soon to be dissolved,
was pressing home its attacks on the Catholic heir to the throne
and the loyal officers of the Crown, while the great Marquis of
Ormonde, shot at on all sides, was at his old task of keeping
Ireland quiet ' with all the vigour time had left him and all the
faithfulness time could not take.'   The ' long tedious ' Habeas
Corpus Bill referred to is said to have finally passed into law
through a jest in the House of Lords, the teller for the ayes
counting one fat peer as ten.   Ned Howard, mentioned towards
the end of the letter, was a younger son of the first Earl of
Berkshire and brother-in-law to Dryden.   A poet and play-
wright, his contemporary Dorset summed him up in the revealing
phrase, ' Thou damn'd Antipodes to common sense.'*

*As every reader of seventeenth century domestic correspondence
knows, coursing and greyhounds were seldom long out of men's
thoughts.   ' Your Reach,' wrote one countryman to another,*

' *is now one of the very best greyhounds in the country, hedges well and tops better and bears pretty well. Few hares can stand before him.*' *Even the dry-as-dust figures of the economist's solemn data are frequently invaded by such sporting irrelevancies: thus the Governor of Chester's accounts for 1665 include such entries as:*

For liver and sheep's feet for the greyhounds . . . *6d.*
. . . To the man that brought the greyhound whelps . . *5s.*
. . . For more liver for the dogs . . . . . *6d.*

TO THE MARQUIS OF ORMONDE FROM COLONEL EDWARD COOKE.

London, 30 *April,* 1679.[7]

We were all in an amaze, the King summoning first of all the Lords to come in their robes, and then all the Commons to appear at the Lords' Bar, where all suspicions of at least a prorogation ended in an assurance of His Majesty's favour in the enclosed speeches. If one may infer the heart from the voice, theirs was very joyful, for I never yet heard so loud hums so often repeated as on the occasion of this speech, so that there was a great pause of silence necessitated between every paragraph. After their Lordships had voted their thanks and desired to have each speech printed, they proceeded on that long tedious *Habeas Corpus* Bill sent them up by the Commons, and most elaborately finished it before they rose. Then the weighty considerations of May Day, and a great greyhound match between the Duke of Albemarle and Sir Ralph Dutton, when the latter was the loser, and that the King had an inclination to see Windsor, convinced their Lordships to adjourn till Friday. . . .

. . . As for Thursday, I have little to say of state affairs, the votes speaking for the House of Commons, and the Lords not sitting. Yet that I may not leave an absolute blank on that day, I presume to give your Grace an account of Hampton Court Olympic, where the King honoured the pastimes with his presence, and thousands followed his example, so that the breadth of the paddock course was fain to be divided with stakes and ropes.

The first match was made this time or month between Tom Cheeke and Sir Ralph Dutton. The latter was confined to his single dog *Hog* to run for £200 next May Day, which was Thursday last, with any dog in England. *Hog* held sound till a week before he run, then had a cut on one toe and a kind of boil on the other. Tom Cheeke agreed to £20 forfeiture, but since the Duke of Albemarle laid £100 on his dog *Smoker's* side against *Hog*, Tom Cheeke rather chose to pay his £20 than hazard his £200, and after betted on Dutton's side. For though the main match was off, yet the second part of it was judged by the King to be run, and Dutton's lame dog was beaten five lengths. So that Tom Cheeke, who might have won two hundred guineas, lost forty; twenty he paid as forfeiture and twenty as bets; besides being laughed at sufficiently.

The next match was run between a black bitch of Mr. Dutton's and a fallow dog of that excellent poet, Ned Howard's, whose dog, having better feet than his verses, won his match. But in the third course a little bitch of Mr. Harvey's went by his goodly fallow dog, to the loss of many six to seven.

After the match was over, the King coming that morning from Windsor, dined with the Duchess of Portsmouth at her house, called on the Marquess of Winchester at Teddington, and after crossing that [*illegible*] went a' horseback through the park to avoid the dust, and met the Duchess on horseback also, with whom side by side he rode through Putney, and so entered his barge. . . .

M

A REMARKABLE CATCH

These evidences of the English passion for sport would not be complete without mention of the gentle art which St. Wilfred taught to the South Saxons and which found its noblest exponent in the seventeenth century in Izaak Walton. Fishing was engaged in by both sexes: there is a record of Charles II's Queen angling in the Thames, and Mrs. Dobson, the Cheshire wife who would not be ' throttled into kindnesses,' at the age of seventy used to fish in the still unpolluted rivers of her native county. ' Here,' wrote a happy squire to his wife, ' are abundance of small trouts; myself and another killed ten dozen of them last Tuesday morning in half a mile's fishing.'

A note on the second Duke of Albemarle appears on pp. 115–16. Newhall was the Duke's house in Essex.

TO THE DUKE OF ALBEMARLE FROM JOHN PETRE.

16 *March*, 1683.[8]

My Lord,

I most humbly beg your Grace's acceptance of the biggest fish that ever I did take in my life, being a pig of your own sow coming out of your own pond. I did heartily wish your Grace with me at the taking of him up, for from the time of my taking the line in my hand till I landed him in the boat was an hour by Newhall clock, and my back was ready to crack. For the time I was there, which was but four or five hours, I had very good sport. My Lord, I wish your Grace all success imaginable both at Newmarket and wheresoever your Grace goeth. . . .

TO Peter Shakerley, m.p., at Westminster from
Mrs. Dobson.

Morthwaite, Cheshire, June, 1691.[9]

My dear friend,

I thank God I am come very well home and shall be
truly glad to see you here. I have sent you a dozen cream
cheeses, but have kept enow here to eat when you come
that we go a' fishing. I will get my fishing rods into order
and worms ready: therefore pray make what haste you can
and resolve to stay a great while when you come. I have
leave to fish in pits not far from here that are stored with
carp, tench and pike, and I hope we shall have sport
enough.

Pray give my love and service to your good lady. I
hope she received my last letter which I writ to her from
Warrington before I went into Yorkshire and the money
she laid down for me as well as if I had been in London to
have had measure taken of me.

BAITING A TIGER

*There is only space for a single illustration of the rougher
sports of seventeenth century England. Bear-baiting, like cock-
fighting, was the pastime of every town in England. But baiting
a tiger was something out of the ordinary. In this letter the
physician and scientist who gave his name to Sloane Street
describes such an occasion for the amusement of his friend, John
Ray, the great naturalist.*

TO John Ray from Sir Hans Sloane.

London, 9 *March,* 1699.[10]

Sir,

This day a large tiger was baited by three bear-dogs,
one after another. The first dog he killed; the second

was a match for him, and sometimes he had the better, sometimes the dog; but the battle was at last drawn, and neither cared for engaging any farther. The third dog had likewise sometimes the better and sometimes the worse of it, and it came also to a drawn battle. But the wisest dog of all was a fourth, that neither by fair means nor foul could be brought to go within reach of the tiger, who was chained in the middle of a large cockpit.

The owner got about £300 for this show, the best seats being a guinea, and the worst five shillings. The tiger used his paws very much to cuff his adversaries with, and sometimes would exert his claws, but not often, using his jaws most, and aiming at under or upper sides of the neck, where wounds are dangerous. He had a fowl given him alive, which, by means of his feet and mouth, he very artfully first plucked and then ate; the feathers, such as got into his mouth being troublesome. The remainders of his drink in which he has lapped, is said by his keeper to kill dogs and other animals that drink after him, being by his foam made poisonous and ropy. I hope you will pardon this tedious narration, because I am apt to think it is very rare that such a battle happens, or such a fine tiger is seen here. . . .

CHAPTER VIII

MEN OF THE WORLD

THE MAN ABOUT TOWN UNDER THE COMMONWEALTH

*The Earl of Chesterfield we have already met: at the time
when his sister-in-law wrote him this letter he was twenty-five
years old and a widower. The Puritan experiment under the
Commonwealth did not inaugurate a new age of human virtue:
on the contrary, by loosening the traditional bonds of society, it
undermined it and broke down the slender barriers of convention
that keep men from the unrestrained pursuit of vice. The licence
of the Restoration courtier was the consequence not of the return
of Charles II, but of the Great Rebellion and the Civil Wars.
Had these never taken place, Chesterfield, growing up in an
ordered society, might have acquired habits of restraint and
wisdom; as it was, he was a finished rake in his early twenties.*

TO THE EARL OF CHESTERFIELD FROM HIS SISTER-IN-
LAW, THE COUNTESS OF ESSEX.

1658.[1]

My Lord,

Had I not ever paid your Lordship a very great deal of
kindness and respect I should let this quite alone. For
I am almost discouraged to undertake it, believing that
it will be as little thought on or regarded as you do that
which is most necessary for you to have more in your
thoughts than I fear and believe you have.

Though I live here where I know very little of what is done in the world, yet I hear so much of your exceeding wildness that I am confident I am more sensible of it than any friend you have. You treat all the mad drinking Lords, you swear, you game, and commit all the extravagances that are incident to untamed youths to such a degree that you make yourself the talk of all places and the wonder of those who thought otherwise of you and of all sober people. And the worst of all is I hear there is a handsome young lady (to both your shames) with child by you.

My Lord, these courses must needs undo your person, fortune, and reputation. For out of those wild persons' company you will not be esteemed, you will lose your most considerable friends, and at last make your life miserable, and, which is the saddest of all, ruin your own soul. For be confident that those momentary pleasures will have an end, and a sad one too if you do not speedily consider your condition and heartily repent of it.

You have a person which might make you and a virtuous wife happy, you have wit, fortune and all desirable things in this world, and you abuse them all and turn them to wickedness, and do, I am sure, very unsuitable to what you owe to the memory of my most deserving sister. You have falsified your own words to me, for how often have you told me how honestly you lived both here and abroad? And I believed you all this while, till now that it is impossible to credit more, which truly gives me a very sensible concern. Though now that I have said thus much I will give your Lordship no more trouble nor interruption in your pleasure, but ever pray for your soul as

Your most humble servant
and most affectionate sister.

To the Countess of Essex from the Earl of Chesterfield.

1658.[2]

Madam,

Your Ladyship knows that the world is strangely given to lying, and therefore had I not ever paid your Ladyship a greater respect than to anybody else, I should little care to give either your Ladyship or myself the trouble of my justification. For since your Ladyship has not credited my former professions, I cannot now expect to be more fortunate and therefore must leave this subject to a fitter season. Only let me desire your Ladyship (in the mean time) to forbear censuring upon my account one of the most virtuous persons living.

Madam, the concern your Ladyship expresses for me in your obliging letter has added pride to all my former good qualities, so that I am now a very accomplished gentleman, and have reason to believe that your Ladyship ought not to dislike that so singular a person should profess himself,

Madam,

Your most humble servant.

YOUNG GENTLEMEN ABROAD

At nineteen young Harry Savile, travelling through France to Spain with a couple of friends, wrote to his elder brother, the head of his family, to protest that he was in no danger from the ladies. Eighteen years later, he wrote from Paris (where he was English Envoy) to the same brother, then Viscount Halifax, about the care of the latter's eldest son, Henry, who at much the same age was returning from Spain through France.

TO Sir George Savile from his brother, Henry Savile.

Most dear brother,

. . . I did felicitate you in my last for your new son, and am much concerned that he bears my name. I wish with all my heart that he prove as fat and in as fair-liking as his namesake, and that he may have his health as perfect as it has pleased God to give it me. In all other things I would have him resemble you and be your successor in all your good qualities, for, without flattering you, I am confident the best wish that I can wish him is that he may be like his father.

As for the pleasures that you tell me there are to be had in these parts, I confess they would be very great ones to one that was not of my humour. But neither of them are extraordinary for me, for, as for matter of fruit, I eat as little as anybody of my age that naturally is given to eat a great deal, and as for ladies, the fairest cannot tempt me. For I am as rightly cut out for a bachelor as ever was man, and therefore I am much obliged to nature that made me a younger brother.

In my last to you I sent you word that Lady-day approached, and now that it is past, and you know my rents are not so great as to serve me much above quarter day, so that I do humbly desire you to let me receive that which was due to me the last Lady-day. I suppose you will not refuse me, considering that all the money I spend abroad is only to render me capable to do you service at my return. For I dare say, dear brother, that had you chosen your brother amongst all the men in the world, you would never have found one that would have loved you better or that would desire with more passion to approve himself,

Most dear brother, your most passionately affectionate brother and most humble servant,

HEN. SAVILE.

To Viscount Halifax from his brother, Henry
Savile.

Paris, 17 May, 1679.[4]

. . . Your son is arrived here, and, according to your
orders, I will do my best to find what sort of gentleman
he is, and send you his character with his person: in the
mean time I will satisfy you that his outside is very well.
His complexion is near the same with your own, but will
be a little brighter when the tan of a Spanish voyage is
gone off, but, having as good eyes and as fine teeth as
ever I saw. He has a very good countenance and has a
clean look, and like a man of quality.

He is about my height, and as yet slender enough, so
that, wanting my breadth, he appears tall enough and
probably may yet grow a little more. He has lost his
sheepish shamefacedness quite; and I see already that
Mrs. Beale will run some hazard by being in the house
with him; and so had Mrs. Gregory, if she had stayed,
so it is God's great mercy she is gone.

For his talents, nature, and humour, I shall be more
perfect in them upon a little more conversation with the
gentleman. But already I can see he has a good deal of
wit, and upon the whole matter I see a great deal of what
I like and nothing that is to be disliked. If I find any such
thing you shall have warning of it very sincerely that you
may mend what is amiss, which will be easy for you to do
because I find him prepared to have a thorough deference
for you. And if he does not please you, you will be
very hard to be pleased, for as far as I can yet perceive
you would have an ill bargain to change sons with any
man I know in England. Thus far I can honestly say now
without the partiality of an uncle. . . .

TO VISCOUNT HALIFAX FROM HENRY SAVILE.

St. Germain, 16 January, 1680.[5]

. . . My nephew's coming over is the very best news I have heard since he went hence. His chamber shall be ready and clean sheets, with a promise to you that his privilege in my house shall be only of that kind, and I will never force upon him any of those cruel enemies that come out of the cellar. But, as I know every young man must have a vice, I will not curb him in his inclinations to the sex; and be no otherwise a spy upon him or them, but to examine that all his tackling be sound, and to find good workmen to repair the breaches that may unfortunately happen. And truly I think I owe so much to the stallion of our family, abstracted from the personal kindness I have for him. And since he will come, pray let him not loiter too long at London, but come and take his share of the carnival at Paris. . . .

' NOT ONE SINNER IN ENGLAND NOW OUT OF LONDON BUT YOURSELF '

Harry Savile's most intimate friend was the Earl of Rochester, his junior by five years. In the autumn of 1677 the latter was convalescing at his Oxfordshire home from one of the more serious bouts of the disease which was soon to kill him. His wild excesses of mind and action—the follies of a poet blindly following his impulses without calculation or fear—had given him so ill a reputation that even a naked scamper round a meadow at Woodstock after bathing with some friends was magnified by scandalous tongues into an unmentionable debauch—' a beastly prank of my Lord Rochester,' wrote young Robin Harley, ' and my Lord Lovelace and ten other men, which they committed on that Sabbath day when they were at Estington, which was their running along Woodstock Park naked.'

Savile's letters to Rochester during the ensuing winter and summer give the news of the town and Court. There are references to the sudden alliance with Holland which followed the Princess Mary's marriage with William of Orange and the consequent talk of war with France that set all England arming and so alarmed Paul Barrillon, the French Ambassador.

Sir Carr was the ' purblind knight,' Sir Carr Scrope, a short-sighted man of wit, a poet, and, according to popular repute, a great lady-killer. Mrs. Barry was the actress, already alluded to, whom Otway loved and Rochester kept. Louise de Kéroualle, Duchess of Portsmouth, was from 1671 onwards Charles II's principal mistress. Sir George Downing and Lord Ranelagh, whom the King spoke of in jest as the only persons in the country who could purchase the new French comedienne, were two of the richest and most unscrupulous men in public life : the first started life as a preacher in the Roundhead army and rose to wealth and power by keeping himself steadily on the winning side, the second made himself notorious by his interested mismanagement of the Irish revenue.

George Porter, Gentleman of the Privy Chamber to the Queen, was the eldest son of that picturesque courtier of earlier days, Endymion Porter. Even as a young man during the Civil Wars he had already built up a notable reputation for debauchery—in the view of his brother-in-law, Lord Goring, no ill judge, ' the best company but the worst officer that ever served the King '—and he continued to do his best at a more mature age to maintain it. He is supposed to have been responsible for the famous aphorism, made to a parliamentary officer at the moment of his deserting the beaten Royalist cause, that good wine was of no party.

Fleetwood Sheppard was of the ' merry gang ' of which Rochester and Savile were both members, a kind of steward to Nell Gwynne and of the King's ' companions in private to make him merry.' Nicholas Staggins was Master of the Music to Charles II.

TO HENRY SAVILE FROM THE EARL OF ROCHESTER.
October, 1677.[6]

Tho' I am almost blind, utterly lame, and scarce within the reasonable hopes of ever seeing London again, I am not yet so wholly mortified and dead to the taste of all happiness, not to be extremely revived at the receipt of a kind letter from an old friend, who in all probability might have laid me aside in his thoughts, if not quite forgot me by this time. I ever thought you an extra-ordinary man, and must now think you such a friend, who, being a courtier, as you are, can love a man, whom it is the great mode to hate. Catch Sir G. H. or Sir Carr, at such an ill-bred proceeding, and I am mistaken. For the hideous deportment, which you have heard of, con-cerning running naked, so much is true, that we went into the river somewhat late in the year and had a frisk for forty yards in the meadow to dry ourselves. I will appeal to the King and the Duke, if they had not done as much; nay, my Lord Chancellor and the Archbishops both, when they were schoolboys? And, at those years, I have heard the one declaimed like Cicero, the others preached like St. Austin: prudenter persons, I conclude, they were even in hanging-sleeves than any of the flashy fry (of which I must own myself the most unsolid) can hope to appear, even in their ripest manhood. . . .

The best present I can make at this time is the bearer, whom I beg you to take care of, that the King may hear his tunes when he is easy and private, because I am sure they will divert him extremely. And may he ever have harmony in his mind, as this fellow will pour it into his ears. May he dream pleasantly, wake joyfully, love safely and tenderly, live long and happily; ever prays (Dear Savile) *un Bougre las qui sera toute sa foutue reste de Vie.*

Votre fidèle ami et
très humble Serviteur,

ROCHESTER.

TO THE EARL OF ROCHESTER FROM HENRY SAVILE.
Whitehall, 17 December, 1677.[7]

Out of a quality common to most men of believing easily what they desire earnestly, I have suffered myself to be silent longer not only than kindness but even common manners would have suffered me to be. But the truth is the whole town have so confidently reported your Lordship would every day be in town (nor was this contradicted by your own servants) that I have wearied myself with that expectation and can no longer hold out but I must ask your Lordship how you do, your health being what I am most concerned for when I have not your company, which I value so much that, as usually happens, I prefer that both to your health and my own.

There is not one sinner in England now out of London but yourself. George Porter has been here a fortnight and is already three surfeits before you, one of sprats, one of tripes and the third of Newark ale. The rogue is grown so ravenous that now he surfeits of everything he sees but Mrs. Long and his son Nobbs which he can never have enough on. . . .

Sheppard has been overturned in a coach at Matt Clifford's funeral and broke his head, and a little before was run with a sword under the eye endeavouring to part Bulkeley and Etherege squabbling in a tavern, so that he is absolutely become a man of blood and talks of nothing but a regiment against the French. He has already allotted what estate he will have in France; and for a house at Paris I do not find he will be satisfied under the Palais Royal.

This is a sort of madness now so common here that either to doubt of making war with France, or beating them when it is made, is an offence against the nation. And though the Parliament will occasion your coming up within a month, it were well enough worthy a journey sooner to see how the style of the court is altered in this point, and to see his Majesty so merry with the Confederates in the Queen's withdrawing room whilst poor Barillon stands by neglected.

The greatest news I can send you from hence is what the King told me last night, that your Lordship has a daughter born by the body of Mrs. Barry of which I give your honour joy. I doubt she does not lie in much state, for a friend and protectress of hers in the Mall was much lamenting her poverty very lately, not without some gentle reflections on your Lordship's want either of generosity or bowels towards a lady who had not refused you the full enjoyment of all her charms.

My Lady Portsmouth has been ill to the greatest degree. The King imputes her cure to his drops, but her confessor to the Virgin Mary, to whom he is said to have promised in her name that in case of recovery she should have no more commerce with that known enemy to virginity and chastity, the monarch of Great Britain, but that she should return to a cloister in little Brittany and there end her days. I have not yet heard that her Grace has confirmed this bargain, but there are fools who believe it, and because the physicians have concluded it necessary for her to go to Bourbon and the tenth of March appointed for the day of her going, it is not hard to have wagers laid that she will return no more.

I had almost forgot for another argument to bring you

to town that a French troop of comedians bound for Nimeguen were by adverse winds cast into this hospitable port and do act at Whitehall so very well that it is a thousand pities they should not stay, especially a young wench of fifteen, who has more beauty and sweetness than ever was seen upon the stage since a friend of ours left it. In good earnest you would be delighted above all things with her, and it were a shame to the nation she should carry away a maidenhead she pretends to have brought and that nobody here has either wit or address or money enough to go to the price of. The King sighs and despairs, and says nobody but Sir George Downing or my Lord Ranelagh can possibly purchase her. . . .

TO THE EARL OF ROCHESTER FROM HENRY SAVILE.

25 June, 1678.[8]

I am most infinitely obliged to your good Lordship for your kind remembrance of me, and if the good gentleman who loved sack and sugar so well was so lucky as to bring me into your mind I wish there were more of them. Though methinks since the death of poor Sir Simon Fanshaw that sort of excellent breed is almost extinguished, or at least so far decayed that, except an old cavalier corporal that I believe you have seen begging in St. James's Park, there is no more any such person than a phoenix to be found in these parts.

A true good fellow is like a kingfisher, can only breed in calm weather. The continual noise of horse, foot, dragoons, cuirassiers, grenadiers, guidons, aides-de-camp, and a hundred such words repeated ten thousand times a day in Whitehall gallery have frighted away even the thoughts of the least indulgence to a man's pleasure, and whoever is not now in this hot season in a *drap de Berry* coat with gold galoon enough to load a mule is not thought affectionate to the government or the army, which your House has voted shall stand a month longer than we intended. And if we can come off so and at the end of August say *cedant armatogaque* we senators shall be much lighter at heart than we are at present, how cheerfully soever we may bear our apprehensions in our faces. I will not say how good a time this is to be in the country, how good a time to be sick, nay how good a time to die in, for fear you should either think me near my end or believe I thought you so, and were therefore gathering some philosophical comfort out of Solomon or Seneca or any other who has treated *de vanitate mundi*. But this I will say that my *taille* being now liker Dick Newport's than my Lord's, and I presume my spirits wasted with my flesh, I am troubled with splenetick vapours that make me dislike the world as much as I ever approved it. From the rising of the sun to the setting thereof, I see no thing that pleases my eyes, or hear no thing but what grates my ears; only I am promised a moment's titillation by Mr. Staggins who is come over with great credit and many new airs. His Majesty has already constituted him lord paramount over all the music. He may reign there like Great Turk and cut whose cats-guts he please if the harmony be not to his liking. With what moderation he will use this absolute power, I leave it to fate and the immortal gods to determine.

George Porter about a fortnight since brought a little stock of Berkshire health to town, which he has since swilled away in taverns, and now lies soaking in bed for more breath. He had a great trial on Saturday last at the bar of the Lords where there was an appeal against him, but he came off so victorious that there was not a voice against him. The Purbeck will 'tis thought at last prove as errant a son of a whore as he was always taken for. He carried the difficulty of the fine in your House; but for the bastardy, the Duke of Buckingham has leave to bring in a bill for the confirmation of it. Not being at court I can send you no news of ladies. . . .

' I WEAR FLANNEL, SIR '

The writers of the three letters that follow were both gentlemen of fashion who occupied their leisure by writing brilliant plays for the London stage, at that time almost an appendage of the Court. Sir Charles Sedley was a Kentish baronet, master of ' that prevailing gentle art ' of both poetry and love. Sir George Etherege, author of three delightful comedies, once defined the virtues of a gentleman as being ' to dress well, dance well, fence well, have a talent for love letters, a pleasant voice in a room, to be always very amorous, sufficiently discreet but not too constant.' Both were members of the little group of rips whose youthful escapades so amused and scandalised Restoration society, and whose leading spirits were the Earl of Rochester and George Sackville, successively Lord Buckhurst and sixth Earl of Dorset. The latter, mentioned in the third letter as having given over variety and shut himself within his lady's arms, was the amorous hero of Sir Carr Scrope's lines,

> *None ever had so strange an art*
> *His passion to convey*
> *Into a list'ning virgin's heart,*
> *And steal her soul away.*

At the time these letters were written the days of such wild pranks were over and both men were in their forties. In 1685 Sir George Etherege was sent by James II to represent his country at Ratisbon.

> *And all to preach to German dame*
> *Where sound of Cupid never came.*

*Here he remained like a fish out of water, 'forced from the
shore of delightful Thames,' as he told a correspondent, ' to
be confined to live on the banks of the unwholesome Danube; . . .
the Muses when they were banished Greece travelled westward
and have established themselves in other countries but could
never find in their hearts to dwell here.' But like the philosopher
he had learnt to be, he tried to make the best of it: ' I comfort
myself as well as I can, forget Julia and suit my inclinations to
the divertisements the climate affords.' Toleration was his
supreme virtue, and in this, for all his frailties, he was a representative of the best spirit of his age. ' I have ever enjoyed a
liberty of opinion in matters of religion,' he wrote in the last
great epoch of religious intolerance. ' 'Tis indifferent to me
whether there be any other man in the world who thinks as I do.
This makes me have no temptation to talk of the business, but
quietly follow the light within me.'*

TO LORD CHESTERFIELD FROM SIR CHARLES SEDLEY.

1682.[9]

My Lord,

When your Lordship was last in town you made me
an offer of some venison, which I did not then lay hold
of, having no occasion, neither was it then in season.
But now I would thank you for a buck, though the town is
so empty that with all my bowling, tennis, drinking and
other general acquaintance, I shall have much ado to find
company for a pasty. Besides the distinction of Whig
and Tory doth much add to the present desolation. They
are in my opinion (at least the violent part on both sides)
much of the same stuff at bottom since they are so easily
converted one to another, I mean self-interest. For
instance the Lord Sunderland upon the Duchess of
Portsmouth's arrival is received at Court. The Lord

Anglesey was voted a libeller and his book against the
Duke of Ormonde a libel at the council: so 'tis thought
he will be three-quarters Whig. The Lord Vaughan is
this week to be married to the Lady Ann Savile notwithstanding he voted her father an enemy to King and country
last sessions. Though we are not blest with poets that
can write us comedies equal to the ancients, I believe
never was any age so comical as this, and a laugher
wherever he turns himself will have occasion to hold
his sides.

Madame de Soissons is arrived whom the Lord Crofts
were he alive would call Madame de Soixante, for she is
ten years older than her sister Mazarin. But whether
our Court will have her a beauty, a miss, a wit or a
politician, is not yet known.

Ruinous play is grown the only diversion at Windsor,
and a man without a thousand guineas to venture is an
ass. And on the contrary, as it has ever been the custom
of people of quality that had infirmities to introduce
fashions that might hide them, so they now cover up
their want of sense and conversation with extravagant
play. Some considerable removes are to be made at
Court, but what they are your Lordship can not but
know before me, so I will not trouble you with my
conjectures.

I could wish England were not so large, that it might
fall within my diocese to visit your Lordship, for I know
no man I would speak more freely to nor more willing
hear than your Lordship. Being without compliment
or any regard to the common close of a letter your very

obedient servant.

TO Henry Guy, secretary to the treasury, from Sir George Etherege.

Ratisbon, 3 November, 1687.[10]

Sir,

I have spared you so long, that I begin to fear you may think I grow negligent in paying you the acknowledgement I owe you. It would be a fine thing if, I who am here at school to learn the affairs and interest of princes, should be such a blockhead as to forget my own. I wish I were near the sea or some river which runs your way that instead of this dull tribute I might send you some of our good wine to put you in mind of me in your cheerful hours. As for our women they are a commodity which will turn to no account in England, especially to you who as well as myself have, by a long experience of the frailties of the sex, almost acquired a perfect chastity.

But while we approach this virtue, let us take care our years do not sour us with any of the common vices of age. Let us still preserve our good humour and our good nature to make us welcome near those young people who possess that plentiful estate we have pretty well run out of, that we may help them rail at the morose and cry out with Falstaff, *Down with them, they hate us.* . . .

TO Henry Guy from Sir George Etherege.

Ratisbon, 19 December, 1687.[11]

I was very much surprised, Sir, with your letter; such a proof of being remembered by one I love at this distance is what I have been little used to. In gratitude I should say much on this subject, but I know you will take it as kindly if I only think it; you may without jealousy let me keep my compliments for those whom I know not how to entertain without them.

The women need not rail at our changing; few of us have the gift to be constant to ourselves. Sir Charles Sedley sets up for good hours and sobriety. My Lord Dorset has given over variety, and shuts himself up within my Lady's arms, as you inform me, and, late as it is, Will Richards begins to pretend to secrecy, for the Devil a word he has even writ me about my Lady Morland.

Notwithstanding the ebbing and flowing in the flesh my mind is a kind of lake, and has the same standing pleasures it had in London, wine and women. But our good fellows are far from being wits, and our whores are yet farther from being beauties. The town is too little to hide us, and the liberty of talking is too great, so that poor lovers like hares in relieving time are fain to clicket up and down the gardens at midnight.

I have a very convenient one, belonging to my house. I wish the rent of it may not cost me too dear—sometime or other. I have good horses and often go a' hunting; were I to write to Tom Crud or Roger Wood this would afford me wherewithal to fill one side of paper. I bungle away now and then in the morning at tennis; here is a pretty carré court and players so exactly sized for Sir Charles that were he here, he would live in it.

Here are two very handsome young ladies but their unconscionable price is marriage. Nevertheless were I as capable of a *belle passion* as some at my age are, they would have cost me many a billet and much time in tying my cravat at 'em. But I cannot think of laying a siege wanting a stock of things necessary to carry it on, and strength sufficient to maintain the place in case I should take it. . . .

I wear flannel, Sir, wherefore pray talk to me no more of Poetry. . . .

THE HEALING OF THE DISCONSOLATE WIDOW

The recipient of this entrancing letter was George Villiers,
second Duke of Buckingham, the Zimri of Dryden's 'Absalom
and Achitophel':

> A man so various that he seemed to be
> Not one, but all mankind's epitome.
> Stiff in opinions, always in the wrong,
> Was everything by starts and nothing long,
> But in the course of one revolving moon
> Was chemist, fiddler, statesman and buffoon;
> Then all for women, painting, rhyming, drinking,
> Besides ten thousand freaks that died in thinking.
> Blest madman who could every hour employ,
> With something new to wish or to enjoy.

This letter is dated October 21, 1689, but there must be a
mistake in the year. 'The jolly Duke of Bucks' died in
April, 1687, of a chill contracted while hunting. 'Bellamira'
was first printed in 1687 and the 'Squire of Alsatia' in 1688.

TO THE DUKE OF BUCKINGHAM FROM SIR GEORGE
ETHEREGE.
                                    Ratisbon, 21 Oct.[12]

My Lord,
   I never enjoy myself so much as when I can steal
a few moments from the hurry of public business to write
to my friends in England; and as there is none there to
whom I can pay a profounder respect than to your Grace,
wonder not if I afford myself the satisfaction of conversing
with you by way of letters—the only relief I have left me
to support your absence at this distance—as often as I can
find an opportunity.
   You may guess by my last whether I don't pass my time

very comfortably here; forced as I am by my character
to spend the better part of my time in squabbling and
deliberating with persons of beard and gravity how to
preserve the balance of Christendom; which would go
well enough of itself if the Divines and Ministers of Princes
would let it alone. And, when I come home spent and
weary from the Diet, I have no Lord Dorsets or Sir Charles
Sedleys to sport away the evening with; no Madam I. . .
or Lady A. . . .s; in short, none of those kind, charming creatures London affords, in whose embraces I might
make myself amends for so many hours murdered in
impertinent debates.   So that, not to magnify my sufferings to your Grace, they really want a greater stock of
Christian patience to support them than I can pretend to
be master of.

I have been long enough in this town, one would think,
to have made acquaintance enough with persons of both
sexes so as never to be at a loss how to pass the few vacant
hours I can allow myself.   But the terrible drinking that
accompanies all our visits hinders me from conversing
with the men so often as I would otherwise do; and the
German ladies are so intolerably reserved and virtuous—
with tears in my eyes I speak it to your Grace—that 'tis
next to an impossibility to carry on an intrigue with
them.   A man has so many scruples to conquer and so
many difficulties to surmount before he can promise
himself the least success, that for my part I have given
over all pursuits of this nature.   Besides, there is so
universal a spirit of censoriousness reigns in this town
that a man and a woman cannot be seen at ombre or piquet
together, but 'tis immediately concluded some other
game has been played between them.   And, as this
renders all manner of access to the ladies almost im-
practicable, for fear of exposing their reputation to the
mercy of their ill-natured neighbours, so it makes an

innocent piece of gallantry often pass for a criminal correspondence.

So that, to deal freely with your Grace, among so many noble and wealthy families as we have in this town, I can only pretend to be truly acquainted but with one. The gentleman's name was Monsieur Hoffman, a frank, hearty, jolly companion. His father, one of the most eminent wine merchants of the city, left him a considerable fortune, which he improved by marrying a French jeweller's daughter of Lyons. To give you his character in short, he was a sensible, ingenious man, and had none of his country's vices: which I impute to his having travelled abroad and seen Italy, France, and England. His lady is a most accomplished, ingenious person, and, notwithstanding she is come into a place where so much formality and stiffness are practised, keeps up all the vivacity and air and good humour of France.

I had been happy in my acquaintance with this family for some months, when an ill favoured accident robbed me of the greatest happiness I had hitherto enjoyed in Germany, the loss of which I can never sufficiently regret. Monsieur Hoffman about three weeks ago going to make merry with some friends at a village some three leagues from this place upon the Danube, by the unskilfulness or negligence of the watermen, the boat, wherein he was, unfortunately chanced to overset: and, of some twenty persons, not one escaped to bring home the news but a boy, that miraculously saved himself by holding fast to the rudder and so by the rapidity of the current was cast upon the other shore.

I was sensibly afflicted at the destiny of my worthy friend; and so indeed were all that had the honour of knowing him. But his wife took on so extravagantly, that she in a short time was the only talk both of city and country. She refused to admit any visits from her

nearest relations: her chamber, her ante-chamber, and pro-
ante-chamber were hung with black, nay, the very candles,
her fans and tea table wore the livery of grief: she refused
all manner of sustenance and was so averse to the thoughts
of living that she talked of nothing but death.   In short,
you may tell your ingenious friend Monsieur de Saint
Evremond, that Petronius's Ephesian matron, to whose
story he has done so much justice in his noble translation,
was only a type of our more obstinate as well as unhappy
German widow.

About a fortnight after this cruel loss, for I thought it
would be labour lost to attack her grief in its first
vehemence, I thought myself obliged, in point of honour
and gratitude to the memory of my deceased friend, to
make her a small visit and condole her ladyship upon
this unhappy occasion: and though I had been told that
she had refused to see several persons who had gone to
wait on her with the same errand, yet I presumed so
much upon the friendship her late husband had always
expressed for me, not to mention the particular civilities
I had received from herself, as to think I should be ad-
mitted to have a sight of her.   Accordingly I came to
her house, sent up my name, and word was immediately
brought me that if I pleased I might go up to her.

When I came into the room I fancied myself in the
territories of death: everything looked so gloomy, so
dismal and so melancholy.   There was a grave Lutheran
minister with her, who omitted no arguments to bring
her to a more composed and more Christian disposition
of mind.   'Madam,' says he, 'you don't consider that,
by abandoning yourself thus to despair, you actually rebel
against Providence.'   'I can't help it,' says she, 'Providence may e'en thank itself for laying so insupportable
a load upon me.'   'O fie, madam,' cries the other,
'this is downright impiety: what would you say now, if

heaven should punish it by some more exemplary visitation?' 'That is impossible,' replies the lady, sighing, 'and,
since it has robbed me of the only delight I had in this
world, the only favour it can do me is to level a thunder-
bolt at my head and put an end to all my sufferings.' The
parson, finding her in this extravagant strain and seeing
no likelihood of persuading her to come to a better
temper, got up from his seat and took his leave of her.

It came to my turn now to try whether I was not
capable of comforting her; and being convinced by so
late an instance that arguments brought from religion
were not like to work any extraordinary effects upon
her, I resolved to attack her ladyship in a more sensible
part and represent to her the great inconveniences, not
which her soul but her body received from this inordinate
sorrow.

'Madam,' says I to her, 'next to my concern for your
worthy husband's untimely death, I am grieved to see
what an alteration the bemoaning of his loss has occasioned
in you.' These words raising her curiosity to know what
this alteration was, I thus continued my discourse. 'In
endeavouring, Madam, to extinguish, or at least to
alleviate, your grief, than which nothing can be more
prejudicial to a beautiful woman, I intend a public benefit;
for, if the public is interested, as most certainly it is,
in the preserving of a beautiful face, that man does the
public no little service who contributes most to its
preservation.'

This odd beginning operated so wonderfully upon her
that she desired me to 'leave this general road of compliments and explain myself more particularly to her.'
Upon this, delivering myself with an unusual air of
gravity, which your Grace knows I seldom carry about
me in the company of ladies, I told her that 'Grief ruins
the finest faces sooner than anything whatever'; and

that ' as Envy herself could not deny her face to be the most charming in the universe, so, if she did not suffer herself to be comforted, she must soon expect to take her farewell of it.' I confirmed this assertion by telling her of one of the finest women we ever had in England who did herself more injury in a fortnight's time by lamenting her only brother's death than ten years could possibly have done; that I had heard an eminent physician at Leyden say that tears, having abundance of saline particles in them, not only spoiled the complexion, but hastened wrinkles. ' But, Madam,' concluded I, ' why should I give myself the trouble to confirm this by foreign instances and by the testimonies of our most knowing doctors when, alas! your own face so fully justifies the truth of what I have said to you.'

' How! ' replied our disconsolate widow, with a sigh that came from the bottom of her heart: ' and is it possible that my just concern for my dear husband has wrought so cruel an effect upon me in so short a time? ' With that she ordered her gentlewoman to bring the looking glass to her, and, having surveyed herself a few minutes in it, she told me she was perfectly convinced that my notions were true. ' But,' cries she, ' what would you have us poor women do in these cases? for something,' continues she, ' we owe to the memory of the deceased, and something, too, to the world which expects at least the common appearances of grief from us.'

' By your leave, Madam,' says I, ' all this is a mistake, no better; you owe nothing to your husband since he is dead and knows nothing of your lamentation. Besides, could you shed an ocean of tears upon his hearse, it would not do him the least service: much less do you lie under any such obligations to the world as to spoil a good face only to comply with its tyrannic customs. No, Madam, take care to preserve your beauty, and then let the world say what it pleases; your ladyship may be revenged upon the world whene'er you see fit.' 'I am resolved,' answers she, ' to be entirely governed by you; therefore, tell me frankly, what sort of a course you'd have me steer?' 'Why, Madam,' says I, 'in the first place forget the defunct: and in order to bring that about, relieve nature, to which you have been so long unmerciful, with the most exquisite meats and the most generous wines.' 'Upon condition you'll sup with me,' cries our afflicted lady, 'I will submit to your prescription.' But why should I trouble your Grace with a narration of every particular?

In short, we had a noble regale that evening in her bedchamber: and our good widow pushed the glass so strenuously about, that her comforter, meaning myself, could hardly find the way to his coach. To conclude this farce, which I am afraid begins now to be too tedious to your Grace, this phoenix of her sex, this pattern of conjugal fidelity, two mornings ago, was married to a smooth-chinned ensign of Count Trautmandorf's regiment, that had not a farthing in the world but his pay to depend upon! I assisted at the ceremony: though I little imagined the lady would take the matrimonial receipt so soon.

I was the easier persuaded to give your Grace a large· account of this tragi-comedy, not only because I wanted better matter to entertain you with at this lazy conjuncture, but also to show your Grace that not only Ephesus in ancient and England in later times, have afforded such fantastical widows, but even Germany itself: where, if the ladies have not more virtue than those of their sex in other countries, yet they pretend at least a greater management of the outside of it.

By my last packet from England, among a heap of nauseous trash, I received the ' Three Dukes of Dunstable '

which is really so monstrous and insipid that I am sorry
Lapland or Livonia had not the honour of producing it:
but, if I did penance in reading it, I rejoiced to hear that
it was so solemnly interred to the tune of cat-calls.
The 'Squire of Alsatia,' however, which came by the
following post, made me some amends for the cursed
impertinence of the 'Three Dukes' and my witty friend
Sir Charles Sedley's 'Bellamira' gave me that entire
satisfaction, that I cannot read it over too often.

They tell me my old acquaintance Mr. Dryden has left
off the theatre, and wholly applies himself to the study
of the controversies between the two churches. Pray
Heaven! this strange alteration in him portends nothing
disastrous to the state; but I have all along observed, that
Poets do religion as little service by drawing their
pens for it, as the Divines do poetry by pretending to
versification.

But I forget how troublesome I have been to your
Grace. I shall therefore conclude with assuring you that I
am, and to the last moment of my life shall be, ambitious
of being,

My Lord
Your Grace's most obedient
And most obliged servant
G. ETHEREGE.

A WOMAN OF THE WORLD

The writer of this letter, witty in thought and phrasing,
illiterate to an almost incredible degree in spelling and punctuation, was Nell Gwyn, ' that indiscretest and wildest creature
that ever was in a Court.' Eight years before she had become
the King's mistress, retiring, though not altogether, both from
the stage (which she had long adorned as an irresistible
comedienne) and other men's arms to revive in an unofficial

capacity the office of Jester Royal. To the end of Charles's days she remained as an unaccountable and refreshingly irreverent opposition to the reigning mistress; when the Duchess of Portsmouth went into half mourning for a French prince with whom she claimed kinship, Nelly put on black from head to foot for the Cham of Tartary, and, when the mob hooted her coach under the impression that it was that of her Catholic rival, popped her head out of the window with a ' Good people! I am the Protestant whore! '

About this time Nelly was causing a good deal of heart-burning in ministerial circles by the supper parties she gave to leaders of the Opposition : to make matters worse the King himself sometimes attended these gatherings of the ' merry gang.' Her correspondent Lawrence Hyde—' chit Lorry '—afterwards Lord Treasurer and Earl of Rochester of the second creation, was the somewhat mercurial younger son of the great Earl of Clarendon, and was at this time at The Hague on diplomatic business.

Mrs. Knight, the singer, and Lady Green were rivals in the catholic affections of the King. Thomas Shadwell was an Opposition poet, victim of Dryden's cruel line,

For Shadwell never deviates into sense.

Joseph Harris, the actor, a friend of Pepys, was the chief pillar of the Duke of York's playhouse.

Lord Burford and Lord Beauclerk were sons of Nell Gwyn by Charles II.

TO LAWRENCE HYDE FROM NELL GWYN.

Undated, but probably June, 1678.[13]

Pray dear Mr. Hyde, forgive me for not writing to you before now. For the reason is I have been sick three months, and since I recovered I have had nothing to entertain you withall, nor have nothing now worth writing, but that I can hold no longer to let you know I never have been in any company without drinking your health, for I love you with all my soul. The Pall Mall is now to me a dismal place since I have utterly lost Sir Carr Scrope, never to be recovered again. For he told me he could not live always at this rate, and so begun to be a little uncivil, which I could not suffer from an ugly *beau garçoṇ*.

Mrs. Knight's lady mother's dead, and she has put up a *'scutchin* no bigger than my Lady Green *scunchis*. My Lord Rochester is gone in the country. Mr. Savile has got a misfortune, but is upon recovery and is to marry an heiress, who, I think, won't have an ill time on't if he holds up his thumb. My Lord of Dorset appears once in three months, for he drinks ale with Shadwell and Mr. Harris at the Duke's house all day long.

My Lord Burford remembers his service to you. My Lord Beauclerk is going into France. We are a' going to sup with the King at Whitehall and my Lady Harvey. The King remembers his service to you.

Now let's talk of state affairs, for we never carried things so cunningly as now, for we don't know whether we shall have peace or war. But I am for war, and for no other reason but that you may come home.

I have a thousand merry conceits. But I can't make her write 'em, and therefore you must take the will for the deed. Goodbye. Your most loving, obedient, faithful and humble

Servant,

E. G.

CHAPTER IX

FOOD AND FELLOWSHIP

IN WINE IS TRUTH

The seventeenth century was an age of good fellowship: life was rough and drinking made it pass more easily. Even the children drank small beer, though some, like little Roger North, found it ' disgustful ' to their ' tender palates,' and men of all classes made every occasion of life an excuse to step aside and take a cup of ale or wine. So Anthony Wood, after a visit to Gloucester Cathedral, ' went to the tavern with one or two of the choir, drank a glass of wine and had a song.'

The age's idea of a holiday was usually a debauch, and some places seemed to keep almost perpetual holiday. ' And so,' wrote sober, pious William Blundell during a visit to Liverpool, ' in as good a case as this drunken town will permit at four in the afternoon.' There were drunken men as well as drunken towns. Among the squires of the bottle none was greater than Sir William Scroggs, King's serjeant and later Lord Chief Justice of England. Born in Oxfordshire, the son of a Smithfield butcher and ' a big fat woman with a red face like an ale wife ' and bred at Oriel and Pembroke Colleges, Scroggs was famed for his loud voice, boisterous manners and brazen countenance.

Weald Hall was the manor in Essex which he purchased in 1667. Christopher, first Lord Hatton, was his life-long friend and later married one of his own sons to Scroggs' youngest daughter. Of Scroggs' first letter, Sir Edward Maunde Thomp-

son, the learned editor who transcribed the Hatton correspondence for the Camden Society, wrote, ' Scroggs must have been drinking his Lordship's health pretty freely before he began the letter, to judge from the drunken appearance of the handwriting.'

Wine was mostly imported into England privately in hogshead, terse or runlet and subsequently bottled by the gentry and the keepers of taverns in their own cellars.   Lord Hatton, residing in Guernsey, was well placed to help Scroggs in this respect. The limpets never seen in England, referred to in Scroggs' second letter, were probably ' ormiers ' or ' oreilles de mers,' a species of shellfish.

TO CHRISTOPHER, VISCOUNT HATTON, GOVERNOR OF GUERNSEY, FROM SIR WILLIAM SCROGGS.

12 *September*, 1673.[1]

My Lord,

The worst name I can call you by; for when you were a commoner and an honest man you had plain thoughts, and believed that promises ought to be performed and that he that said: 'I'll send you a hogshead' had but meanly kept his word in sending but two.   But now you, like them that pretend so much to religion that they are above ordinances, think it dishonourable to your title to keep your word, and that by your dignity you must falsify lest you become like that low sort of people that keep faith.   Sir, I am much wronged by you in preventing me from buying of wine at £6 a hogshead that must now cost me £10, depending very foolishly on one that I ought to have known before.   I know now that pirates and the dangers of seas must be your excuse; but why wine could not as safely come as cider I understand not, unless there be articles for apples but not for grapes, or that the vigour of one would make it safe, but the cowardice of wine would turn it into vinegar.

o

My Lord, pray know that I am (though not the best performer) yet the greatest exacter of promises that will never be answered by reason but the thing itself; and think that reasonable to be made into a law that whatsoever is promised ought to be performed, whether it can or no; for though it were sometimes impossible, yet that were better to condemn than suffer the excuses that will ever be made by [your] Lordship.

I can have no better reason for establishing impossibilities by law than my Lord Hatton, who otherwise will make all things impossible. I could willingly rail on, but can write no more than

W. S.

If hogsheads were as cheap as warrants I had received them.

To my Lady my real service; to Saunterer, my love, like hers. In great haste to drink your Lordship's health.

TO Viscount Hatton from Sir William Scroggs.

1673.[2]

My Lord,

You say very true, wine is answered with nothing but wine. If anything or anybody else could have done it otherwise, it must have been your Lordship, in whom there is much art, but in wine is truth. Your present was spoiled before your brother received it. We broke ope the coffin at his house, wherein we found only the furniture of a coffin, corruption. Those limpets that were never seen in England lack wine to make 'em taste; and I will take it that your Lordship keeps your word, that you send what was yet never seen in England when you send the next hogsheads.

My Lord, you must not take it ill if I write of nothing

but wine, for there is nothing I want more nor of which I can better write or more willingly—with this difference only, that wine wrote for has not half that elegancy as wine thanked for.

I am glad to hear your Lordship is like to come over, because then you will bring wine infallibly; for you know you must show your face and see Weald Hall. In short, I rely upon you in that matter and let Christmas take its fortune accordingly.

Having vented my passion of love to wine, my next good subject is of railing against women, and in the first place at your sisters, who, by the conduct of your brother and his lady, haunt my chamber oftener than a pauper and with much greater trouble, for they only [do] not give, but these plunder what others give. I want your company to redress that too. Prithee, my dear Lord, make haste . . . and that's an answer to the compliment you gave him that is too much a friend to need one, because I am all love and all yours.

W. S.

DRINKING WILL THESE DOUBTS DISPEL

In the next two letters, two very different men breathe their love of wine: the Earl of Rochester, fast approaching the end of his brief tragic life in country retirement, and William Blundell, the poor, prudent, persecuted Catholic squire of Crosby, Lancs. The ' black and fair Countess ' of Rochester's letter was almost certainly Barbara, Countess of Castlemaine and Duchess of Cleveland.

William Blundell's letter was probably addressed to his grandson's tutor, ' a lay gentleman of good parts and reputation,' with whom he had just left the boy at the Jesuits' College at La Flèche in France.

TO HARRY SAVILE FROM THE EARL OF ROCHESTER.

Bath, 22 June [1679?].[3]

Whether Love, Wine or Wisdom (which rule you by turns) have the present ascendant I cannot pretend to determine at this distance; but good nature, which waits about you with more diligence than Godfrey himself is my security that you are [not] unmindful of your absent friends. To be from you and forgotten by you at once is a misfortune I never was criminal enough to merit since to the black and fair Countess I villanously betrayed the daily addresses of your divided heart. You forgave that upon the first bottle, and upon the second, on my conscience, would have renounced them and the whole sex.

Oh! that second bottle, Harry, is the sincerest, wisest and most impartial downright friend we have; tells us truth of ourselves and forces us to speak truths of others; banishes flattery from our tongues and distrust from our hearts, sets us above the mean policy of court-prudence which makes us lie to one another all day for fear of being betrayed by each other at night. And, before God, I believe the arrantest villain breathing is honest as long as that bottle lives, and few of that tribe dare venture upon him, at least, among the courtiers and statesmen. I have seriously considered one thing, that [of] the three businesses of this age, Women, Politics and Drinking, the last is the only exercise at which you and I have not proved ourselves arrant fumblers. If you have the vanity to think otherwise, when we meet let us appeal to friends of both sexes, and, as they shall determine, live and die their drunkards or entire lovers. For, as we mince the matter, it is hard to say which is the most tiresome creature, loving drunkard or the drunken lover.

If you ventured your fat buttock a'gallop to Portsmouth, I doubt not but thro' extreme galling you now lie bedrid . . ., and have the leisure to write to your country-acquaintance, which if you omit I shall take the liberty to conclude you very proud. Such a letter should be directed to me at Adderbury, near Banbury, where I intend to be within these three days.

> Bath, the 22nd of June, from
> Your obedient humble servant,
> ROCHESTER.

PROBABLY TO MR. WASHINGTON AT LA FLÊCHE, FRANCE, FROM WILLIAM BLUNDELL.

Crosby, 29 *December*, 1681.[4]

Worthy Sir,

I am now at home, just as you may imagine a man who has left your good wine and purer air of France for the grosser liquors and thick fogs of a cold northern climate. No such thing as health as yet have I met with here for as much as concerns myself. My cough became most violent, my bed was intolerable to me and I spent whole nights in my chair. At the present I can stand on my own lame legs again; but if my cold be pleased to leave me with the first of the next spring it is full as much as I look for. You see what penance I am now doing for my late excess at La Flêche. Yet if you be wise, defer that painful point of piety for as much as concerns yourself till you come to another world, and leave not the spot you stand on for a purgatory so painful here. I do give you an account of my ill that you may measure your own good by it, and accordingly value the same.

. . . Sir, I desire you to present my respects to all my good friends and benefactors. And when you are resolved to enjoy yourself and your friends, and that the

pretty maid of your house brings out that lovely white
bottle of sparkling wine, remember—oh! remember then
the miseries that muddy ale have brought upon mortal
man! Be thankful for your own condition, commiserate
this of mine, and take one glass extraordinary to the better
health of

Your much discomposed,

Yet constant friend and servant,

W. B.

IN VINDICATION OF ALE

*The miseries of muddy ale that so distressed sixty-year-old
William Blundell did not lie heavy on all Englishmen. Ale
was the national drink of England, and it was generally held
that the further north one went the better it was. In this letter
a Cheshire squire reminds a young relative in London of the
virtues of his native liquor.*

TO GEORGE SHAKERLEY IN LONDON FROM HIS
BROTHER-IN-LAW, CHARLES HURLESTON.

Circa 1700.[5]

Dear Brother,

I am sorry to hear that our Chester ale hath so ill
a report there, but do not at all wonder at it, by reason
that noble liquor has so many enemies. I mean such as
cannot compass it at so great a distance or your stumared
claret drinkers that lies languishing under so many distempers and advances your Bills of Mortality to such a
prodigious quantity. Here we are free from any distemper at all, unless it be such as yourself, that get a heat
and a cold in the playhouse or the puny coffee drinkers.
But such as myself that sits still and takes a cup of
Cottingham, he is fit for hunting, setting, coursing or any

noble recreation, and not to stay at home in their chambers to receive messages from the ladies to desire to know how they do and they hope you are no worse for staying out so late, etc. These and many other arguments I could use in vindication of our Chester ale, but know it needless to urge it to one that knows the goodness of it so well. . . .

GOOD FELLOWS IN STATE

The chapter would not be complete without an example of the state feasting and drinking which was so important a part of seventeenth century ceremony. Robert Paston, first Lord Yarmouth of Oxnead, Norfolk, who figures as the hero of this letter, was High Steward of Great Yarmouth and Vice-Admiral of Norfolk. A little earlier in the year he had entertained the King at Oxnead, and here we see him receiving the loyal entertainment of his own little kingdom of Great Yarmouth.

TO LADY YARMOUTH FROM JOHN FISHER.

Oxnead, 1 October, 1675.[6]

. . . About one o'clock yesterday after breakfast as they called it, but more truly a very great dinner, my Lord and all the gentlemen with him, the old and new Bailiffs, and several of the Aldermen (who never left his Lordship) marched off in the same way and like parade as we came in (though not with as many horse), passing by a new great ship just fitted to be launched as we came away. And thus we went along the market side of the town, the new Bailiffs and several of the townsmen riding before my Lord's coach, and the old Bailiffs, with the knights of the town and others, following in my Lord's coach, in their own, and without the gates, an honest gunner (who

saluted my Lord at his alighting at the Bailiff's door, when
he came in with above 20 potguns), bade his Lordship
farewell again with the like number. And thus we were
sent away with a powder, which is one signal testimony
of the affection of the town. . . .

Lest my Lord should not be satisfied or well pleased
with the variety of provisions, for which they had ransacked the earth, water, and air, they would not let the
fourth element escape, but before his Lordship was quite
risen from dinner, or just turning about from the table,
for a fourth course they brought in a man to show his
Lordship the experiment how fire might be eaten without damage or hurt for such whose stomachs were prepared for it or were not satisfied with those dainties we
had received. But this countryman of ours gave us our
fill of this immediately, and we left him to his own
peculiar diet, nobody that I saw being willing to taste
on't. . . .

I must not omit their generosity in clearing my Lord
and all his followers of all charges for horse meat and other
expenses in the several inns, which was an additional
demonstration of their kindness and the more acceptable,
by being unexpected. My Lord would have gratified
several officers of the town, but we were informed it
would not be accepted, nor the offering it well taken,
so his Lordship ordered £5 to the servants in the Bailiff's
house where he lay and had received all their civilities,
and £10 more for the poor. And now I am got on to
the Downs again, where, at the rails, being the extent
of their jurisdiction a mile out of the town, the old
Bailiffs and Knights with Sir William Adams and others
took their leaves of my Lord, the new Bailiffs and several
Aldermen, Justices, etc., riding on still a mile further
to Caister (where we first met them on Tuesday), and
would have attended his Lordship yet further (he

persuaded them to the contrary), and there with mutual embraces and a bottle of excellent wine, they sang *Loth to depart.* But by this time it was two o'clock, and the length of my Lord's journey made us break up, and so with their hearty good wishes for his Lordship's health and prosperity, they returned back to the town and we hastened hither. . . .

CHAPTER X

TRAVELLING

The epoch that began with the Restoration and closed with the accession of Queen Anne was the last in which travel in England was a major adventure. In the next age the turnpike road, the canal and the fast mail coach were to begin that unification of the island which the railway was to complete. But in the later seventeenth century the soft unmetalled highways, subjected to an ever-growing volume of wheeled traffic, were as bad as ever they had been in the Middle Ages and in many places considerably worse. ' I had a sad mischance coming from London with my wife and servants in the Aylesbury coach,' wrote one traveller, ' for the coach overturned and fell on the side I sat of, and those in the coach fell on me, and thereby put one hip out of joint and mightily strained the joint of my other hip and my back bones are displaced.' Even the London streets were sometimes impassable; Charles II was forced to beg Parliament for legislation to repair the highways round Whitehall lest his bride should find her new home surrounded by water, while seven years later, in 1669, the Bishop of Durham complained that, though his town stable, coach and horses were very costly, he could not use them, ' for I am come to that pass that I cannot endure to go upon the stones in these streets, which are so full of broken holes and gutters that I am fain to use a chair every day to Whitehall and Parliament.' *

* Correspondence of John Cosin, Bishop of Durham (Surtees Soc., 1870), ii. 209–10.

Private coaches, usually drawn by six shire horses or Flemish mares, had been a feature of the roads since the beginning of the century. But as the two letters which follow show, they were an uncertain and expensive form of travel, especially when they began to grow old: ' I wish the new wheels had come up with my coach,' *wrote one magnate,* ' for these old wheels break every time they go out. On Saturday I was at Little Chelsea and they cost two shillings mending. Yesterday I was at Islington and they cost me three shillings for broken strakes.'

For those who wished to travel quickly the post horse was the swiftest and safest medium. Post horses could be hired from the government postmasters along all the main roads at threepence a mile, with an extra fourpence for the guide at each stage, and thus mounted one could hope to cover a steady ten or twelve miles an hour. Many, like young Ralph Verney, who was always sick in a coach, far preferred to travel this way. In the third letter a servant of the Duchess of Ormonde, wife of the Lord-Lieutenant of Ireland, describes to the Duke's secretary a journey made post along the winter roads from Holyhead to Stone in Staffordshire.

TO SIR RALPH VERNEY AT CLAYDON FROM MRS. MARGARET ELMES.

Covent Garden, 24 October, 1661.[1]

Dear Brother,

To say so much as your favours commands me is beyond my reach and altogether impossible for me to do, so I beg your excuse for all errors in me and to accept of my real thanks.

For the disasters in our journey to London, they were so many and so great that I know you would a' laughed sufficiently at me had you but seen them. In the first place our horses tired as soon as we came out of Chalfont, for there was no fresh ones to be had. It was near eight o'clock before we got to Leicester House corner. When we were in all that fine puddle, we had like to a' been overturned but escaped it by having the coach held up while we alighted in that clean place. And when we were out, the coachman made shift to drive his coach into such a place as he could not pass through for posts. Neither could he put back again, so we were forced to walk from that place to Covent Garden afoot, and not only so, but to take out all that was had in the coach along with us, for the coach was likely to stand in the fields all night. My brother Harry was with us, but the Squire and Martin were gone home a' horseback. Harry was loaded like a porter between his own things and his dame's. You may guess what a cleanly case I was in, and how she was pleased with it that is, dear brother

Your affectionate sister and servant
M. ELMES.

To WILLIAM COLEMAN FROM SIR J. VERNEY.

16 June, 1697.[2]

. . . I'd not have it known but to yourself, I reckon to be at Claydon between the 7th and 11th of July. . . . There will come in my coach myself, my wife and my three daughters, Perry behind and to ride on horseback by Hodges and Wallis, besides the keeper that may come up with the horses, but you must consider who shall look to the Park a' night in his absence. . . . There will be three maids to come down, they must go in the Stage Coach, but then I know not how to get them from Aylesbury. We can't spare 'em until we go ourselves, and then when we come there my wife will want her maid, so they must not stay long after us neither.

So pray consider whether you can hire three horses

for 'em that would carry double, and men to go fetch 'em
and open the gates for 'em. . . . I write so long before
that I may have your thoughts of it. . . . All my horses
will be on the road to bring me down; that's the reason
that I shall be so put to it to get the maids to Claydon. . . .

TO SIR GEORGE LANE FROM JAMES BUCK.

Stone, 18 *January*, 1663.[3]

As I remember you were so kind as to command me
to give you an account of my landing, upon which
score I shall do it and to let you know how far I am in
pursuit of those commands laid upon me, else it could
not be worth your trouble. Upon Thursday night,
about ten o'clock, I landed at Holyhead, and that you may
see duty has wings, I did immediately (without the fond
assistance of caudle or buttered ale) take horse and make
no stay till I came to Stone this day, being about two
o'clock.

So that I rode, the ways being very bad, a hundred miles
in less than two days. And you may say 'twas well rode
little gent., being now within twenty miles of the place
whither I am commanded, but thought it unfit to go
thither in an unseasonable hour of the night to give them
an alarm, but stay and rest myself till Monday to be there
in a more fitting hour and appear with all cheerful kindness from their friends. And then I shall give a just
account to those that are most concerned.

But give me leave to return a little to my journey.
Yesterday, betwixt Denbigh and Chester, I met a gentleman riding post in his shoes and stockings, a close coat
with a high-crowned hat and a falling band, the post-boy
blowing his horn very fiercely all the way before him.
And being something curious to know what knight errant

this was, by enquiry at the next stage I came to I found him to be one indeed, for he told the people there that he came from the Countess of Chesterfield, daughter to the Duke of Ormonde, and that he was going to the Duke in a great concernment, and was to stay but five hours in Ireland. All which in my opinion did look as madly in its kind as any thing that was done before. By this time I suppose you know more of him, but I supposed his business to be very good or very bad. But had the two knights errant known each other upon the rencontre, 'tis hoped the knight of the spurs might have had the better of it by way of discovery, and made some advantage of it. But I resolved to take no notice of any such person, who put me in mind of St. George that relieved the distressed damsel.

And now, Sir, I hope you will desire me to write no more to you upon so slender an occasion as my particular safety, but if you please you may let her Grace know how far I am got, and how near I am to give her Grace an account of her commands. . . .

[Postscript.]—The last night here fell a great deal of snow, and now 'tis very cold and travelling will be very bad.

THE PUBLIC COACH

Stage coaches were the principal contribution of the seventeenth century to the amenities of English travel. After the Restoration they sprang up all over the country. Judged by modern standards they were neither fast nor comfortable— clumsy, boxlike vehicles, usually made of black leather and swung on leather straps, with wooden shutters or flaps for windows, they jolted at thirty or forty miles a day up and down every main road in England. But to those who remembered the country before the Civil Wars they appeared almost unbelievably fast: ' in four days and a half from Garswood to London,' wrote Lancashire William Blundell, ' it seems to be almost incredible.'

Every coach had its own particular inn of call in the towns along its route, where horses were changed, travellers taken up or set down, and where would-be patrons could engage their places and obtain particulars of the times of service.

The query about Lord Craven's fire spies during Charles Hatton's search for his inn is an allusion to William, Earl of Craven, the old Cavalier, who made it his life's work to organise fire-fighters in Restoration London. Mr. Ebriel was a North-ampton saddler, who took in letters and parcels for Lord Hatton and his family.

The two letters from John Dryden describing his journeys by coach were sent to his cousin, Mrs. Steward, after staying with her at her Northamptonshire home, Cotterstock. The fat woman in the coach who so often reminded the company in the coach of the frailties of her mortal nature, still, by the virtue of the poet's genius, remains flesh and blood, like the Wife of Bath or Juliet's nurse or Sairey Gamp. To ' smicker ' is defined in Kersey's Dictionary of 1708 as ' to look amorously or wantonly.'

To Christopher Viscount Hatton from Charles Hatton.

14 Dec., 1676.[4]

My Lord,

Last Monday I received yours of the 9th inst. and was very glad to hear you got so safe to Easton. According to your order therein, I desired Mademoiselle de la Chappele to see the Lady Anne Grimston, and accordingly she did. And I desired her to be at an hour's readiness, whensoever she should receive your orders to go down.

But, your Lordship taking no notice in your letter when you would have her go, made me imagine you did not design it left this week.   But last night, at eleven of the clock (the extremity of bad weather occasioned the delivery of the letters so late), I received yours of the 12 inst., wherein you desired Mademoiselle should go down as to-day.

It was too late then either to advertise her or take a place in the coach.   But this morning, betwixt three or four of the clock, I got up and was to go to White Hart Yard in Drury Lane; whereabouts in Drury Lane I knew not.   There was so great a fog and it was so extremely cold that betwixt my house and Drury Lane I met no living creature.   And when I was in Drury Lane, that I might be directed to White Hart Yard, I was forced to knock up somebody, and over against Drury House I knocked at a door.   And everybody in the house being fast asleep, I was necessitated to knock very loud.   And at last a man clapped his head out at a window, and (that which was very pleasant) he, imagining I was one of my Lord Craven's fire-spies, the first words he said to me was: ' Where is the fire, Sir, where is the fire? '   I humoured him in his error, for fear of warm water being flung on my head, and told him in Southwark.   He then asked whether my Lord knew of it.   I told him I could not tell, but I was going to inform one who was concerned that lived in White Hart Yard, which how to find he gave me very punctual directions and desired to know who it was.   But I thought it not convenient to name anybody, but left him, and found Mr. Housdan's house; and, when I had knocked them up, I acquainted them with the reason of my disturbing them.

But Mademoiselle la Chappele would very desirously have deferred going down till the next opportunity of the coach, which I thought might have been displeasing to your Lordship. And I fully satisfied her that it was absolutely necessary she should go this day, for, should it thaw, perhaps the coach might not be able to pass of a week or ten days. And when I had prevailed with her to resolve to go as this day, I went to Smithfield and it was but five of the clock when I got thither. And, when I had taken a place in the coach, I went and fetched Mademoiselle, and, with an address to Mr. Ebriel, I recommended her to the care of the passengers and saw her trunk delivered to the carrier. I gave her twenty shillings in money, paid fifteen shillings for her passage, and for coach hire, porter, and breakfast I paid four shillings and sixpence more.

Your truly affectionate Brother to serve you,

C. HATTON.

To Mrs. Steward from John Dryden.

Tichmarsh, Northants. 23 *November,* 1698.[5]
Madam,

To take acknowledgements of favours for favours done you, is only yours. I am always on the receiving hand; and you, who have been pleased to be troubled so long with my bad company, instead of forgiving, which is all I could expect, will turn it to a kindness on my side. If your house be often so molested, you will have reason to be weary of it before the ending of the year and wish Cotterstock were planted in a desert, an hundred miles off from any poet.

After I had lost the happiness of your company, I could expect no other than the loss of my health, which followed according to the proverb that misfortunes seldom come alone. I had no woman to visit but the parson's wife; and she, who was intended by nature as a helpmeet for a deaf husband, was somewhat of the loudest for my conversation, and for other things, I will say no more than that she is just your contrary and an epitome of her own country.

My journey to London was yet more unpleasant than my abode at Tichmarsh, for the coach was crowded up with an old woman fatter than any of my hostesses on the road. Her weight made the horses travel very heavily. But, to give them a breathing time, she would often stop us, and plead some necessity of nature, and tell us we were all flesh and blood. But she did this so frequently that at last we conspired against her and, that she might not be inconvenienced by staying in the coach, turned her out in a very dirty place where she was to wade up to the ankles before she could reach the next hedge. When I was rid of her, I came sick home and kept my house for three weeks together. . . .

TO Mrs. Steward at cotterstock near oundle in northamptonshire from John Dryden.
28 *September*, 1699.[6]

Madam,

Your goodness to me will make you solicitous of my welfare since I left Cotterstock. My journey has in general been as happy as it could be without the satisfaction and honour of your company. 'Tis true the master of the stage-coach has not been over civil to me, for he turned us out of the road at the first step and made us go to Pilton. There we took in a fair young lady of eighteen and her brother, a young gentleman; they are related to the Treshams, but not of that name. Thence we drove to Higham, where we had an old serving-woman and a young fine maid: we dined at Bletso and lay at Silso six miles beyond Bedford. There we put out the old woman and took in Councillor Jennings his daughter; her father going along in the Kettering coach, or riding by it, with other company. We all dined at Hatfield together and came to town safe at seven in the evening.

We had a young doctor, who rode by our coach and seemed to have a smickering to our young lady of Pilton, and ever rode before to get dinner in a readiness. My son, Charles, knew him formerly a Jacobite; and now going over to Antigua, with Colonel Codrington, having been formerly in the West Indies.

Which of our two young ladies was the handsomer, I know not. My son liked the Councillor's daughter best: I thought they were both equal. But not going to Tichmarsh Grove, and afterwards by Catworth, I missed my two couple of rabbits which my cousin, your father, had given me to carry with me, and could not see my sister by the way. I was likewise disappointed of Mr. Cole's Ribadavia wine. But I am almost resolved to sue the stage-coach for putting me six or seven miles out of the way, which he cannot justify.

Be pleased to accept my acknowledgement [for] all your favours, and my cousin Steward's; and by employing my son and me in anything you desire to have done, give us occasion to take our revenge on our kind relations both at Oundle and Cotterstock. Be pleased, your father, your mother, your two fair sisters and your brother may find my son's service and mine made acceptable to them by your delivery; and believe me to be with all manner of gratitude, give me leave to add, all manner of adoration,

Madam,
Your most obliged obedient servant,

JOHN DRYDEN.

CROSSING THE THAMES

Bridges in the seventeenth century were the exception rather than the rule, and travellers had constantly to negotiate streams, the smaller by ford, and the larger by ferry boat. Even London had only one bridge, and the Thames at Westminster had to be negotiated by boat. The 'Westminster Bridge' referred to in Wallis's letter was only a pier projecting into the water.

Dr. John Wallis, the mathematician and one of the original founders of the Royal Society, was eighty-three at the time of writing this letter and had been Savilian Professor of Geometry at Oxford for half a century.

TO SAMUEL PEPYS FROM DR. JOHN WALLIS.

Oxford, 24 *October,* 1699.[7]

Sir,

In a letter of yours to Dr. Charlet I find you are pleased to speak kindly of me. . . .

Of your queries to Mr. Hudson, I doubt he will be able to give you but a small account from old historians. I doubt scarce any better than that of Acts XXVII. I can partly guess, by a little experience I once had in a short voyage, if I may so call it, from Stangate Hole (I think it is so called) to Westminster Bridge. I had one Sunday preached for Mr. Gataker at Redriff, and lodged there that night. Next morning I walked with him over the fields to Lambeth, meaning there to cross the Thames to Westminster. He showed me in the passage divers remains in several places of the old channel which had been heretofore made from Redriff to Lambeth for diverting the Thames while London Bridge was building (all in a straight line, or near it, but with great intervals, which had been long since filled up). Those remains, which then appeared very visible, are, I suppose, all or most of them filled up before this time, for it is more than fifty years ago, and people in those marshes would be more fond of so much meadow grounds than to let those lakes remain unfilled. And he told me of many other such remains which had been within his memory but were then filled up. But thus much by the way.

When we came to Stangate Hole (over against Westminster Bridge) we took a boat in a thick mist, intending for Westminster Bridge, just across the water. When we had been at sea (for so I must call it) three times as long as would have been sufficient for the voyage, we made land, and discovered a shore with flags and reeds, and found ourselves within a bow-shot of the place from whence we first launched. We then put to sea again, and when we had a second time spent about as much time, we met another vessel just on head of us; we hailed the boat and asked whither they were bound; they said to Westminster (in a course directly opposite to ours), and found, upon discourse, that we were going directly to London Bridge and were about as low as Whitehall or further. I expostulated with our seamen how it was possible they could so mistake, and thought they might at least know whether they rowed with tide or against tide. They told me, no; if they were at anchor they could see which way the stream ran; but, being in motion, they could only know what strokes they made with their oars, but knew not what way they made at each stroke unless they could see the shore; nor was there any wind stirring whereby to direct their course. I then told them, if they could now set themselves right, I would be their steersman to hold on the same course. It was now winter, and a thick mist, and in such case (though little wind stirring) we might discern the motion of our own breath; and, by observing this, I could see when we varied from the course designed, and accordingly directed them to row more to the right or left hand as there was occasion; and by this steerage we came within the noise of the people at Westminster Bridge, and then made up to them.

Now if we had thus been wandering (for about half an hour or more) in so short a passage as just across the Thames, we may well conjecture at what pass those must be who, in the wide sea, without sight of land, had no help from sun, moon, or stars to direct their course, when as the magnetic helps were not yet known. . . . What better information Mr. Hudson may give you from ancient circumnavigations, I leave to him. And (having begged your pardon for the impertinences of a tedious letter), remain, Sir, your very humble servant,

JOHN WALLIS.

WAITING ON THE WIND

Those who wished to travel out of England were dependent on wind and tide for the time of their departure. This is amusingly illustrated by two letters from young John Jackson to his uncle, Samuel Pepys, who with the help of his old friend and man of business, Will Hewer, had just despatched him for a grand tour of France, Spain and Italy.

TO SAMUEL PEPYS IN LONDON FROM JOHN JACKSON.

Shoreham, 6 at night, 14 *October,* 1699.[8]

Honoured Sir,

With all the advantage which Mr. Hewer's kindness gave us in setting-out so early yesterday morning, we arrived not here till past 8 at night, but very safe and well,

I thank God. I found the master of the passage-boat at my inn and disposed to sail with the first fair wind; but that being contrary, and so continuing, I am still detained here, and God knows how much longer I may be so. I have made a shift to while away this day with unpacking and repacking my things to more advantage, and viewing what little there was to be seen of the town, etc.; but this being over, I fear I shall find every day I stay longer here more tiresome to me than my 50 miles riding yesterday.

There is nothing like a gentleman in the town. Mr. Luck, to whom Mr. Sergison recommended me, is one of the principal, and very civil in his way, but I not being capable of accepting his offers of a dram of cherry brandy or smoking a pipe, our conversation was very soon at an end; and I have no thoughts of qualifying myself for resuming it.

Twas a real affliction to me that the hurry of my departure allowed me not an opportunity of acknowledging in more particular manner my infinite obligations to you; but my hopes, Sir, are that you are in no doubt of my grateful sense of them, of which I shall yet labour more fully to convince you by my conduct on this occasion.

The Custom-House officers unexpectedly interrupting me, I am obliged to break off with begging your blessing and acceptance of my most humble duty, remaining, honoured Sir, Your most obliged and most dutiful nephew,

J. JACKSON.

I beg the favour of your giving my humble service to Mrs. Skinner, and to Mr. Hewer's and Sir James Houblon's families, and the rest of my friends.

TO SAMUEL PEPYS FROM JOHN JACKSON.

Shoreham, 17 October, 1699.[9]

Honoured Sir,

The wind coming-about this morning to the N.E., I was in great hopes we should have got off to-day; but it soon returned again to the S., and left me under greater affliction than ever. They tell me 'tis now (about 7 in the evening) near due East; and though this affords but few points for our course, yet if it stands there and the fair weather continues, I am assured we shall sail at high water to-morrow, which will be about noon.

I pray God we may. For when I consider the mien of my captain, I can doubt of anything that depends upon him. I am made to believe by all hands that he is indeed an able seaman, but I am sure he has one of the meanest tarpaulin-aspects, and the most of a sot in his looks, that I ever saw. And were it not that I am hourly informing myself by other seamen here, I should suspect he lost his opportunities, or had some by-ends in not going; wherein I see no authority to control him, or obtain the least satisfaction if it were so. Which may be reckoned amongst the inconveniences of this by-passage. His name is Wynne, one concerned in the transport-vessels during the war, and (as he owns to me himself) often laid by the heels for conveying over obnoxious persons.

I had destined this night for going to see the herring-fishing; but have been disappointed by my fishermen. Should it be my misfortune to be kept here to-morrow, I will not be prevented (with God's leave) in going out with them.

I humbly salute all my friends, and begging your blessing, remain, honoured Sir, Your most dutiful and obedient nephew,

J. JACKSON.

FOREIGN TRAVEL

In the next five letters we see Englishmen engaging in foreign travel—Samuel Pepys himself advised by that prince of virtuosos, Mr. Evelyn, on the rarities to be seen during his forthcoming holiday in France—the one which followed the close of his Diary and ended in the death of his wife; Sir Thomas Browne, corresponding with his sons during their studies abroad; and Sir Henry Chicheley, Governor of Virginia, writing to his niece in Cheshire from that ' barren part of the world.' The last letter shows the reverse of the picture—a poor Plymouth sailor captive in Algiers, one of the many thousands of unhappy English merchant seamen captured by Moorish pirates and kept as slaves under the African sun until death or, far more seldom, a ransom released them.

TO Samuel Pepys from John Evelyn.

Sayes Court, Deptford, 21 *August,* 1669.[10]

Sir,

I send you my rhapsodies, but know, that as soon as I had set pen to paper, I was diverted by a thousand accidents. Then I followed Mr. Cowley's funeral, but I sneaked from church, and when I came home (which was near five o'clock) an army of workmen (your wall-builders) and others, besieged me for money and to reckon with them. So as what I send you is snatches and night-work, and unconnected, which you must pardon, and if you judge it worthy it cause to be transcribed, for my running hand is an Arabic not to be endured.

But yours is a running voyage and desultory, and therefore you will the easier pardon me. There may be likewise diverse gross omissions, which you will best judge of when you come to Paris and begin to traverse the town, so as it is from you I shall expect to be paid with fresh and more material observations.

I could have set you down catalogues of many rare pictures and collections to be seen in that city, but you will every day meet with fresher intelligence. It is now many years since I was there, *et mutantur tempora, et mores, et homines.* Pray forget not to visit the *Taille-douce* shops, and make collection of what they have excellent, especially the drafts of their palaces, churches, and gardens, and the particulars you will have seen; they will greatly refresh you in your study, and by the fireside, when you are many years returned.

Israel, Sylvestre, Morin, Chauveau, are great masters, both for things of the kind extant, and inventions extremely pleasant. You will easily be acquainted with the best painters, especially Le Brun, who is the chief of them; and it would not be amiss to be present at their Academy, in which Monsieur du Bos (a principal Member) will conduct you. For the rest, I recommend you to God Almighty's protection, augur you a happy journey, and, kissing your Lady's hands, remain,

Sir,

Your most humble and obedient servant,

J. EVELYN.

TO THOMAS BROWNE FROM HIS FATHER, [SIR] THOMAS BROWNE.

Norwich, 21 *September*, 1661.[11]

Honest Tom,

I understood lately that you are come to Rochelle and intend to continue there for some months: do therein as you shall find it advantageous unto your intentions. We are all exceeding obliged to Mr. Bendish, to whom

I pray commend my respects; I shall be studious to find out some way of return unto him. Study the French language and help yourself by the grammar, forget not limning and perspective and daily practise arithmetic. Endeavour an handsome garb and laudable boldness, be courteous unto all, and betime practise patience. You may see the Isle of Rhé before winter and the salt works, observe the manner of the making of wine, both white and claret, and also of making oil, enquire whether it be usual to go up the Loire against the stream, for so you may go from Nantes or thereabouts to Orleans and so by coach to Paris, or over land with the messenger, when you shall be advised by friends to remove. I hope this box will come safe unto you. Serve God with all fidelity and God protect you. I rest your ever loving father,

T. B.

TO HIS FATHER, DR. THOMAS BROWNE, FROM MR. EDWARD BROWNE.

Genoa, 14 November, 1664.[12]

Sir,

I wrote to you the last week from Turin. I am now come to Genoa. Travelling in this country is more expensive than I could imagine, but the hopes of seeing the most remarkable places in Europe, and attaining that sweet language here spoken, doth still encourage me. I have been here already four days, and intend to-morrow or next day to go by sea to Lerici, a port of this state, about seventy miles off. Genoa is one of the best ports in these seas; hath a noble tower or pharo, the most stately one I ever beheld; the inhabitants exceeding rich; many palaces exceeding those of kings and princes in other parts. At Signor Imperiale his palace, I saw fish ponds built of marble and set about with statues; fish come upon whistling and follow one as he walks upon the side of the ponds. The orange and lemon trees are delightful and come to better perfection than in France. The water works are not to be expressed, they having a great convenience of the hill to make their water rise. This Imperiale hath five daughters, to every one whereof he gives in marriage about thirty thousand pound sterling. Out of his window he can see so much of his own as is of value unto him fifty pound sterling a day. The palace of Prince Doria is the most famous in the city; where is an aviary or bird cage of fourscore paces long and eighteen broad, very high, so that many trees grow under it. There are also fountains and many strange birds, where I saw an hen of Grand Cairo, &c. In the garden of this house is a fountain with Neptune riding upon three sea horses, one of the noblest in Italy. Strada Nova, or the new street, hath eleven palaces, and is reputed the fairest in Europe. I saw Francesco Maria Balbi his palace, furnished with pictures of old masters, also del Negro and the Duke of Genoa his palace, the senate house and the manner of choosing their officers. Their galleys much delighted me, but the poor slaves, and their miserable life, is a very pitiful spectacle.

ED. BROWNE.

TO MRS. LEGH OF LYME FROM SIR HENRY CHICHELEY, GOVERNOR OF VIRGINIA.

16 *February*, 1674.[13]

Dear Niece,

I had the good fortune (for all the dangers of the seas) to receive the hare's wool cloth for a petticoat for my wife, for which I return you many thanks. And had not the ship come in so late that all tobaccos had been in last, I had returned you what you desire in tobacco, but

this year I'm not so good as my word. The next shall
not fail to send you a parcel sorted out for your husband.

For news I suppose you expect none from this barren
part of the world, and for birds and squerritts, what is
sent by the seamen is so abused that seldom few or none
come to hands, they pretending the rats kill them, which
I confess are so numerous that I wonder they don't fall
foul of the ship's gang. I was glad to hear my cousin
Sarah was married, but I hear since (though it were with
her father's consent) yet he proves not so good either in
estate or condition as was expected.

I hope all your pretty little ones are in health, which
God grant they may long so continue, that shall always
be the prayers of, dear niece,

> Your affectionate uncle and humble servant
> HENRY CHICHELEY.

TO R. MITCHELL AT HIS HOUSE IN MOON LANE,
NEAR THE GREAT TREE, FROM RICHARD MITCHELL,
A POOR PLYMOUTH CAPTIVE IN ALGIERS.

14 *January*, 1679.[14]

My dear,

With my unspeakable love to thee and our poor
children, and my kind love to our parents and to all the
rest of our friends and acquaintance in general, having
now an opportunity to write I would not neglect it,
hoping of your good healths, as blessed be God I am in
at the present writing. My dear, to hear of your healths
and welfares would administer a great deal of comfort to
me in this my comfortless and destitute condition it hath
pleased the Lord to cast us into, I being with many
hundreds more taken by the Turks and brought into this
place, being sold.

To relate the sadness of our condition is beyond the

tongue of man to express, and little or no hopes of redemption. Oh! how it would make a heart of stone to weep to see the barbarous and inhuman usage of Christians in this place, some drawing carts like horses with irons of great weight upon their legs, with many a blow, and some, a hundred at a time, upon the bare soles of their feet with a thick rope; others carrying of dirt; others digging in the vineyards, with very small allowance of bread and water. And many others more barbarous usage than I am able to set down. The Lord bear up our spirits if it be His blessed will, and in His due time redeem us out of the hands of those unreasonable men.

There is a hundred and five English ships taken, sunk and burnt this war, and what will be the event of all God in his infinite wisdom knows best. If it would please the Lord to put into the King's heart, or the hearts of the country, to contrive some way for our redemption, it would be a happy thing, before the pestilence begin, which is every summer. It swept away last summer above eighteen hundred Christians. If it were the will of God I could heartily desire to see my native country once again, but if He have otherwise ordained it, the Lord satisfy all our spirits, and help us to live so in this world as we may meet together with joy and comfort in the world to come is the prayer of thy faithful and ever loving husband till death in captivity,

RICHARD MITCHELL.

THE MAILS

A chapter on travel would be incomplete without a reference to the mails. By Charles II's reign the principle, adopted early in the century, of giving the government the sole responsibility and profit of carrying letters had become firmly established, and

an adequate system was in operation on the main roads radiating from London, though little had yet been done to meet the needs of remote districts or to provide a cross-country post. Letters were usually paid for on delivery on a scale which involved a complicated and, as this letter reveals, somewhat uncertain calculation as to distance and the number of sheets used. A single sheet could be carried up to eighty miles from London for twopence.

A few of the drawbacks of our early postal system are here illustrated in the familiar form of a letter of complaint to the Postmaster.

TO THE COMPTROLLER OF THE POST OFFICE, LONDON, FROM WILLIAM BLUNDELL.

17 *December* [1673?].[15]

Sir,

I am the meanest of many thousands who enjoy the convenience of the post; yet do I adventure to tell you that I think there is some defect in these parts by the want of due order therein. We do sometimes find it needful to pay the post at Liverpool for such letters of ours as are to go thence to London, whereby it comes to pass that our letters do not seldom miscarry. And the cause I have found to be this: when our letters are paid for at Liverpool, according to what is there required, and are carried from thence to Warrington (as in their usual way to London) exception is often taken *there* against the payment endorsed, and our letters returned back for a pretended defect in the same, as being 6*d*. or 7*d*. less than is due for the bulk. Sundry of these letters from me and from others of my family have casually come back to our hands and the utter loss of divers other of our packets we do ascribe to the same cause.

Many years ago I made my verbal complaint of the very

same miscarriage. Your office in London, where I had a gentle hearing, gave promise of future redress. But the grievance hath been nothing abated, neither can there in my opinion be any amendment of the same unless the Master of the Post House at Liverpool may have such power to charge our letters upwards when we pay for them there, as that he may answer for the fact at your Office and our letters pass to London without control. For the present that very mean (as I take it) fellow himself who carries the letters from Liverpool is (or lately was) the post and the postmaster there. How suitable these things are to the profit and repute of the Office I submit to your better skill. . . .

CHAPTER XI

FRIENDSHIP

*The English in the seventeenth century were a quarrelsome race.
' If you said any such thing,' wrote one polite gentleman to
another, ' I would advise you to eat your words immediately,
else—by the living God—I'll cram them down your throat with
my sword—and that very shortly.' But though they swaggered
and bullied in their cups and were far too touchy about what
they called their honour and far too free with their swords in
affirmation of it, they had, as the following letters show, a
genius for true friendship.*

*In the first letter a London barrister refuses out of affection to
accept the fees of a poor provincial squire. Both were Roman
Catholics, and one of them, Richard Langhorne, was seventeen
years later to die a martyr to the intolerance of English Protestants
and the wickedness of the politicians who goaded them on. The
second letter, in which Samuel Pepys thanks his old friend James
Houblon, the Huguenot merchant, for his staunchness to him
during his imprisonment in the Tower and Marshalsea, refers to
the same fevered period, when none but the stoutest friendship
could stand the test of perjured informers, brow-beating judges
and howling mobs. The third and fourth letters, written ten
years later when the country was in the throes of a Revolution,
illustrate the same theme.*

*The mention of the lions in Pepys' letter recalls that the
London Zoo of the seventeenth century shared the same grim
home as the Crown Jewels and prisoners of State. Scott was*

the villainous informer whom his enemies had employed to accuse
Pepys of treason. Will Hewer, writer of the fourth letter, now
become a man of great substance—though ready in his friend's
behalf to endanger it all—was the same Will Hewer who had
come as a boy to Pepys' house one July day twenty-eight years
before and had been even then so obedient that his master was
'greatly glad of him.'

TO WILLIAM BLUNDELL FROM RICHARD LANG-
HORNE.

1662.[1]

. . . I am now, Sir, to thank you again and again and a
thousand of million of times again for your last exceeding
kind letters and care of your poor friend.   But in truth
did I not very well know your excess of charity and had
I not daily occasions to see my own defects, many such
letters from so sober a person as yourself would endanger
my running mad with pride, and make me think myself
something, whereas (God knows) I am the most inconsiderable and in truth the worst of all your servants as
being the most modest.   But you are a perfect friend to
all intents and purposes, and that is a jewel rarely found
in this world.   You are that person whom I must love
and honour with all my might.

Will you not allow me so to do?   In good earnest, Sir,
I do not compliment at this time nor at any time with my
friend.   There is nothing in this world within my
power but you have a title to command it, and shall at
your pleasure find me obedient as becomes a true and
grateful friend to every command of that welcome kind.
And if this be not plain I will unriddle all by (not begging
but) claiming a friendly favour from you wherein you
must complete and seal this demonstration to me (which
in truth I doubt not), *that you love me.*   It is this: that
from this day forward you will give me leave on all

occasions of your own to be of Counsel for you upon the score of true and noble friendship and without not only offering, but without making mention of any other fee than that of your love and affection. Do this and I am your eternally cheerful grateful friend. If you deny me this I must still be eternally your friend, but as melancholy as unkindness from my friend can render me.

Well, friendship tells me you do consent. And therefore as to what is now past and done by me for your son since I last took fees, must go upon this account, for during his present hard condition and so long as he lies upon you without his own estate, all fees from him I reckon fees out of my friend's purse, and therefore will take none: what you give from henceforth must be out of your better part. . . .

TO JAMES HOUBLON AT WINCHESTER STREET, LONDON, FROM SAMUEL PEPYS.

Brampton, 14 *November*, 1680.[2]

Sir,

My last said I should be in town the beginning of this week. But, to tell you the truth though there be no place, I thank God, where I dare not show my head, yet there is one where I am ashamed to show my face again till I have done something (that ought long since to have been done) for securing the remembrance of what I am owing there, though I can never hope to discharge it, and that is at a namesake's of yours in Winchester Street.

But don't mistake me, that his forgetfulness I am jealous of, and not my own. For it is no less possible for me or just to forget myself as him, without whom I am not sure I should, ere this, have been myself. But he, you must know, is one of so tender a memory that there is no good deed of his own that will stick in it, for he shall do you twenty good offices before he will think them one; nay, and do them with more thanks than he will endure to take from him he does them to.

To supply which, I have bethought myself of fastening my picture as a present upon him, in hopes that when he sees that it will be out of his power not to recollect his errands on my score to Westminster Hall, his visit to the lions, his passings over the bridge to the Patten in Southwark, and a thousand other things which, by his good will, he would never come within the hearing of. Nay, in my conscience, if he knew this were the design of my present, he would turn his head a' one side every time he comes in sight on't.

And even, lest he should do so, I have been fain to think of an assistant device; and that is, to send a small bribe to every one of his family to get them in such a case to be putting in some word or other as he passes by to make him look upon it; as thus: ' Was Mr. Pepys in these clothes, father, when you used to go to the Tower to him? ' Or thus: ' Lord, cousin, how hath this business of Scott altered my poor cousin Pepys since this was done! ' Or thus: ' What would I give for a plot, Jemmy, to get you laid by the heels, that I might see what this Mr. Pepys would do for you.' With these helps, I don't doubt but it will do; at least so far as to stick an impression upon the young ones of what, in their father's right (if he won't), they may challenge from me as they shall grow big enough to make work for me, and find me become not too little to do them any.

I make it, therefore, my request, that by your hand these small mementos may be distributed to the end and use aforesaid. Upon notice whereof from Mr. Hewer I shall appear in town again, and not sooner. I am, dear Sir,
Your most obliged
and most affectionate humble servant,
S. PEPYS.

TO SAMUEL PEPYS, SECRETARY OF THE ADMIRALTY,
AT YORK BUILDINGS, LONDON, FROM JOHN EVELYN.
Sayes Court, 12 *December,* 1688.[3]

Sir,

I left you indisposed, and send on purpose to learn
how it is with you, and to know if in any sort I may serve
you in this prodigious Revolution. You have many
friends, but no man living who is more sincerely your
servant, or that has a greater value for you. We are
here as yet (I thank God) unmolested; but this shaking
menaces every corner, and the most philosophic breast
cannot but be sensible of the motion. I am assured you
need no precepts, nor I example so long as I have yours
before me. And I would govern myself by your commands to, Sir,

> Your most humble, faithful servant,
>
> J. EVELYN.

TO SAMUEL PEPYS FROM WILLIAM HEWER.

Wednesday Night, 19 *December,* 1688.[4]

Honoured Sir,

I humbly thank you for yours of this afternoon, which
gives me great satisfaction, and hope this afternoon or
evening's Audience will prove to your satisfaction,
which I do heartily wish and pray for. If not, I know
you will cheerfully acquiesce in whatever circumstance
God Almighty shall think most proper for you, which
I hope may prove more to your satisfaction than you can
imagine. You may rest assured that I am wholly yours,
and that you shall never want the utmost of my constant,
faithful, and personal service, the utmost I can do being
inconsiderable to what your kindness and favour to me
has and does oblige me to. And therefore, as all I have

proceeded from you, so all I have and am is and shall be at your service.

I have no reason to complain as yet of any hardship, but to-morrow I shall know the utmost and then I shall wait on you, remaining in the meantime

Your ever faithful and obedient servant,

WILLIAM HEWER.

[Endorsed by Pepys], ' a letter of great tenderness in a time of difficulty.'

A GIRL'S FRIENDSHIP

A very different type of friendship is the subject of the next three letters. Frances Apsley, daughter of Sir Allen Apsley, M.P., Treasurer of the Household to the Duke of York, was born in 1653 and was thus nine years older than the Princess Mary, the Duke's eldest daughter, with whose childhood she was intimately associated. The two girls pretended to be husband and wife, and assumed romantic names in their correspondence with one another. Frances as the elder was the husband or ' Aurelia,' and Mary the wife, ' Mary Clorine.'

The first two letters appear to have been written in 1676, a year before Mary's marriage to William of Orange: Mary was then fourteen and her correspondent twenty-two. The last shows how the friendship continued after Mary's marriage to the Prince of Orange and her departure from England.

TO FRANCES APSLEY FROM THE PRINCESS MARY OF ENGLAND.

Circa 1676.[5]

My dearest, dear husband,

If you suspect your true wife, I should take it ill, but that as you say there is no true love without jealousy and, having it from your own mouth, I do believe and forgive if you can be so good to do both to me: pray God you may. Your crying when you write will easily be believed from me. I did so too in my last letter, but did not tell you so because I thought you would not believe me, and I fear you will not now but think I say so because you said so in your letter. But if you will not believe I swear by all our loves 'tis true. That body I guess you suspected me with I love very well; next you I love her better than any young woman. . . . But to think I loved her better than you, sure you could not.

You say you have shed tears for me before and wish this might be the last time you shed for me. I wish so too and I'm very sure it will be your own fault if you do. There is nothing in the world that I know but my Aurelia should know too but this, for this is a thing I could not have told for all the world; now it is over and I hope will never come again. I confess you had a great deal of reason to take it ill, but I hope you have so much goodness as to forgive and believe that henceforward there is nothing in this heart or breast, guts or bowels but you shall know it.

I am sure if you blame me for want of love you are much in the wrong, for to express my love it must be less. It is impossible for me to say half what I think of you: I have so much love for my dear, dearest, dear Aurelia that it is impossible for me to say anything. I love you, I love you, I love you, till you would be weary of hearing of my love. I'm sure to answer your letter to the full, I must call one of the Muses, for nothing ever had so much in it to my Aurelia but a Muse.

I am afraid to tire you with too long a letter, therefore here I end. Pray believe that there is nothing in the world I love better than my dear, dear husband. Doctor Lake is just come to break off my letter, I think, but pray believe me your obedient wife

MARY CLORINE.

T O Frances Apsley from the Princess Mary of
England.
                                            Circa 1676.[6]

Who can imagine that my dear husband can be so love-
sick for fear I do not love her. But I have more reason
to think that she is sick of being weary of me, for in two
or three years men are always weary of their wives and
look for mistresses as soon as they can get them. But I
think I am pretty well assured of the love of my dear.

But if I had all that is to be had in the world I should
never have enough. If my dearest, oh dearest Aurelia did
but show half the love to me as I, if I had speech to declare,
should do to her, I should be the happiest creature in the
world, as now I am but in indifferent happiness. For
nothing in the world, I am sure, can so much add to my
pleasure as to love and to be loved again. For my part
I have more love for you than I can possibly have for all
the world besides.

You do not expect from me a letter like your own this
morning, for I am sure Mr. Dryden and all the poets in
the world put together could not make such another.
I pretend to nothing in this world but, if it be possible, to
tell my love I have for my Aurelia, to my dearest, dearest
husband, and ever beg of her to accept me as her most
obedient wife

                                            Mary Clorine.

T O Frances Apsley from Mary of Orange.

                              Honslerdyck, 9 *August* [1678].[7]

I have a hundred thousand pardons to beg of my dear,
dear husband who, if I did not know to be very good and
hope she loves me a little still, I could not so much as
hope to be forgiven. But those considerations make me,

though very criminal for not having writ since I was well again, begin to believe that so charitable a body as yourself can't know how sorry I am for the fault, and continue long angry. But if anything in the world can make amends for such a fault, I hope trusting you with a secret will, which though in itself 'tis not enough, yet I tell you 'tis one. Yet I would hardly give myself leave to think on it nor nobody leave to speak of it, not so much as to myself, and that I have not yet writ the Duchess word, who has always charged me to do it in all her letters.

It is what I am ashamed to say, but seeing it is to my husband I may, though I have reason to fear because the sea parts us. You may believe it is a bastard, but yet I think upon a time of need I may make you own it since 'tis not out of the four seas. In the mean time if you have any care of your own reputation, consequently you must have of your wife's too, you ought to keep this a secret, since if it should be known you might get a pair of horns and nothing else by the bargain. But dearest Aurelia, you may be very well assured, though I have played the whore a little, I love you of all things in the world.

Though I have spoke as you may think in jest all this while, yet for God sake, if you love me, don't tell it, because I would not have it known yet for all the world, since it cannot be above six or seven weeks at most. And whenever you do hear of it by other people, never say that I said anything of it to you. In the mean time I beg of you to say nothing as you hope ever to be trusted another time.

OLD AND LEARNED FRIENDS

The last letter upon this score of friendship belongs to the beginning of a new age, but seems fitting here as linking two of the best known and most pleasing figures of the latter

*seventeenth century. At the time of its writing Evelyn was
eighty-one and Pepys sixty-eight, and their friendship had lasted
for thirty-six years. It had still a further eighteen months to
run before Evelyn, with three more years before him, had sadly
to record the news of his fellow diarist's death.*

TO JOHN EVELYN FROM SAMUEL PEPYS.

Clapham, 19 November, 1701.[8]

Dear Sir,

As much as I am (I bless God!) in perfect present ease
here, as to my health, 'tis little less, however, than a
very burial to me, as to what of all worldly goods I put
most price upon, I mean, the few old and learned friends
I had flattered myself with the hopes of closing the little
residue of my life in the continued enjoyment of, and at
the head of them all, the most inestimable Mr. Evelyn.
But Providence, that must not be repined at, has thought
fit to part us; yet not without a reserve, I trust, of another
place of meeting for us, and better, and more lasting, for
which God fit us!

Not that I mean this for a final God-b'-w'-you! for,
one way or other, I hope we shall see one another before
the winter be over, and possibly a great many other sights
that we don't think of. In the [mean] time, in return
for your most kind enquiries after me, I make this my
messenger on the same errand after your health and my
ever honoured lady's, which I shall never want a more
particular concern for.

'Twere endless to talk at this time of public matters,
and not to much more purpose to think of them, if one
could help it; but he is a much abler philosopher than
I that can do it under the aspect they now seem to bear
towards both Church and State.

Mrs. Skinner is my Lady's most obedient servant and yours; and my nephew most dutifully the same; and all of us Mr. Evelyn's, your grandson and my friend, with all respect.

I am, dearest Sir,
Your most faithful and ever most affectionate
humble servant,

S. PEPYS.

CHAPTER XII

GROWING OLD

A FRIEND BY THE FIRESIDE

' *My ancient kind friend,*' *wrote William Blundell to John North in 1692, ' I have been lately told that thro' the great goodness of God you have weathered all the storms and that you do still remain fixed upon the same old spot. I thank God for it that I have in some tolerable sort done the same myself, and that now I have little to do with the world but to leave it in a happy hour.'* It was the good fortune of our ancestors of the seventeenth century that after all the changes and vicissitudes of their troubled lives, the ' old spot ' was usually still theirs at the end. The letters which follow are in the same vein. The first is from that ageing roué, the second Earl of Chesterfield, now grown into a philosopher. After the Revolution he retired altogether from Courts and politics and lived mainly on his Derbyshire estates, surviving till his eightieth year. He became the patron of Dryden, who dedicated to him his translation of Virgil's ' Georgics.' The correspondence between this nobleman and the great poet, fallen on somewhat evil days, reflects as much credit on the second Earl of Chesterfield as the more famous correspondence between Johnson and the fourth Earl fails to do on the latter.

TO MR. BATES FROM THE EARL OF CHESTERFIELD.

Bretby, 5 November.[1]

Sir,

I received yours of the 18 instant and was in hopes to have been in town almost as soon as this paper, but a feverish distemper has confined me these eight days to my house. And truly I am not yet in a condition to go abroad, though thanks be to God I am much better than I was, and shall now prepare for my London journey and to make my accounts for my summer's building, which when I come to examine, I doubt that I shall think it time to fly my country without the help of other inducements to carry me to town. To which place (as Denham says) most men do run, some to undo and some to be undone, but as I desire not to share with the former, so I hope to avoid the latter, for a mate at chess, a bottle of Burgundy and a friend by the fireside, are the remaining pleasures that can now justly be pretended to by

Sir,

Your &c.

TO THE EARL OF CHESTERFIELD FROM JOHN DRYDEN.

London, 17 February, 1696.[2]

My Lord,

I have hitherto wanted confidence to give your Lordship the trouble of a letter which I designed almost a year together, and am now forced to take this opportunity or wholly lose it. My translation of Virgil is already in the press and I cannot possibly defer the publication of it any longer than Midsummer Term at farthest. I have hindered it thus long in hopes of his return, for whom and for my conscience I have suffered, that I might

have laid my author at his feet.   But now finding that
God's time for ending our miseries is not yet, I have been
advised to make three several Dedications, of the
Eclogues, the Georgics, and the Æneids.

The Eclogues have been desired a year ago by my
Lord Clifford, whose father, the Treasurer, was my Patron,
the Æneids by the Marquess of Normanby, and if I durst
presume so far, I would humbly offer the Georgics to
your Lordship's patronage.   They are not I confess the
most specious part of Virgil, but in revenge they are his
masterpiece in which he has not only outdone all other
poets, but himself.   Accordingly I have laboured and
I may say have cultivated the Georgics with more care
than any other part of him, and as I think myself with
more success.   'Tis suitable to the retired life which
you have chosen, and to your studies of Philosophy.
From the first hour since I have had the happiness of
being known to your Lordship I have always preferred you
in my poor esteem to any other nobleman and that in all
respects.   And you may please to believe me as an
honest man, that I have not the least consideration of any
profit in this address, but only of honouring myself by
dedicating to you.

By this time, my Lord, you may perceive why I have
been solicitous to procure the favour of your being one
of the subscribers to this work.   And, to return to the
beginning of my letter, 'twas upon a just diffidence of my
success in this presumption that I have humoured my
natural bashfulness in not addressing to you sooner.   But
as teeming women must speak at last or lose their longing,
so I am constrained to beg that I may not miscarry of my
translation, who am with all manner of humility

'Your Lordship's

most obedient servant,

JOHN DRYDEN.

TO JOHN DRYDEN FROM THE EARL OF CHESTERFIELD.

10 *August*, 1697.[3]

Sir,

Tho' I have never been ambitious of being obliged by many men, yet I am very much pleased with the being so by Mr. Dryden. Not out of vanity in having my inconsiderable name placed (by so great a man) in the front of one of his works, but because it gives the world a testimony of his friendship to me. I confess that I have always esteemed you the Homer of this Age, and I am sure that you have had that one advantage far above him, for he never shined much but in the dark, I mean till he was dead, and you have had that glory the greatest part of your life. But I do not pretend to offer the incense of praise to him who is the best teacher of others how to give it; my intention being only at this time to express some part of my resentments for the invaluable present that you have made me; and to desire your acceptance (by this bearer) of a small mark of those respects which shall ever be paid you by

Sir, Your most humble servant

CHESTERFIELD.

' THE GENERAL DISEASE OF LOVING HOME '

The older the great Lord Halifax became, the fonder he grew of Rufford, the abbey in the Nottinghamshire forest which was the home of his race. At the time of writing this remarkable letter he had not yet reached his fiftieth year, but his exquisite and balanced mind was already beginning to feel the strain of the revolutionary politics of his age. Later in that very year, during the session of Charles II's fourth Parliament, he was to stem the republican tide by his cool yet heroic opposition to the Exclusion Act:

Jotham *of piercing wit and pregnant thought,*
Endow'd by nature and by learning taught
To move assemblies, who but only tried
The worse a while, then chose the better side ;
Nor chose alone, but turned the balance too ;
So much the weight of one brave man can do.

Perhaps something of the calm judgment that twice in ten
years saved his country from civil war and caused hot-headed
fools to dub him by the name he cherished of ' Trimmer,' was
derived from the peaceful hours he spent in ' his old tenement.'

TO HARRY SAVILE FROM HIS BROTHER, THE EARL
OF HALIFAX.

Rufford, 2 Feb., 1680.[4]

I am once more got to my old tenement, which I had
not seen since I had given order to renew and repair it.
It looketh now somewhat better than when you was last
here; and, besides the charms of your native soil, it hath
something more to recommend itself to your kindness
than when it was so mixed with the old ruins of the abbey
that it looked like a medley of superstition and sacrilege.
And, though I have still left some decayed part of [the] old
building, yet there are none of the rags of Rome remaining. It is now all heresy, which in my mind looketh
pretty well, and I have at least as much reverence for it
now as I had when it was encumbered with those sanctified ruins. In short, with all the faults that belong to
such a misshapen building patched up at so many several
times, and notwithstanding the forest hath not its best
clothes at this time of the year, I find something here
which pleaseth me, whether it be the general disease of
loving home, or whether for the sake of variety, since
I have been so long absent as to make my own house a
new thing to me, or by comparing it to other places where

one is less at ease, I will not determine. The best reason
I can give is, that I grow every day fitter for a coal fire
and a country parlour, being come now to the worst
part of my elder brothership in having so much a greater
share of years than you that it may make amends for the
inequality of the division in other respects.

The greatest pleasure I have now to hope for dependeth
much upon the good advice you will give your nephew,
who never shall have any injunctions from me but such as
he ought for his own sake to impose upon himself. I
think him so capable of succeeding well in the world
that it is pity he should miscarry by a wrong setting out
at first. Therefore pray let us have a care of his launch-
ing, for there is the greatest danger for young men in
this age. . . . I have great reason to be pleased with
your kindness to him, but you have drawn an unnecessary
encumbrance upon yourself by taking him into your house.
Pray make him no compliments that give you any trouble,
and therefore let him be in some lodging near you,
where he may be enough under your eye without giving
you the inconvenience of an inmate. It may be a real
kindness to inform him sometimes of such things as pass
through your hands as are not great secrets, and yet may
give him a taste and quicken his appetite to know what
passeth in the world. He promised me to read books of
treaties and negotiations, in which you may not only
encourage but direct him very much to his advantage.
It is a great matter for a growing man to apply himself
to read what may be of some use, which may be done
with as much pleasure at least as in losing time upon
nouvelles and *entretiens*, things only fit for young fellows
and their wenches to read till the hour of assignation
cometh for a more substantial entertainment. . . .

R

'ALL MY OLD FRIENDS DROP AWAY'

William Sancroft, after a scholastic youth, became Dean of St. Paul's in 1664. He was thus more than any other man, save its architect, responsible for the rebuilding of the Cathedral, and it was in his company that even before the Great Fire Evelyn, Wren and others viewed the tottering fabric and decided on a ' noble cupola, a form of church building not as yet known in England, but of wonderful grace.' In the winter of 1677/8, after the death of Archbishop Sheldon, to everyone's surprise he was preferred to the Primacy, largely on the initiative of the King, who recognised his genuine piety and saintliness:

> Zadock the priest, whom, shunning power and place
> His lowly mind advanced to David's grace.

In 1688, at the age of seventy-two, he led the opposition of the Seven Bishops against James II's Declaration of Indulgence, and suffered imprisonment and trial. Yet in the winter of the same year, after the expulsion of the royal master who had injured him, he refused to take the oath to King William and was suspended. After his expulsion from Lambeth in 1691 he retired to Fressingfield in Suffolk, the home of his birth and of his own yeoman forbears. Here he lived quietly till his death in August, 1693. ' It touched my spirit,' wrote his friend Roger North, ' to see the low estate of this poor old saint, and with what wonderful regard and humility he treated those that visited him, who were not worthy to serve him.'

TO SIR H. NORTH FROM WILLIAM SANCROFT, NON-JURING ARCHBISHOP OF CANTERBURY.

Fressingfield, 7 October, 1691.[5]

Dear Friend,

How kind and obliging is that complaint of yours, that I give you not so much trouble as you would be well pleased to have for my sake! You call it business: but, alas! Sir, I have little of that, and if we can get off my nephew's bonds, shall have every day less at London, where (as we had it yesterday in the psalm) I am become like a dead man, out of mind, and like a broken vessel, of no use at all.

Yet that honourable and excellent lady (it seems), even in the midst of her inexplicable sorrows, is pleased to think of me and mention me: the God of heaven comfort her in the one and reward her for the other. The Sunday after I received from you that doleful news, I had just occasion to remember her in reading the gospel for that day, concerning the good widow of Nain and her only son, which is so parallel to the present case. And though we cannot at present expect the miraculous event, yet the time will come, when our merciful Lord will say to the son, Young man I say unto thee arise; and in the mean[time], I most humbly beseech him to have compassion on the mother, and to say to her effectually Weep not.

Alas! for honest old John Cook! all my old friends drop away, one after another, and I shall stand alone, I think, ere long, of those of my time; but in the course of things it cannot be long. God fit me for that hour; and (if it be his good pleasure) from sudden death deliver me. . . .

'AN OLD DECREPIT MAN'

The remaining letters in this chapter are written by John Dryden in the last two years of his life, both to his young cousin, Mrs. Steward of Cotterstock House, Northamptonshire. It is pleasant to recall that this talented lady was the daughter of Pepys' early friend, John Creed. In 1698 she was twenty-six and Dryden sixty-seven.

TO MRS. STEWARD AT COTTERSTOCK, NORTHANTS,
FROM HER COUSIN, JOHN DRYDEN.

Saturday, 1 October, 1698.[6]

Madam,

You have done me the honour to invite so often, that it would look like want of respect to refuse it any longer. How can you be so good to an old decrepit man, who can entertain you with no discourse which is worthy of your good sense, and who can only be a trouble to you in all the time he stays at Cotterstock? Yet I will obey your commands as far as possibly I can and give you the inconvenience you are pleased to desire; at least for the few days which I can spare from other necessary business, which requires me at Tichmarsh. Therefore, if you please to send your coach on Tuesday next by eleven o'clock in the morning, I hope to wait on you before dinner. There is only one more trouble which I am almost ashamed to name. I am obliged to visit my cousin, Dryden of Chesterton, some time next week, who is nine miles from hence, and only five from you. If it be with your convenience to spare me your coach thither for a day, the rest of my time till Monday is at your service; and I am sorry for my own sake it cannot be any longer this year, because I have some visits after my return hither, which I cannot avoid. But if it please God to give me life and health, I may give you occasion another time to repent of your kindness by making you weary of my company. My son kisses your hand. Be pleased to give his humble service to my cousin Steward, and mine, who am,

Madam,
Your most obedient obliged servant,
JOHN DRYDEN.

TO MRS. STEWARD FROM JOHN DRYDEN.

Candlemas-Day, 1699.[7]

Madam,

Old men are not so insensible of beauty as it may be you young ladies think. For my own part, I must needs acknowledge that your fair eyes had made me your slave before I received your fine presents. Your letter puts me out of doubt that they have lost nothing of their lustre, because it was written with your own hand; and not hearing of a fever or an ague, I will please myself with the thoughts that they have wholly left you. I would also flatter myself with the hopes of waiting on you at Cotterstock some time next summer; but my want of health may perhaps hinder me. But if I am well enough to travel as far northward as Northamptonshire, you are sure of a guest who has been too well used not to trouble you again.

My son, of whom you have done me the favour to enquire, mends of his indisposition very slowly; the air of England not agreeing with him hitherto so well as that of Italy. The Bath is proposed by the doctors, both to him and me: but we have not yet resolved absolutely on that journey, for that city is so close and so ill situated, that perhaps the air may do us more harm than the waters can do us good. For which reason we intend to try them here first; and if we find not the good effect which is promised of them, we will save ourselves the pains of going thither.

In the mean time, betwixt my intervals of physic, and other remedies which I am using for my gravel, I am still drudging on: always a poet, and never a good one. I pass my time sometimes with Ovid and sometimes with our old English poet, Chaucer, translating such stories as best please my fancy; and intend, besides them, to add somewhat of my own; so that it is not impossible, but ere the summer be passed, I may come down to you with a volume in my hand like a dog out of the water with a duck in his mouth. As for the rarities you promise, if beggars might be choosers, a part of a chine of honest bacon would please my appetite more than all the marrow puddings; for I like them better plain, having a very vulgar stomach. My wife and your cousin Charles give you their most humble service, and thanks for your remembrance of them. I present my own to my worthy cousin, your husband, and am, with all respect,

Madam,
Your most obliged servant,
JOHN DRYDEN.

CHAPTER XIII

RELIGION

'WE ARE BUT STRANGERS AND PILGRIMS'

Religion was the common background of seventeenth century England. Its necessity was constantly stressed by the uncertainty of life in an age when families were large and early mortality frequent. ' This is no place to sit down in,' declared Jeremy Taylor, ' but you must rise as soon as you are set, for we are people but of a day's abode; we must look somewhere else for an abiding city, a place in another country to fix our house in, whose walls and foundations is God.' ' At the beginning of this month,' recorded the Rev. Philip Henry in his diary, ' Mr. John Broughton died aged seventy. About the middle a son of Randle Meredith's aged about thirty. Towards the end a child of Mr. Lloyd of Halghton aged fourteen months. I see no age secures from the stroke of Death; he comes sometimes at midnight; sometimes at noon, sometimes at cock-crowing.'

The Rev. Philip Henry was the son of a minor court official, who was brought up by a mother of Puritan mind, who ' looked well to the ways of her household, prayed with them daily, catechised her children and brought them daily to public ordinances.' After a period in the Church of England, he became a Nonconformist. He was the kind of man, by no means uncommon in that age, who found a religious meaning in every incident of life, however trivial: a gift of £10 from

*a noble patron at the University was 'a seasonable mercy,'
recovery from a fever 'a signal answer of prayers,' and a
lost letter 'an afflicting providence.'*

TO MATTHEW HENRY AT GRAY'S INN FROM HIS
FATHER, PHILIP HENRY.

                                        13 *November*, 1685.[1]

Son Matthew,

We are glad to hear of God's goodness to you in your
journey, going out and coming in, and of the pleasing
circumstances which he hath brought you to in the place
where you are. Concerning which you do well not to
call it settlement, for our present state here below is and
must be a tabernacle-state; we are but strangers and
pilgrims, as all our fathers were; the world is our inn,
and the place wherein you are, bearing that name, it
should mind you daily what your condition is in it. You
are to count upon being there but a while and to manage
yourself, your time, your affections, your conversation
accordingly. Whilst you reckon you have no continuing
city here, you are the more concerned to make one sure
that is to come.

It pleases God to lengthen out his displeasure towards
us in this neighbourhood in the continuance of the smallpox which hath taken away many. Ours are yet preserved; to His name be the praise, in whose hand our
times are and at whose dispose are all our ways.

Tho. Hensh. was here to-day, paying his rent, honestly;
the rest, I hope, will be had ere long. But the general
complaint is that nothing takes money. The price of
cattle and corn is low, and pity 'tis that plenty should be a
grievance; 'tis but a little while, I am sure, since the
complaint was high and loud the other way. God in
mercy secure the gospel to us, though he feed us with

the bread of adversity and give us tears to drink in other
matters! The Doctor gave them a good sermon,
Nov. 5, from 2 Cor. i. 10. There was generally in all
the country hereabouts, especially on the Welsh side,
greater expressions of joy than ordinary, and many
pulpits full of sharp reflections upon the people concerned;
only one I hear of whose text was, Go teach all nations,
baptizing them: what he inferred from thence suitable
to the occasion I know not.

My love to your chamber-fellow unknown; help one
another what you can especially for Heaven, remembering
wherein two are better than one.   When you have leisure
and can conveniently, go see your aunts, but not by
water lest you catch cold.   However write to them, if
there be such a way thither, by the penny-post. . . .

TO Mrs. Lyttleton from her father, Sir Thomas
Browne.

15 September, 1681.[2]

Dear Betty,

Though it were no wonder this very tempestuous and
stormy winter, yet I am sorry you had such an uncomfortable sight as to behold a ship cast away so near you.
This is no strange though unwelcome sight at Yarmouth,
Cromer, Winterton, and sea towns.   Though you could
not save them, I hope they were the better for your prayers,
both those that perished and those that 'scaped.   Some
wear away in calms, some are carried away in storms:
we come into the world one way, there are many gates
to go out of it.   God give us grace to fit and prepare ourselves for that necessity, and be ready to leave all when
and howsoever he shall call.

The prayers of health are most like to be acceptable;
sickness may choke our devotions, and we are accepted

rather by our life than our death: we have a rule how to lead the one, the other is uncertain and may come in a moment. God, I hope, will spare you to serve him long, who didst begin early to serve him. There died thirty-six last week in Norwich. The smallpox very common; and we must refer it to God's mercy when he pleaseth to abate or cease it; for the last run of the smallpox lasted much longer than this has yet done.

Your brother Thomas went once from Yarmouth in the evening and arrived at the Isle of Wight the next day at one o'clock in the afternoon, but it was with such a wind that he was never so sick at sea as at that time. I came once from Dublin to Chester at Michaelmas, and was so tossed that nothing but milk and possets would go down with me two or three days after. Yourself is not impatient, you will have no cause to be sad: give no way unto melancholy, which is purely sadness without a reasonable cause. You shall never want our daily prayers, and also our frequent letters. God bless you both.

I rest your loving father,

THOMAS BROWNE.

' AN HIDEOUS AND PORTENDING THING '

In an age when religious feeling was so strong as to amount almost to an obsession, men were ready to see the hand of God in every happening, especially in anything out of the ordinary like a storm and a comet. Such superstition was not confined to the common people. Sir Robert Harley and Edmund Verney were both men of education. The great storm of November, 1662, referred to in the first letter, all but destroyed Dover: one urgent message to the capital was endorsed: ' In haste, post haste, or all's lost; port, town and people.'

To Sir Edward Harley from his brother, Sir
Robert Harley.

Dover, 12 November, 1662.[3]

This morning I was awakened with the coming of the
sea into the town of Dover. I cannot judge but that one
such other tide will wholly destroy the town and harbour.
You know Dover lieth almost east and west, so that a
south-east or south-west wind is most dangerous for
bringing in the sea. But the wind was now at north-
west which makes a calm water in this road, so that it
was a very extraordinary thing to have the sea so tempestuous. Besides it was no spring tide, yet it was an
higher tide and the sea more raging than ever was known
in the memory of man. It was an hideous and portending
thing. I pray God we may learn the voice of these
things.

To John Verney at mr. roberts's, a merchant's
house, in carpenter's hall near london wall,
from his brother, Edmund Verney.

East Claydon, 3 August, 1674.[4]

Dear Brother,

I received your story how that in Holland the winds
were loosed and the Heavens opened, showering down
much mischief . . . destroying both man and beast and
building. Which indeed (if true) is very wonderful and
terrible to behold, and ought to be a warning unto that
people more in particular to repent. And most commonly
such dismal accidents are forerunners of an alteration at
least, if not total subversion, of Church and State where
they fall. . . . Your affectionate brother,

Edmund Verney.

GOD'S SEVERE MERCIES

To the seventeenth century mind far more than to the mind
of to-day affliction was a blessing sent from God to test a
man's spirit and teach him the divine lessons of patience and
resignation. The measure of a good Christian was the extent
to which he was able to overcome his natural feelings in
adversity and submit himself cheerfully to the inevitable, which
was held to be only God's mercy in disguise. This attitude
was not confined to the Puritans, as is sometimes supposed;
the following letter was written by a Roman Catholic squire.

TO A FRIEND AT LONDON DURING THE GREAT PLAGUE
FROM WILLIAM BLUNDELL.

[1665.]⁵

My very dear good friend,

I was truly glad to receive one from you of the 16th,
by which I understand that you and your husband were
then in health. For all your respects to me I do kindly
thank you, and will not fail to recommend you daily to
God during that dreadful visitation which lies so heavy
upon you.

Whatsoever state you are in, if you think it fit to write,
I dare venture to read it. As for the writing of news I
do give you many thanks for that you have writ already,
but you need not to trouble yourself any further upon that
account, for I fail not to be furnished constantly twice a
week with the printed news book. If you please to write
to me once again concerning the present state of yourself
and your little family, you will do me a great pleasure if
you will satisfy my mind in one great doubt. It is reported by some persons in these parts concerning the
state of London, that the famine kills more than the

plague and that the price of all manner of victuals is excessively high: whether this be so or no you will please to tell me.

For the rest I do exhort you to patience and to resign your own wills to the blessed will of God. If you be taken away by this dreadful pestilence, you have had a fair warning and a very long time to prepare yourselves for Heaven. But if God be pleased to favour you with longer life, the memory of this dismal time will be an antidote for your future against all temptations to sin. It seems to me that every day at London is now (as it were) a Day of Judgment, and that all your thoughts are placed on death, on Hell, on Heaven, and upon eternity.

These are meditations which cannot go out of your mind, and will certainly much advance your happiness if you use them right. So that all those things which seem to us severities from God Almighty are mercies, in very truth, as long as we are chastised for sin and have time allowed us for repentance.

I have suffered something myself in former times and this, as yourself can best witness, in an extraordinary manner, yet that I take now to be the greatest favour that ever God bestowed upon me since I came to the use of reason. And without that favour I have great reason to believe that all my temporal and eternal expectations had been utterly lost. Affliction gives great understanding; and the pains of death itself patiently and religiously borne may procure us eternal life. Thy will be done on earth as it is in Heaven is the balsam that cureth all. As long as you can heartily say this your better part is safe whatsoever becomes of your body. Sweet Jesus dispose of all to his own honour and hear our prayers and let our cries come to him.

I am your affectionate and very solicitous friend

W. BLUNDELL.

A MINISTER'S REBUKE

John Maitland, second Earl and first Duke of Lauderdale, was famous as a young man for the strength of his Presbyterian convictions, and throughout an exceedingly worldly career retained a wide knowledge of divinity, based on early reading. Until the end of the first Civil War he was one of the leaders of the Scottish Covenanters, but afterwards revolted against the dominance of the bigots of the Kirk, attached himself to Charles II and was taken prisoner while following his standard at Worcester. After nine years' imprisonment, he came into his own with the Restoration, when he was made Secretary of State for Scotland, of which country he became virtually dictator. In this position, and during his attendance at the Court of Charles II, he appears to have given himself more and more to debauched courses.

Richard Baxter, who had been born in 1615, a year before Lauderdale, was the most distinguished figure among the English Presbyterians. At the Restoration he was offered a Bishopric, but refused, and two years later on the passing of the Act of Uniformity withdrew from the Church of England. He remained, however, a powerful influence in the religious life of the time, preaching whenever he was able and, despite occasional persecutions, constantly writing. Like most of his co-religionists he found some difficulty in expressing himself in a small compass, and it has been necessary to cut much of his letter to Lauderdale.

TO THE EARL OF LAUDERDALE FROM THE REV. RICHARD BAXTER.[6]

My Lord,

Your extraordinary respects and favours have made it my duty to be more than ordinarily tender of your soul and honour. Having of late been often put upon serving

you as to the latter behind your back, according to my
capacity, I am assured (with respect to both) it is my
duty to let you know the occasion. And faithfulness
forbiddeth me to conceal from you the words of great
dishonour that are (I doubt not) injuriously spoken of
you. For as your defence against an adversary behind
your back is difficult, though you were acquainted with
his proceedings, so, when you know nothing of them,
it is next to impossible. And the course of the world
tells me, that it's like enough that a thousand will speak
against you to others before one or two will faithfully
acquaint you with it. However no man being more
obliged than I, no man can be expected to be more
willing.

The first aspersions I told you of. Since then it is
given out in general that you are so fallen from all that
can be called serious religion as that sensuality and com-
pliance with sin is your ordinary course. In particular
that you use to take your cups unto excess, and sometimes
unto drunkenness (and they instance when you went with
the King to see a ship) and that the sensualists are hardened
by you, and that unto scorn, because of your former professions of piety. And (to use their own words) that you
are not only corrupted but a corrupter; and they have
made it too commonly half-believed that you serve others
in an odious vice, which because of the quality of the
persons, and the greatness of the sin, I must not name,
but by this much you may understand. And that in your
drunkenness (I must use their words) you have offered
your service in such words, which are not to be uttered,
but are thus secretly made the matter of your reproach.

It wounded me to hear of things so odious whispered
against those whom you and I are so much bound to honour.
And (for the Nation's sake, as well as their own) God
forbid it should be true of them. But of yourself I have

still with confidence and detestation affronted such de-
tractors, and rebuked their reports as base and odious
slanders. . . .

And yet knowing the danger of your station, I am not
without some jealousy lest flesh and worldly wisdom
should too much get advantage over you: but these
jealousies carry me not to censure you, but to pray the
more for you and thus to warn you. My Lord, as slanders
are permitted by God in Mercy to teach you what to
prevent and to avoid, so I know you have the common
enemies of mankind to conflict with and to conquer if
you will be saved; and I know your temptations are many
and strong; and you must be more than man, if you keep
your ground, without some more than ordinary care and
watchfulness and resolution. And, God forbid that you
should lose that in prosperity which you gained in adversity! and that God who was near you in a prison,
should be put far from you in a Court! . . .

My Lord, I am not persuading you for the securing of
your soul to leave the Court that you may escape temptations (though if there were no other remedy, it were
better cut off a right hand or pull out a right eye than
perish). I know if all good men should do so on that
pretence, they would but desert their trust and the
commonwealth and the interest of Christ, as cowardly
soldiers that will quit the field for fear of being wounded,
or slothful workmen that will quit the vineyard for fear
of doing their work amiss. This were to give up all as
deplorate. But I beseech you Watch and *Walk with God !*
Lose not your hatred of sin, your zeal for God, and tenderness of his honour. Never do that intimateth your
approbation of known sin; or tendeth to encourage
any in it. . . .

I beseech you, my Lord, grow not strange to God and
Heaven. Let not the greatness of your employment

seem an excuse to you (ordinarily) for the restraint of
prayer and some fit proportion of reading and meditation.
It were indeed a miserable life that should imprison your
soul in smoky vanity and shut you out from your com-
munion with God.   This were to be debased below those
poorest Christians, that in a cottage and in rags have daily
access to God in prayer and holy meditation.   It were a
miserable honour that should thus depress you! and a
miserable gain that should bring upon you so great a loss.

O, my Lord, do I need to tell you, that the fashion of
this world doth pass (and hastily pass) away, and that it
is only God that must shortly be your peace and comfort,
or you will be swallowed up in sorrow and despair!   Do
I need to tell you that all this glory will quickly set in
the shadows of death, and that all this sweating will turn
sour! and how little it will comfort a departing soul to
look back on prosperity, and how terrible it will be to
reflect on a life of covenant breaking and unfaithfulness
to God!   I hope I need not mind you of such common
truths!   But I find it so hard myself to be indeed what I
resolve in sickness and distress to be, that I am thereby
induced to beseech you, for the Lord's sake, to remember
all your promises and pay your vows, and requite not
your deliverer with forgetfulness, neglect or dishonour.
And remember that many eyes are upon you and that God
deserveth at our hands that all creatures and interests
should stoop to his honour, interest and will, and keep
the friend that must stand by you when all worldly
friendship fails.

My Lord, it is the assurance of your favourable acceptance of plain and faithful words which inviteth me to use
this freedom.   My chief end is for God's honour and
your everlasting peace, to desire you to make advantage
of detraction and avoid the appearances of evil.   My
next end is, that I may receive such full information and

s

direction from you by which I may be enabled most successfully to use my small abilities and interest for the just vindication of your honour when back-biters and slanderers make it necessary. I have not let any living soul be acquainted with this free address to you. But I acquainted one of your most faithful friends with the endeavours of the calumniators, who told me so much of the malice at the bottom as further enabled me to refell them. My Lord, all this trouble is only from the sense of my great duty to approve myself

Your Lordship's faithful servant to

his power,

R. B.

PERSECUTION

Feeling as strongly about religion as they did, it was only in accordance with human nature that the people of seventeenth century England should have persecuted one another. A man whose fundamental beliefs differed from one's own was accounted more dangerous than a thief or a murderer, for he might well by his influence or persuasion pervert one's neighbours or even children to his heretical views and so condemn them to eternal perdition. No sect that attained political power showed itself exempt from this particular failing: Anglicans, Presbyterians, and Independents have an equally black record in the matter of persecution, albeit an equally golden one in the constancy which they showed in the hour of adversity and proscription. In this last they were equalled, if not surpassed, by the Quakers and Roman Catholics, who never achieved their opportunities for persecuting others but were given their full share of those for patiently enduring persecution.

In the first letter the Quaker, William Penn, then a young man of twenty-six, informs his father, the Admiral, of his third arrest for publicly expounding his unpopular religious

*views. The letter which follows, written to a Westmorland
magistrate, helps to explain the dislike and fear in which so
harmless a sect was held by contemporary opinion. In the third
a curious light is thrown on the intolerance of the Protestant
populace, and in the fourth the non-juring Bishop of Bath and
Wells, the saintly author of the Evening Hymn, refers to the
persecution which he and his fellow loyalists suffered after the
Revolution of 1688.*

TO ADMIRAL SIR WILLIAM PENN FROM HIS SON,
WILLIAM PENN.

Second-day morning, 15th, 6th month (August), 1670.[7]

My dear Father,

This comes by the hand of one who can best allay the
trouble it brings. As true as ever Paul said that such as
live godly in Christ Jesus shall suffer persecution, so for
no other reason am I at present a sufferer. Yesterday I
was taken by a band of soldiers, with one Capt. Mead, a
linen draper, and in the evening carried before the Mayor;
he proceeded against me according to the ancient law.
He told me I should have my hat pulled off, for all I was
Admiral Penn's son. I told him that I desired to be in
common with others, and sought no refuge from the
common usage. He answered, it had been no matter if
thou hadst been a commander twenty years ago. I discoursed with him about the hat; he avoided it, and
because I did not readily answer him my name, William,
when he asked me in order to a *mittimus*, he bid his clerk
write one for Bridewell, and there would he see me
whipped himself, for all I was Penn's son, that starved
the seamen. Indeed these words grieved me, as well as
that it manifested his great weakness and malice to the
whole company, that were about one hundred people.
I told him I could very well bear his severe expressions

to me concerning myself, but was sorry to hear him speak those abuses of my father, that was not present, at which the assembly seemed to murmur.   In short, he committed that person with me as rioters; and at present we are at the sign of the Black Dog in Newgate market.

And now, dear father, be not displeased nor grieved. What if this be designed of the Lord for an exercise of our patience?   I am sure it hath wonderfully laid bare the nakedness of the Mayor.   Several Independents were taken from Sir J. Dethick's, and Baptists elsewhere.   It is the effect of a present commotion in the spirits of some, which the Lord God will rebuke; and I doubt not but I may be at liberty in a day or two to see thee.   I am very well, and have no trouble upon my spirits, besides my absence from thee, especially at this juncture, but otherwise I can say, I was never better; and what they have to charge me with is harmless.

Well, eternity, which is at the door (for He that shall come will come, and will not tarry) that shall make amends for all.   The Lord God everlasting consolate and support thee by His holy power, and preserve to His eternal rest and glory.   Amen.

Thy faithful and obedient son,

WILLIAM PENN.

My duty to my mother.

TO DANIEL FLEMING AT RYDAL HALL FROM THE REV. WILLIAM WILSON.

Windermere, 26 December, 1666.[8]

Honoured Sir,

I am bold to trouble you (and yet I am too bold in terming those businesses of trouble to you, seeing it is not more your duty than delight to approve your faithfulness in the service of God and your Country, which

is not only your great honour but known character) I am
bold, I say, to trouble you with an information against a
Quaker woman, who this last Christmas Day in the middle
of Divine Service, before a great and solemn assembly in
God's own house, did not only disturb me their Minister,
but the whole Congregation by her most irreverent
gesture, standing in the midst of the church, where with
a loud strange inarticulate noise she did drown the sound
of my voice and words to the amazing of my hearers.
And at last, not containing her furious passion, in the time
of prayers she spake aloud and delivered herself in a great
impetuous rabble of slanderous language against my own
person, calling me covetous and greedy, a deceiver of the
people, whilst we were presenting our devoutest requests
unto God in His holy Church.

Sir, I know you will take cognisance of this her disturbance of me in my sermons, of her chiding in the
Church and in the Churchyard where she abused several
of the best of the parish, whose joint desires with mine
are to inform you of these her misdemeanours. Indeed,
Sir, it was a great offence to all my auditors, and a strange
spectacle here to us of a furious woman, we having, I
believe, not one native in our parish of this Sect. This
woman and her husband came but into the parish this
last year, and they may well be called Puritan or Jesuit
Quakers. By this fact, it is verily feared, she hath given
an example to all others of her faction whereby they will
be encouraged to those former insolences whereby they
were wont to abuse Churches and disturb Ministers and
congregations, if by the authority of Magistrates they be
not timely suppressed and restrained.

As the law hath always had a special regard to those
persons, places, and times, that there should be no breach
of the peace to such which be dedicated to the service of
God, so I know, Sir, you will be careful to preserve the

privileges of the Clergy, and the reverence of God's
house according to several statutes in that case provided.
Thus with my best respects and service to you and your
virtuous wife

I rest your humble servant,

WILLIAM WILSON.

TO CHRISTOPHER, VISCOUNT HATTON, FROM HIS
BROTHER, CHARLES HATTON.

22 November, 1677.[9]

. . . No Archbishop is yet declared. The persons
most spoken of are the Bishop of London, the Archbishop
of Dublin, the Dean of Paul's, Sir Lionel Jenkins, the
Bishop of Oxford, but those who are not friends to the
Coventry family oppose him. The Dean of Paul's was
nominated when the Bishop of London was the sole
candidate; and they who were not friends to the Bishop
of London nominated the Dean of Paul's, not out of kindness to him, but, in opposition to the Bishop of London,
set him up as a person highly qualified, beyond exception,
both for the gravity of his years, his profound learning,
exemplary piety, approved prudence, and recommended
above most others in one circumstance very considerable,
that he was without the dependences of relations, hath
no nephews and nieces to provide for. And some say it
is as convenient for the Church of England that *alterius
orbis papa* should have no relations as it is for the Church
of Rome that *papa Romae* should have none. But, if the
Bishop of London misses it, he hath gained this great
fame: that he was judged most worthy in the vogue of
the greatest of the King's Protestant subjects. It is very
wonderful that so many should appear so zealous for him;
but the Popish party are full as zealous for the Archbishop
of Dublin. The general report amongst the vulgar

yesterday was that the Bishop of London was Archbishop;
the Bishop of Rochester, Bishop of London; my cousin
North, Dean of Westminster; and Doctor Outram,
Bishop of Rochester. . . .

Last Saturday the coronation of Queen Elizabeth was
solemnized in the city with mighty bonfires and the burning of a most costly pope, carried by four persons in
divers habits, and the effigies of two devils whispering in
his ears, his belly filled full of live cats who squawled
most hideously as soon as they felt the fire; the common
saying all the while it was the language of the Pope and
the Devil in a dialogue betwixt them. A tierce of
claret was set out before the Temple Gate for the common
people. Mr. Langhorne said he is very confident the
pageantry cost £40. . . .

TO ROBERT NELSON FROM THOMAS KEN, NON-
JURING BISHOP OF BATH AND WELLS.
2 *March*, 1696.[10]

Sir,

I received the book which I imagined came from you,
and for which I return you many thanks; and since that,
your obliging letter came to my hands. You have done
an honour to the memory of our dead friend, which we
all ought to acknowledge; and I am very glad that his life
is writing by another hand, as you tell me. He was
certainly as saintlike a man as ever I knew; and his books
are demonstrations of it, which are full of as solid and
searching a piety as ever I read. God was pleased to take
him from the evil to come, to his own infinite advantage,
but to our great loss. His blessed will be done.

Since the date of your letter, a new scene has been
opened: and if the act passes which is now on the anvil,
I presume the prisons will be filled with the malcontents;
and your friend, though innocent and inoffensive, yet

apprehends he may share in the calamity; and foreseeing
it, it will be no surprise to him. In respect of that sort
of men I have been always of the mind of the Prophet,
that their strength was to sit still. And so it will be
found at the long run. And 'tis the wisest and most
dutiful way, to follow, rather than to anticipate,
Providence. . . . I commend you all to God's most
gracious protection.

Good Sir,

Your very affectionate servant,

THOS. BATH AND WELLS.

A CUP RUNNING OVER WITH MERCY

*Sir Edward Harley of Brampton Bryan had been an ardent
Presbyterian since childhood. He had fought against the King
and suffered persecution under the Commonwealth. He was
the author of several religious works. His second wife, Abigail,
was the daughter of Nathaniel Stephens of Essington, Gloucestershire, and bore him as her first son the famous Robert Harley,
first Earl of Oxford.*

*Lady Rachel Russell was the widow of the Whig leader,
Lord William Russell, who had suffered on the scaffold for high
treason in 1683. She was a daughter of the great Cavalier
Earl of Southampton and at the time of writing this letter was
fifty-nine years old. She was a woman of noble character, and
the spirit of cheerful resignation in which she writes is as fine a
testimony as any to all that was best in the religious outlook
of seventeenth century England.*

TO LADY HARLEY AT ESSINGTON, GLOUCESTERSHIRE,
FROM HER HUSBAND, SIR EDWARD HARLEY.

St. George in Ross, 21 October, 1662.[11]

It is my birthday, therefore, I am bound to entertain
you. This may come as seasonably to you as it doth

from me to divert after dinner or supper. I would gladly
have spent this day with you, but I was content it should
pass as the years it hath summed up have for the most
part done before it, in labour and travel and recreation,
in sunshine and showers, upon land and water, in embracing
my dearest comforts, in parting with them, in health,
and in the remembrances of mortality. Thirty and eight
years which have passed over my head have perhaps
sprinkled more grey hairs there than in many others;
but there is not a white stroke there that I would part
with, for there is not one I could be without. I have
tasted of many troubles, but my God hath given me
always a cup running over with mercy. One letter of
the name of Jesus Christ allowed me as my Lord, is more
than a world of comfort. Next to the mercies of my
soul you come in, and then the children, and then a
wonder that God should bestow so many favours upon so
mean a servant, and then an adoration of free grace,
which is above all. . . .

TO LADY ROOS AT HADDON FROM HER MOTHER,
LADY RACHEL RUSSELL.
Sunday, 29 *September*, 1695.[12]
. . . Take it well, my love, I remind you of your duty,
and let it be your part to strive to do it. To whom asks
it shall be given; you shall be contented if you desire it.
I have experienced it, and just at your years, I bless God
I can say—without vanity—what pleased me I enjoyed,
what crossed me had not power to torment me long.
I strove to think if my lot had not been what it was it
might have been worse for me in regard to my eternal
interest, and this might pass and other days come, or
however the day of vexation would end. And I can't
commend a better reflection than this, the troubles or

pleasures that end with time are not to be affecting at so high a rate; a year or two to some seems long, but twenty past as nothing. I have felt many days of bitter grief, as well others of lesser trouble and provocation, and many of great and true happiness, which was made up by love and quiet at home, abroad friendships and innocent diversions, and yet, believe me, child, life is a continual labour checkered with care and pleasure. Therefore rejoice in your portion, take the world as you find it, and you will I trust find heaviness may endure for a night, but joy comes in the morning. It grows dark, your sister is to close this.

CHAPTER XIV

DISEASE, DEATH AND BURIAL

SICK CHILDREN

The jargon of disease and of those who minister to it varies from age to age, though the symptoms remain much the same. The seventeenth century 'fell into an extreme cough,' or had 'a grievous pain in its belly,' not infrequently with ladies 'mixed with the vapours.' Sometimes, like poor, fashionable, horse-racing Colonel Henry Verney, it was 'deeply gone in the glanders,' and more often of 'a quartan ague in the back.' The language of its cures was as distinctive: 'I took a vomit,' wrote Anthony Wood, 'having been some days before and then possessed with great melancholy and distraction.'

Probably more than fifty per cent. of the population died in early infancy, and only a small proportion survived childhood. In the first letter Sir Thomas Browne, who was a practising doctor as well as a philosopher and an author, writes about the complaints of his little granddaughter to his son, also a practising physician—such a one as Sir Richard Blackmore described himself, 'a hard worked doctor, spending my days in coffee houses, receiving apothecaries or driving over the stones in my carriage visiting patients.' The next letter is about the smallpox, the pestilence that threatened every family of children in the land and frequently carried off or disfigured such of their elders as had had the doubtful fortune to escape having it in their own

*infancy. Because of its greater mortality among adults, some
parents deliberately put their children in the way of taking the
disease, thus anticipating the practice of vaccination.*

*Despite the frequency with which they were called upon to
fight smallpox, the doctors of the seventeenth century were able
to make little headway against it, and it continued to keep down
the population of England until vaccination and the sanitary
improvements of a later age did the physicians' business for
them. Sir Thomas Browne was of the opinion that chewing
rhubarb helped. ' Mr. Richardson, an exciseman near Bath, a
serious young man,' recorded Dr. Glegg in his diary, ' was
seized with the smallpox. When I came to him, I prescribed a
vomit which succeeded well. The smallpox appeared on the
fourth day of the confluent kind and very malignant, with many
purple spots intermixed. On the twelfth day, the second fever
was very high and on the following day he was delirious. I
prescribed opiates and alexipharmicks and two episparick
plaisters. Through God's assistance he recovered.' It was
an assistance on which seventeenth century medicine relied
greatly.*

TO DR. EDWARD BROWNE IN SALISBURY COURT,
NEXT THE GOLDEN BALLS, LONDON, FROM HIS
FATHER, SIR THOMAS BROWNE.

24 *January,* 1681.[1]

Dear Son,

My daughter Betty had a letter from Nancy, wherein
she writ concerning her daughter, little more than two
months old, which she saith is a fair full faced child, great
headed and but short winded, which showeth that she is
like to be rachitical, and, as they speak here, is set for
the rickets. And these are early signs of what may be
expected or feared. Being a full child, you did well to
appoint her syrup of rhubarb sometimes, and an issue,
and that being but lately made, she cannot expect much

from it, though she be yet over forward. To make it run
much she useth a little orange for a pea, and probably that,
or orrice or elder, may quicken, when the running
slacketh. But if it might suffice, it were well if it would
run with a pea; for that lieth quietly, nor so much
hazards inflammations.

The midwife or nurse persuaded her to give oxym.
scillit., a spoonful, and that made her sick, but is a good
medicine. She is somewhat too young and unable yet
to take drinks or decoctions of china, sarsa, eryngium, rad.
osmundæ, agrimonie, hartstong, betonica, and antirachi-
tical ingredients; except a syrup or distilled water, or
both, be made, of which she may be able to take some
spoonfuls, and the mild chalybeates do excellently well.
The bleeding at the ear no hurt, sometimes good: care
would be taken that the nurse keep a good diet; many
do well who are bred up by the spoon. As soon as you
have time, write a kind word unto her, for she perplexeth
herself night and day about the child. . . .

Dr. Burnett's book, in 8vo., is come to Norwich,
of the life and death of my Lord of Rochester. Love
and blessing to my daughter Browne and little Susan.
Tom, God be thanked, is well, though I wonder he falls
into no cough, wearing his hat and gloves so seldom.

Your loving father,

THOMAS BROWNE.

TO FRANCES BLUNDELL AT KILKENNY, IRELAND, FROM
WILLIAM BLUNDELL.

La Flêche, France, 9 October, 1681.[2]

Dear Sister,

. . . On the 24th of September . . . my dear charge
E. B. was seized with a pain in his back. On the 26th he
raved and said and did things extremely extravagant.
I removed him that night to a doctor's house. On the

28th the smallpox appeared, which grew in six days to cover his whole face in a very horrid manner. The soles of his feet, his head, his hands were dressed in the same sort, but yet a little thinner . . .; much smart he endured till they begun to die, which was two or three days since. He is now void of pain and I trust quite free from danger; yet the charge will be somewhat high! We hope his visage will suffer little, the doctor in that particular being said to be skilful and fortunate. The patient is inwardly well and his appetite towards his victuals is now as good as ever. The wife and daughters of the house attend him with the greatest love and diligence, all which, and the apothecary's bill especially, is like to be somewhat. You may expect good things of this Edmund. His judgment is very sound, and his observation both of men and things is no worse than the best I have known at the entrance to the 18th year.

It is now the 13th day, and Edmund grows daily better. We hope for considerable advantages from his present distemper; that his body will be more vigorous and his face less troubled with red spots which did blemish before, but not greatly deface his visage. His hair is now cut off, and herein I do purpose to send you an unclean small lock of the same. The charge of peruques is now added to a thousand other expenses. . . .

CURES

Seventeenth century cures make curious reading to modern eyes, though they were often founded on greater knowledge of human needs, and especially of the remedial value of herbs, than is generally realised. ' I took early in the morning a good dose of elixir and hung three spiders about my neck, and they drove my ague away: Deo gratias,' wrote learned Elias Ashmole. Every notable housewife kept a household book of

*recipes and cures to which guests were expected to contribute, and
constant toll was laid on the surrounding gardens and meadows
for the simples which were held, often rightly, to restore the
healthful balance of the body : cowslip flowers, borage, bugles,
lilies of the valley, rosemary, sage, betony flowers, ' each
flower in its season,' balm, motherwort, spike flowers, bay
leaves, orange leaves. Many of these cherished cures, however,
were more romantic than effective : pigeons in the bed for smallpox to extract the venom and bring on sleep, a live sheep or an
application of treacle for the measles, and a cold marble stone
on which the sun had never shone applied to the belly to relieve
the colic. One of the most curious cures was a ' restorative
electuary ' composed of ' parrots' tongues and hawks' livers.'*

*John Dolben of Segroit was a humble Welsh squire, one of
whose cousins rose to the Bench and another of whom became
Archbishop of York. Dr. Robert Plot, who describes so amusing
a cure for the bite of a mad dog, was one of the leading anti-
quaries and collectors of curiosities of his age. His ' Natural
History of Oxfordshire ' and ' Natural History of Staffordshire '
were written as part of a larger work, never completed, of a
Natural History of England. He was Secretary of the Royal
Society and Professor of Chemistry at Oxford. A Kentish man
himself, he was writing in this letter on his native heath. His
correspondent, the Master of University College, Oxford, was
one of the learned friends of Pepys' old age.*

TO MRS. DOLBEN AT GWERSILT, DENBIGHSHIRE, FROM
HER SON, JOHN DOLBEN.

21 *February*, 1684.[3]

Ever honoured and most dear Mother,

I was at Plas Coch upon Monday last, where my uncle
and aunt were much troubled to hear of your indisposition. And my uncle upon serious consideration hath
ordered for you as followeth: viz: to take three of the
pills over night and three in the morning for two or three

days together: then intermit a day or two, then take three spoonfuls of the never-failing over night and as much in the morning for two or three days if you can bear it.

There are in the great box some cordial lozenges which you are to take as often as you please: they are very good against the wind. There is likewise a bottle of Juniper water, which you are to take at any time, if you find yourself anything fainty; this is also very good against the wind. You have there some French barley which you are thus to use: viz: half a handful of it with a handful of each of the herbs in two quarts of water to be boiled to a quart, then to be sweetened with a little sugar and some juice of lemons or rather orange. This is to be your most ordinary drink. All which my uncle judgeth to be most proper for your condition.

My dear Mother, I humbly entreat you not to be frightened with the basket but to make use of the means, and I hope God will give the blessing. . . .

TO DOCTOR ARTHUR CHARLETT, MASTER OF UNIVERSITY COLLEGE, OXFORD, FROM DOCTOR ROBERT PLOT.

Rochester, 18 *August*, 1693.[4]

Good Master,

According to my promise I here send you word that I have reached this place, having been as successful in my journey as I could expect. But the greatest rarity that I met with has been here, viz: a medicine for the bite of a mad dog, which was applied here to Doctor de Langley, Prebend of Canterbury, his wife and fair daughter who were all three dipped in salt water, a little below the bridge, without fig-leaves, last Friday morning by two lewd fellows of this town, the spectators, you may be sure, being very numerous. That the reverend Doctor was really mad I hope you will not doubt; but whether

the medicine had its due effect, I guess I shall hear by
that time I reach Canterbury, when you shall be sure to
hear again from

Your most faithful friend,

ROBERT PLOT.

' BRING OUT YOUR DEAD '

*The bubonic plague visited London on a grand scale for the
last time in 1665 and the English provinces in the following
year. Against its might medical science was practically
powerless. Its ravages were chiefly confined to the poor, whose
insanitary and crowded hovels made an ideal breeding-ground
for the black rat whose parasites carried the disease. The rich,
living under cleanlier conditions and able to fly from the
pestilence, were almost immune: of the leading figures of
seventeenth century politics, society and literature scarcely one
perished in the Great Plague of 1665, even those who, like
Pepys and the Duke of Albemarle, remained in the heart of the
stricken town, escaping. But among the poor the plague raged
with every gruesome attendance of horror.*

*Neither Sir Thomas Browne nor William Blundell requires
further introduction. The latter's correspondent, Roger
L'Estrange, the Cavalier journalist, was at that time State
Surveyor of the Imprimery and editor of the ' Intelligencer,'
which supplied Blundell with his news. L'Estrange remained
in London throughout the Plague.*

TO JOHN HOBART IN ST. GILES'S PARISH, ESQ., FROM
[SIR] THOMAS BROWNE.

Great Melton, 31 *August*, 1666.[5]

Worthy and honoured Sir,

I am extremely troubled to hear that some have had the
sickness in your house. As you shall all have my daily
prayers, so I cannot give myself any satisfaction unless I

T

confer my mite unto the preservation of a person whose friendship I highly value and whose true worth I have so long and truly honoured. And, therefore, in order to prevention you may please to use two fumes, one of vinegar, wherein rue, angelica, wormwood, scordium, juniper, bay leaves and savin are steeped, which may be used often in the day and in the chambers. Another of an higher and stronger nature twice or thrice a day in the hall, parlour and other rooms; and if anyone hath had it, before he cometh to communicate with others his chamber may be fumed, the doors being shut close. Of this you may have, if you please to send to Mr. Day, the apothecary, where you may also have a preventive, and also an antidotal electuary of no mean nature, whereof give a dram and half in posset drink unto any that falls sick, and to be in bed, and again the next night, and so again the third night, and to drink possets of scordium, wood sorrel, and angelica. If you have no issue, to make one may be of singular effect, though it be stopped up two months hence, or to keep a blister always on some part, sometimes on the arm, sometimes on the leg.

From the report made of some who have been sick in your house and escaped, I am very hopeful that the malignity was not so great as in other places. And I have one observation set down by a learned man, and confirmed to me by Dr. Witherley, in the late sickness of London, which affordeth me much comfort, and I hope will be verified in your family; that in houses where the first that falleth sick escapeth, the rest either fall not sick, or, if sick, escape; of this I would not omit to inform you, because I comfort myself much therein, and I am sure it holds *ad plurimum* if not always. Good sir excuse me.

I rest your most faithful friend and unworthy kinsman,

THOMAS BROWNE.

T O ROGER L'ESTRANGE FROM WILLIAM BLUNDELL.

2 October, 1665.[6]

My very dear and good Sir,

I have yours of the 26th last with a paper of fresh
intelligence. But I am now more solicitous than ever
till you pass your quarantine. You stayed too long in
that unhappy place. And if nothing worse do attend you,
your dreams must be of graves and corpses for this many
a day. I have the horror upon myself at this great
distance, and that dismal churchyard will not go out of
my mind. God Almighty protect you and the remainder of your good family, and send you soon and safe
together. . . .

Yours to love and serve you,

WILL: BLUNDELL.

'THE NASTY SPA'

*From the plague-pit to the fashionable watering-place is a
long leap, but both belong to the medical phenomena of the
seventeenth century. Sea-bathing was a mystery still to be
revealed, but there was a widespread belief in the virtues
of inland waters, both for internal and external use. Besides
famous spas like Bath—whence Pepys emerged from the bath
' parboiled ' and sweating profusely—Tunbridge Wells and
Harrogate, there were innumerable springs in the vicinity of
humble villages like Hogshaw in Buckinghamshire and Astrop in
Oxfordshire which were exploited by enterprising local land-
owners and doctors and resorted to by the faithful in great
numbers.*

*Peg Elmes was a sister of Sir Ralph Verney and the wife of a
sulky Northamptonshire squire, Mr., afterwards Sir, Thomas
Elmes. She was a great ' malade imaginaire,' and her family*

(at least those members of it who did not have to pay for it) regarded the ' chargeable diversion ' of her constant resort to some new physician with much amusement. Her fashionable complaints of the horrors of Harrogate, or Knaresborough Spa as it was still called, are in keeping with a type as old as civilisation. It was at Harrogate, ' the Yorkshire Spa,' that dawn used to be made hideous for visitors by the appearance in their lodgings of importunate water-women with sulphur-stained faces selling pots of the healing waters.

TO SIR RALPH VERNEY AT SIR NATHANIEL HOBART'S HOUSE IN CHANCERY LANE, OVER AGAINST LINCOLN'S INN, FROM HIS SISTER, MRS. ELMES.

Knaresborough Spa, 4 June, 1665.[7]

Dear Brother,

The 1st instant we arrived at the nasty Spa and have now began to drink the horrid sulphur water. Which, although as bad as is possible to be imagined, yet in my judgment pleasant to all the doings we have within doors, the house and all that is in it being horridly nasty and crowded up with all sort of company which we eat with in a room as the spiders are ready to drop into my mouth. And sure hath neither been well cleaned nor aired this dozen years. It makes me much more sick than the nasty water. Did you but see me you would laugh heartily at me.

But I say little of it to what I think. Then to mend all this, they go to supper at half an hour after six, so I save a bit and sup by myself two hours after them, which is the pleasantest thing I do here. We are sixteen of my uncle and aunt's family, and all in pension at 10s. a week for ourselves, and 7s. for our servants with lodgings in.

I have not heard from you I know not when, so in

my opinion live here as if there were nobody else in the world, but just what I see of these bumpkins. We met the Lady Compton and her sister the Lady Ann Compton at Doncaster, who assured me the Blackamore's Head in Chancery Lane was shut up of the plague, which makes me in a very great fear of you, and the rest of your family, so am the more impatient to hear of you. Which is all from

Your truly affectionate sister
and servant
M. Elmes.

A CONVALESCENT

The remedies of the seventeenth century were not always unsuccessful, as the following letter from Thomas Ken shows. Lord Weymouth was the patron who befriended Ken after the Revolution of 1688 and who gave him the use of his own house Longleat as a home. The invalid was possibly one of the Misses Kemeys of Naish, Somerset, who were also devoted friends of the little Bishop.

TO Viscount Weymouth from Thomas Ken, bishop of bath and wells.

[1686?] [8]

All Glory be to God.

My very good Lord,

I can now, God's holy name be praised, give your Lordship a better account of the good Lady than I did in my last. She is now in all appearance past danger and sleeps well, and eats an egg, and sits up for two or three hours, and has taken steel . . . a week which agrees very well with her, so that she recovers daily, and it is visible in her looks. She has a great mind for asparagus, and there is none in all the country. If your Lordship has any, this messenger will wait on you to-morrow, and they will be a most acceptable present; and the physicians do very gladly indulge her that sort of diet. She presents her humble service to yourself and to my Lady, with abundant acknowledgements of your great concern for her. I cannot yet be permitted to leave her; only I made an excursion to Wells for two nights, and I am very glad Mr. King came not thither.

God in His infinite goodness multiply His blessings on yourself, on my Lady, and on your family,

My good Lord,

Your Lordship's most humble and affect. servant,

THO. BATH & WELLS.

DEATH SUMMONS THE EARL OF ROCHESTER

When the doctors of medicine had done their best to save the body and had been beaten, the doctors of religion were called in to save the soul. Of the great deathbed struggles for salvation of that age none made so deep an impression on the imagination of England as that which Gilbert Burnet waged for the soul of John Wilmot, second Earl of Rochester. Stricken down by a terrible illness, the result of his own excesses, Rochester at the beginning of the last winter of his life called in Burnet, then a rising preacher, to resolve his religious doubts. Nine months later, after four days of intensive theological argument, he died on July 26, 1680, in his thirty-fourth year, at his home in Woodstock Park, confessing and calling himself a Christian.

TO THE LADY ST. JOHN AT HER HOUSE AT BATTERSEA FROM ANNE, DOWAGER COUNTESS OF ROCHESTER. 19 *June* [1680].⁹

I must, dear sister, give you an account of the first hopes of comfort I have of my son Rochester; who, tho' he is still very weak, yet these two days has produced

strange alterations in him.   He sleeps very well, is but
little feverish, his great tortures of pain almost abated,
gathers some strength, tho' but little yet.   But God is
infinitely merciful, upon all accounts, both to his soul and
body.   'Tis my great hopes he will persevere, in the way
God has put him in, for his soul's happiness.

I cannot omit one passage lately.   Mr. Fanshaw, his
great friend, has been here to see him; and as he was
standing by my son's bedside, he looked earnestly upon
him and said, . . . ' Fanshaw, think of a God, let me
advise you; and repent you of your former life, and
amend your ways.   Believe what I say to you; there is a
God, and a powerful God, and he is a terrible God to
unrepenting sinners; the time draws near that he will
come to judgment with great terror to the wicked;
therefore, delay not your repentance: his displeasure will
thunder against you, if you do.   You and I have been
long time acquainted, done ill together.   I love the man;
and speak to him out of conscience, for the good of his
soul.'   Fanshaw stood, and said never a word to him,
but stole away out of the room.   When my son saw him
go, ' Is 'a gone? ' says he, ' poor wretch!   I fear his heart
is hardened.'   After that, Fanshaw said to some in the
house, that my son should be kept out of melancholy
fancies.   This was told my son again: upon which says
he, ' I know why he said that; it was because I gave him
my advice; but I could say no less to him than I did, let
him take it as he pleases.'

Dear sister, my hope is great: and God is good, on
whom I depend for good, both for his soul and body.
I believe I have tired you with my discourse.   I have
nothing more at present, but to assure you

I am, Madam,

Your faithful friend and servant,

A. ROCHESTER.

You must not let Mr. Fanshaw know what I have told you. Before I sealed this, I received yours, and two waters for my son Rochester; he and his lady give you thanks, and present their service to you. I thank God my son continues, at all times, very devout, ever since God struck him with a sense of his sins. He is very tender and fearful, but it does not carry him to despair. He is sensible the satisfaction of Christ is his support, and relies wholly upon Christ's merits for his salvation. This day has not been so good a day with him as yesterday ; he has had some faint fits.

' THIS IS THE END OF DAVY '

The next four letters record the deaths of three men, one of them famous and two obscure. David Whitford, who ' died hard ' as the seventeenth century phrase was, was the son of a Bishop who fought as a lad for the King in the Civil Wars and was made a prisoner after the Battle of Worcester. He was a student of Christ Church and chaplain to Lord Lauderdale. The Hon. Robert Boyle, the subject of the second letter, was the greatest chemist of the age, a man of universal and curious genius who elicited admiration from almost everyone who knew him. He died at the end of 1691 at the age of sixty-four. The Lord Rochester, who was one of his friends, was Lory Hyde, the first Earl of a new creation and no relation to the ill-fated poet whose death was the theme of the last letter; the Bishop of Salisbury who preached his funeral sermon, however, was no other than Gilbert Burnet, the bustling Scots divine who had officiated at Wilmot's deathbed. The second letter has the additional interest of describing a very different kind of death— a murder. Its writer, Sir Edmund King, was the physician who first attended Charles II after the seizure which heralded his last illness.

Edmund Verney of the White House, East Claydon, and his sons, Ralph and Mun, were introduced in our first chapter. Edmund senior was to follow his eldest son to the grave two years later and Edmund junior was to die in 1690 at the age of twenty-two.

TO JOHN ELLIS FROM THE REV. HUMPHREY PRIDEAUX.

Oxford, 27 October, 1674.[10]

By reason of the multiplicity of business Mr. Dean hath at present cast upon me, I have only time to tell you that if you intend to take your degree this term it is full time you were already here; and that yesterday, at 10 in the morning, David Whitford was found dead in his chamber having been the night before and that very morning at 8 very well. He had not one farthing in his pocket, although he had received £9 within 10 days before; but all was spent in ale, he having been drunk almost every night since he came hither. He was found fallen back upon his bed half dressed, with a brandy bottle in one hand and the cork in the other; he finding himself ill, as it seemeth, was going to take a dram for refreshment, but death came between the cup and the lips: and this is the end of Davy. Mr. Dean coming into his chamber upon the noise of this accident, we searched to see what he had left; among his papers I by chance light on a bond ready drawn up to be sealed, by which Davy bound himself to give £500 for a parsonage by such a day or resign it again. The horror of this crime joined to the rest of his lewd life hath made death appear very dismal unto me. . . .

To Christopher, Viscount Hatton, from Sir Edmund King.

2 January, 1692.[11]

My Lord,

My being out of my bed two nights together with Mr. Boyle, whose death I foretold the first day he complained of an alteration, which was Tuesday. And that day I told my Lord Rochester and others of his friends and desired another physician to be sent for, which was that night. And at ten, as I told your Lordship, I was sent for to be in the house all night, but did not let him know it, for fear of surprising him (he was up all Tuesday). Wednesday morn was much better, but exceeding low and faint; would rise in the afternoon, and at five we met and desired him to go to bed at seven. Doctor Stokeham was to sit up; but at ten or eleven he grew worse, so that my Lord Ranelagh and Lady Thanet Dowager, etc., was sent for, and they sent for me. I was just hot in my bed, after something I had taken for my great cold; and, though I had not a grain of hope he would live till I came, yet, considering it was the last attempt I could make to serve one who for many years past had great affection for me and relied under God, as he often told me, upon my care, I was resolved to go to him. It was one o'clock in the night; but he was dead before I came. His lamp went out for want of oil; so did his sister's, too.

He was buried last night at St. Martin's, and lies by his sister. The Bishop of Salisbury preached his funeral sermon, and gave a large and true character becoming so great a man as he was and whose second in universal knowledge, etc., 'twill be hard to find. The Bishop said he had a conversation with him the better part of twenty-nine years; but mine has been above thirty years, and, the last ten or twelve, not four days together from him, if in town. It would make me look vain to relate his affectionate expressions to me. He has been kept alive, by God's blessing, upon the dint of care several years, to a wonder. But I ask your Lordship's pardon for being so long upon this subject. Seeing the subject will bear it, I hope you'll excuse it.

I suppose your Lordship has heard of the barbarous murder of Doctor Clenche? He lived in Brownlow Street in Holborn. Monday night last about nine at night, two men came in a hackney coach to call him to one not well ; but he was not at home, and they said they'd come again. About ten the same night they came to the end of the street and sent the coachman for him. He, poor man, took his cloak and went to them into the coach; they bid the coachman drive to the *Pie* without Aldgate. But, as soon as they had him, they began their villainies ; for his hat was found in the street near Barnard's Inn, and we believe he was soon dead. And there, to blind the coachman, they enquired for a man there near Aldgate nobody knew. By this time the dead man began to be cold and stiffish, that they were sure he was dead. When they came back as far as Leadenhall Street, they called the coachman and gave him 3/6 to buy two pullets for supper. The man got them quickly, and, when he came back, there was only the doctor dead and almost cold; the murderers gone.

About fourteen days since, two huffing men came at night for me in a hack; but I was abroad. They came a second time and were angry I was not at home. Then my wife sent them word they had best get another doctor (there's enough), for she believed if I did come home I would not go with them, nor should not if she could help it; so they went away much out of humour.

But, before this, I escaped an imminent danger of the

kind, I bless God, which has stuck by me ever since. But this of Doctor Clenche is a terrible thing. It was reported in the city it was me, to the great concern of many of my friends; but my coach being in the city that morning gave them another account, which was too true. My Lord Falconberg came to my house himself and several others.

Since I wrote this, we are informed those taken upon suspicion are the very persons that murdered him; one Harrison especially.

Just now the doctor's wife and the Vice-president of the College send to me to come in my gown to assist with him at the pall this Saturday night. I am not well, yet intend to go, to pay the last respect to him.

TO MUN VERNEY AT TRINITY COLLEGE, OXFORD, FROM HIS FATHER, EDMUND VERNEY.
16 *February*, 1686.[12]

Child,

. . . My dearly beloved son Ralph departed this transitory life yesterday morning about 11 o'clock. . . . My heart is so incurably pierced with grief for the loss of my dear child that I can no more be comforted than Rachel was who wept for her children. . . . My poor son is this day to be put up into three coffins, two of wood and one of lead and is to be drawn to his dormitory in my father's vault in Middle Claydon. I shall not stir out of doors till he is gone. He is to be drawn in a hearse with six horses and scutcheons and one coach more with six horses accompanies him, my brother and Jack Stewkeley go down in it as chief mourners, and four men in mourning ride by on horseback along with the body all the way. . . .

TO EDMUND VERNEY FROM HIS SON MUN VERNEY FROM TRINITY COLLEGE, OXFORD.

23 *February*, 1686.[13]

Most honoured Father,

I received both yours, that of the 16th and that of the 18th, and by the former I understand that it was the pleasure of Almighty God to take unto himself the soul of my dearest and only brother. But I hope the thoughts of the happiness which he enjoys in Heaven will in a great measure lessen the sorrow which I undergo by losing so near and so dear a relation. Now seeing it has pleased Almighty God to make me acquainted with the sorrows and afflictions of this world by taking from me my only brother, I hope it will be a means to make me fear God and honour you and my mother, and by so doing I hope I shall render both you and myself happy. I have made me a new black cloth suit, and a new black mourning gown, which with new muslin bands and cloth shoes will stand me in very near ten pounds. . . .

I present my duty to you and my grandfather and my love to my dear sister, and so I subscribe myself

Your most dutiful son

EDMUND VERNEY.

THE LOSS OF A WIFE

The subject of the two letters that follow, the first written to Ralph Thoresby, the antiquary, is the death of a wife after long years of marriage. With Sir Robert Southwell, the retired Clerk of the Privy Council, we are already familiar. His correspondent, Sir William Petty, one of the most remarkable men of his age, had begun life as the son of a humble clothier, had served at sea as a common sailor, amassed a fortune and established a great reputation as a mathematician, inventor and statistician.

TO Ralph Thoresby from the Rev. Richard
Stretton.

London, 4 May, 1695.[14]

Dear Sir,

This brings you the most sad disconsolate tidings that
ever I had occasion to send you. It hath pleased the only
wise God, with one stroke of His hand, to remove the
desire of mine eyes and the delight of my heart, my
tender, loving and dearly beloved wife from me yesterday
between seven and eight at night, after four or five days
of pain and sickness. With a cheerful, sweet, composed
countenance, without so much as one sigh or groan, she
resigned up her soul into the hands of a tender Redeemer
who loved her and washed her from her sins in His own
blood. She had no pangs in her death: she is got to
rest, and I have not the least hesitation or doubt in my
own heart but that she is as well as heart can wish; but
we are left in a sad, desolate and disconsolate estate.

But God hath spoken, and He also hath done it, and
what shall I say? I will be dumb and not open my
mouth, because He hath done it; it is fit to be silent
before God, when God puts us to silence. He had a
greater right in her than I had; His did precede and excel
mine and He hath better provided for her than ever I
could have done. My lease of her was expired and for-
feited long before; and as a Sovereign He may dispose of
His own as He pleaseth. She lived desired, and dies as
much lamented as most women of her rank ever were.
She will be missed by more than near relations. I have
lost as loving, tender, prudent a wife, and my son as
tender, careful a mother as ever any could enjoy. Oh!
what arrears of thankfulness are due that we enjoyed
her so long, and so much sweetness and comfort in her;
help us with your prayers (and engage all our friends to

beg) for support under, and a sanctified use and improve-
ment of this severe providence. I have known what it is
to part with sweet hopeful children, and it is hard enough
to bear it; but to part with a wife, and such a wife,
cuts deep and reacheth the very soul. Mine, and my
son's hearty love and service to you and yours, and to all
friends. I commit you to God and rest

Your sorrowful, afflicted friend and servant,
RICHARD STRETTON.

TO SIR WILLIAM PETTY FROM SIR ROBERT SOUTH-
WELL.

Kingsweston, 28 *February*, 1681.[15]

Dear Cousin,

You were not only my comforter upon the death of an
excellent father, but you exercised great skill to prevent
his death. And now, by yours of the 31st past, you do
not only condole the great loss I have sustained in a wife,
but you seem to think it reparable. As to the loss, 'tis
true 'twas but of a mortal thing, and so I must submit.
He that hath an unlimited Jurisdiction did it, for we
wanted nothing that human aids could give. And perhaps
I ought not to repine that one who had so many prepara-
tions for Heaven, was taken to the rewards thereof.

But when by 19 years' conversation I knew the great
virtues of her mind, and discover since her death a more
secret correspondence with Heaven in acts of piety and
devotion (which before I knew not of), you will allow
me, at least for my children's sake, to lament that they
have too early lost their guide.

I have had many other close trials since my father's
death—the loss of a good mother, of an only sister, two
nephews educated by my care, and a beloved son who died
three years before. And yet I may say he died but even

now; for by what steps and motions he declined towards
his grave, just the same were now gone over again by his
dear mother to the observation and sorrow of all that
beheld. So that a tragedy of the greatest past affliction
I ever had, was that repeated upon me, and I leave you to
judge whether I had not load enough.

But I hope all these rugged paths will best conduct me
to my journey's end. 'Tis certain the earth becomes less
worthy for the good who leave it, and weak natures may
be allowed to think Heaven the more desirable for their
friends who are gone before.

There is but one strong motive in me to respite such
desires, which is the consideration of four young children
who will hardly find so good a friend as myself in the whole
world. They deserve well from me, and with application may be led into the path of a virtuous life. They
are all parcels of their mother, acting in small different
resemblances the tenor and habit of her life. So that,
as to your expedient, I look upon it under correction
but as a mere knocking these four in the head; and I
cannot think myself out of the bonds of wedlock while
they live. Your own case and mine (about this age) was
quite upon a different foot and without any proportion.

I speak not this in sorrow, for I have wiped that away
and am cheerfully entertaining myself here with my
children, and cannot wish for a better employment of my
life. My son either walks or rides about with me,
repeating at a time an hundred of your verses (of the
104th Psalm) with such accent and delight as would
perhaps give you entertainment to hear him. The load-
stone, Mercury, the bees, the four small animals and so
to the stars etc., are all to him as the mariner's compass. And would you have me forget this boy, who
remembers with pride the kiss you gave him for demon-
strating at eight years old an equilateral triangle? Well of

this I have said enough to justify my rejection of any salve that can ever be thought of on this side Heaven; and I will only add, as to myself, that being wonderfully troubled with the scurvy in my nerves, I am under all the trials I can bear to get some deliverance from it.

As to your good sentence lately obtained in the Exchequer, I am sure I take real comfort in it and wish from my heart that you may see a short and prosperous event of that great perplexity; that so the world may have the fruit and treasure which your leisure and tranquillity would afford.

My blessing to my godson and to his hearty brother. My boy puts his humble service to his fine cousins, and I am ever Sir, Your most humble servant

R. S.

THE FUNERAL

The seventeenth century mind was never more characteristically occupied than when contemplating its own end. It prepared for it with every circumstance of pomp and solemnity. ' 'Tis an object I will fix and charge upon my memory,' wrote William Sancroft to his brother, ' and often represent to my thoughts my dear father lying buried betwixt his two wives; and though I am now ready to wander further from you, yet will I hope one day to return and find my last home at his feet.' That a man might lie at peace till the day of Judgment in his own place and beside his own folk was a dear thought that robbed death of half its terrors.

'Walking on Thursday last,' wrote a Londoner to a country friend, ' I saw the carcass of the great Coke of Norfolk conveying to his long home, which to one of you that dwell a hundred miles off methinks should not be so grievous being all your lives accustomed to the mortification of going to your long homes.'

Such funeral cortèges, followed by a train of coaches as they made their way into the distant shires, were a familiar sight to the Londoners of the day. So Peter Shakerley, losing his wife of a summer's fever in London, made arrangements to carry her body into Cheshire, two hundred miles away, and lay it in the vault of his fathers in the little wooden church of Nether Peover. It was his hope, as his letter to Mrs. Dobson tells, that later he should one day rest there himself. But thirty years later he took the body of his long lost wife a further journey and laid it under the chancel of Somerford Chapel, fifteen miles distant, that he and she might lie together close to the great house, now desolated by the estate breaker, which he had built for his family.

The elaborate ceremony of a seventeenth century funeral is illustrated by the two following letters. At that of a man or woman of any consequence, the whole countryside took part. At one such—of a middling country squire—seventy of the neighbouring gentry were given mourning gloves and scarves, another seventy gloves at half-a-crown a pair, while doles of 2d. or 3d. each were distributed to upwards of seven hundred poor persons.

TO Mrs. DOBSON AT MORTHWAITE, CHESHIRE, FROM PETER SHAKERLEY, M.P.

Westminster, 5 September, 1691.[16]

My dearest Friend,

It has pleased God to deprive me of my only earthly joy, my dear, dear wife, who departed this life the 1st instant. I intend to inter the corpse at Lower Peover upon Saturday the 12th of this month (being this day sevennight) and in order to that I have sent to acquaint all the gentry in the country (not excepting any) that I desire they will be at Peter Yates's house at Hulmes Chapel upon Saturday the 12th instant by 10 of the clock forenoon, for I intend to set out thence by 12 that the gentlemen and their ladies may have time to return home. My own house Hulme is so full of cheese I cannot possibly use it on this occasion; therefore must have the treatment as well as I can at Peter Yates's house, which will not be very inconvenient because I must lodge the corpse there Friday night, at which time and place I should be glad to see you who are my true friend, and so my poor dearest did faithfully esteem you.

I have written to Peter Yates to take care that sufficient accommodation and provision be made for all that come (viz: very good and plentiful collations of cold meats in two good by-rooms near the great room for the gentry that come from far and will be out early, with voiders of biscuits and white wine, claret and sack for them; and bakers' biscuits and burned ale good store for the tenants and neighbours of Peover, Hulme, Byley, etc., to whom I desire John Eaton will send. And lest my letter to Peter Yates should miscarry I write this to you and desire you will acquaint him with it, and desire John Eaton to be one of the servitors and I hope Mr. Hobson will be there for another. You would be very kind if your occasions would permit you to go there meantime and see that all things be ordered decently and well, suitable to that respect and love which is most justly due to this my most entirely beloved, who has left her text for her funeral sermon (viz: the last Chapter of the second Epistle to the Corinthians and the eleventh verse). I have written to Mr. Richardson the minister at Lower Peover to prepare a sermon upon it against the time, and lest that letter miscarry I also desire you to send to him and acquaint him with it. The neighbouring clergy should also be invited, but how that is to be done I know not, so leave it to Mr. Richardson to order. I have been near

two hours in writing this; what's omitted please to help
out, and in this my miserable condition let me have your
prayers for

Your truly afflicted friend,

P. SHAKERLEY.

Mr. Richardson must also order the clerk or sexton at
Peover to make the place of interment at the east end
of my own chancel, but so as that when it shall please God
to call me hence my body may lie by this my dearest,
which was her inclination (as well as 'tis mine) as I am
told, for I could not reach time enough to see my dearest,
which is a great addition to my misery.

TO ROBERT SOUTHWELL FROM VALENTINE SAVAGE.

Dublin, 27 November, 1669.[17]

Mrs. Katherine Perceval was very handsomely buried.
There were twenty-three poor women in gowns and
kerchiefs, after them the maids that watched with her
in her sickness, which were some thirty-six, in white
gloves and scarves, then John Leyland and the butler in
black, after them two doctors of divinity and two bishops,
then the corpse, the pall being borne by six knights'
daughters, and they led by six knights' sons, who had all
white scarves and black cyprus over, after them all the
ladies and gentlemen, their relations, in mourning on
foot, led by knights and squires in long black cloaks, and
made at least thirty couple, after them the Lord Mayor
and Aldermen and other gentlemen and gentlewomen,
not in mourning, and then a number of coaches. And so
to the church, where they were met with the choristers.
And afterwards there were at her funeral as many tears as
ever I think at one time were shed in that place.

CONSOLATION

The last two letters treat of consolation. Jeremy Taylor was the first preacher of his age. A royalist, he had recently suffered imprisonment and proscription. His letter to Evelyn is the more touching in that he also had just suffered the loss of his ' two sweet hopeful boys.'

The Duchess of Ormonde had been married to her husband at fourteen, and her death at the age of sixty-nine ended an association that had continued for over fifty-four years.

TO JOHN EVELYN FROM JEREMY TAYLOR.

17 *February*, 1657.[18]

Dear Sir,

If dividing and sharing griefs were like the cutting of rivers, I dare say to you, you would find your stream much abated; for I account myself to have a great cause of sorrow, not only in the diminution of the numbers of your joys and hopes, but in the loss of that pretty person, your strangely hopeful boy. I cannot tell all my own sorrows without adding to yours; and the causes of my real sadness in your loss are so just and so reasonable that I can no otherwise comfort you but by telling you that you have very great cause to mourn; so certain it is that grief does propagate as fire does. . . .

But, sir, I cannot choose but I must hold another and a brighter flame to you. It is already burning in your heart, and if I can but remove the dark side of the lantern, you have enough within you to warm yourself and to shine to others. Remember, sir, your two boys are two bright stars, and their innocence is secured, and you shall never

hear evil of them again.   Their state is safe, and Heaven
is given to them upon very easy terms; nothing but to be
born and die.   It will cost you more trouble to get where
they are; and amongst other things one of the [hardest]
will be, that you must overcome even this just and
reasonable grief.   And, indeed though the grief hath but
too reasonable a cause, yet it is much more reasonable
that you master it. . . .

Sir, if you do not look to it, time will snatch your
honour from you, and reproach you for not effecting
that by Christian philosophy which time will do alone.
And if you consider, that of the bravest men in the world
we find the seldomest stories of their children, and the
apostles had none, and thousands of the worthiest persons,
that sound most in story, died childless; you will find
it is a rare act of Providence so to impose upon worthy
men a necessity of perpetuating their names by worthy
actions and discourses, governments and reasonings.
If the breach be never repaired, it is because God does
not see it fit to be; and if you will be of this mind, it will
be much the better.

But, sir, you will pardon my zeal and passion for your
comfort.   I will readily confess that you have no need of
any discourse from me to comfort you.   Sir, now you
have an opportunity of serving God by passive graces;
strive to be an example and a comfort to your lady, and
by your wise counsel and comfort, stand in the breaches
of your own family, and make it appear that you are more
to her than ten sons.   Sir, by the assistance of Almighty
God, I purpose to wait on you some time next week, that
I may be a witness of your Christian courage and bravery,
and that I may see that God never displeases you as long
as the main stake is preserved—I mean your hopes and
confidences of Heaven.   Sir, I shall pray for all that you
can want—that is, some degrees of comfort and a present

mind; and shall always do you honour, and fain also would do you service, if it were in the power, as it is in the affections and desires of

Dear Sir,
Your most affectionate and obliged
friend and servant,
JER. TAYLOR.

TO THE MARQUESS OF ORMONDE, LORD-LIEUTENANT OF IRELAND, FROM MICHAEL BOYLE, ARCHBISHOP OF ARMAGH.

Dublin, 29 July, 1684.[19]

You have now shot the gulf, and have passed the greatest difficulty of your life. You have lost the noblest person, the wisest friend, and the best of wives that ever lived; one of such an universal goodness that her death doth worthily challenge not only your Grace's, but the kingdom's lamentation. But all the glories of this world must have an end, and God in his divine wisdom hath [thought] fit to put a determination unto this.

The news thereof was a surprise and indeed of great astonishment; but I hope it may not be unseasonable for your Grace on this occasion to consider how long God hath been pleased to afford you the enjoyment of this great blessing. If my computation fails me not, it is about fifty-five years that you have been happy in each other. What an age of mercies have you possessed together! How have you supported each other through all the changes and varieties of fortune, and have made even your sufferings easy to you both by your mutual assistances! God hath been infinitely kind and indulgent to you both all those past years of your life, and I know your Grace to be so much a Christian as not to repine that now, at the latter end of your days, he should make that separation which mortality cannot avoid.

Pardon me, my Lord, that I presume to become your Grace's remembrancer in this great matter, though I cannot in the least doubt but that your great and good thoughts have fully discoursed more than I am able to write on this occasion. I can think a thousand things more which may not be improper for your Grace upon this subject but really, my Lord I cannot speak them: *vox faucibus haeret*. I shall not therefore any further press upon your Grace's retirements, but shall heartily pray that all the methods of God's providence may be so sweetened unto you by a free resignation of yourself to his good pleasure, that you may be ever happy to yourself and yours in this world, until he shall think fit to translate you from this vain being of mortality to an eternal and an immortal one in Heaven.

NOTES

CHAPTER I

1 Roger North, *The Lives of the Right Hon. Francis North, Baron Guilford; the Hon. Sir Dudley North; and the Hon. and Rev. Dr. John North.* Ed. Augustus Jessopp (1890), iii. 215.

2 *The Works of Sir Thomas Browne,* ed. Geoffrey Keynes (1931), vi. 244–5.

3 *Collected Works of John Wilmot, Earl of Rochester,* ed. John Hayward (Nonesuch Press, 1926), 296.

4 *Collected Works of John Wilmot, Earl of Rochester,* ed. John Hayward (Nonesuch Press, 1926), 296.

5 *Hist. MSS. Com., Portland* (14th Rep., App. II) (1894), iii. 317.

6 *Bradshaigh Papers, Shakerley MSS.*

7 *Bradshaigh Papers, Shakerley MSS.*

8 *Bradshaigh Papers, Shakerley MSS.*

9 *Bradshaigh Papers, Shakerley MSS.*

10 *Bradshaigh Papers, Shakerley MSS.*

11 *Bradshaigh Papers, Shakerley MSS.*

12 *Bradshaigh Papers, Shakerley MSS.*

13 *Bradshaigh Papers, Shakerley MSS.*

14 *Verney Memoirs* (1925 ed.), ii. 309.

15 *Verney Memoirs* (1925 ed.), ii. 312.

16 *Hist. MSS. Com., Kenyon* (14th Rep., App. IV) (1894), 91–2.

17 *Bradshaigh Papers, Shakerley MSS.*

18 *Shakerley MSS.*

19 *Verney MSS.*

20 *Verney Memoirs* (1925 ed.), ii. 311.

21 *Verney MSS.*

22 *The Works of John Dryden,* ed. Sir Walter Scott (rev. by George Saintsbury, 1893), xviii. 99–100.

23 *The Works of John Dryden,* ed. Sir Walter Scott (rev. by George Saintsbury, 1893), xviii. 100–2.

24 *Cavalier : Letters of William Blundell to his Friends,* ed. Margaret Blundell (1933), 176–7.

25 *Letters and the Second Diary of Samuel Pepys,* ed. R. G. Howarth (1932), pp. 170–1.

CHAPTER II

[1] *Hist. MSS. Com.*, *Pine Coffin* (App. to 5th Rep.) (1876), 374.

[2] *The Flemings in Oxford*, ed. J. R. Magrath, D.D. (1904), i. 535–6.

[3] *The Flemings in Oxford*, ed. J. R. Magrath, D.D. (1904), i. 536–7.

[4] *Verney MSS.* (partly printed in *Verney Memoirs* (1925 ed.), ii. 413).

[5] *Verney Memoirs* (1925 ed.), ii. 415–16.

[6] *Verney MSS.* (partly printed in *Verney Memoirs* (1925 ed.), ii. 416).

[7] *The Flemings in Oxford*, ed. J. R. Magrath, D.D. (1904), i. 296–9.

[8] *The Flemings in Oxford*, ed. J. R. Magrath, D.D. (1904), i. 320–1.

[9] *Verney Memoirs* (1925 ed.), ii. 426.

[10] *Verney Memoirs* (1925 ed.), ii. 428–9.

[11] *Shakerley MSS.*

[12] *Shakerley MSS.*

[13] *Shakerley MSS.*

[14] *Shakerley MSS.*

[15] *Shakerley MSS.*

[16] *Shakerley MSS.*

[17] *Shakerley MSS.*

[18] *Shakerley MSS.*

[19] *Shakerley MSS.*

[20] *Verney Memoirs* (1925 ed.), ii. 426.

[21] *The Flemings in Oxford*, ed. J. R. Magrath, D.D. (1904), i. 299–300.

[22] *The Flemings in Oxford*, ed. J. R. Magrath, D.D. (1904), i. 300–1.

[23] *Letters of Humphrey Prideaux*, ed. E. M. Thompson (Camden Soc. 1875), 5–8.

[24] *Letters of Humphrey Prideaux*, ed. E. M. Thompson (Camden Soc. 1875), 9–14.

[25] *Letters of Humphrey Prideaux*, ed. E. M. Thompson (Camden Soc. 1875), 23–4.

[26] *Letters of Humphrey Prideaux*, ed. E. M. Thompson (Camden Soc. 1875), 47.

CHAPTER III

[1] *Letters of Philip, Second Earl of Chesterfield* (1829), 88–9. (Also printed in G. Steinman Steinman, *A Memoir of Barbara, Duchess of Cleveland* (1871), 11–12.)

[2] *Letters of Philip, Second Earl of Chesterfield* (1829), 86–7. (Also printed in G. Steinman Steinman, *A Memoir of Barbara, Duchess of Cleveland* (1871), 10.)

[3] *Letters of Philip, Second Earl of Chesterfield* (1829), 91. (Also printed in G. Steinman Steinman, *A Memoir of Barbara, Duchess of Cleveland* (1871), 13.)

[4] *Letters of Philip, Second Earl of Chesterfield* (1829), 103. (Also printed in G. Steinman Steinman, *A Memoir of Barbara, Duchess of Cleveland* (1871), 17.)

[5] *Letter Book of Philip Stanhope, Earl of Chesterfield, Brit. Mus. Add. MSS.* 19253, f. 24.

[6] *The Complete Works of Thomas Otway,* ed. Montague Summers (Nonesuch Press, 1926), iii. 242–3.

[7] *The Complete Works of Thomas Otway,* ed. Montague Summers (Nonesuch Press, 1926), iii. 245.

[8] *The Complete Works of Thomas Otway,* ed. Montague Summers (Nonesuch Press, 1926), iii. 244.

[9] *The Correspondence of the Family of Hatton,* ed. E. M. Thompson (Camden Soc. 1878), i. 21.

[10] *The Correspondence of the Family of Hatton,* ed. E. M. Thompson (Camden Soc. 1878), i. 68–9.

[11] *Letters of Philip, Second Earl of Chesterfield* (1829), 167–9.

[12] *Hist. MSS. Com., Cowper* (12th Rep. App. II) (1888), ii. 362.

CHAPTER IV

[1] A. L. Cust, *Chronicles of Erthig on the Dyke* (1914), i. 96–7.

[2] A. L. Cust, *Chronicles of Erthig on the Dyke* (1914), i. 18.

[3] A. L. Cust, *Chronicles of Erthig on the Dyke* (1914), i. 26–7.

[4] *Verney MSS.* (partly printed in *Verney Memoirs* (1925 ed.), ii. 272).

[5] *Hist. MSS. Com., Stewart* (10th Rep., App. IV) (1885), 137.

[6] *Letters of Eminent Men addressed to Ralph Thoresby, F.R.S.* (1832), i. 64–5.

[7] *Shakerley MSS.*

[8] *Shakerley MSS.*

[9] *Verney MSS.* (partly printed in *Verney Memoirs* (1925 ed.), ii. 234).

[10] *Verney MSS.* (partly printed in *Verney Memoirs* (1925 ed.), ii. 188).

[11] *Verney MSS.*

[12] *Verney MSS.*

[13] *Verney MSS.*

[14] *Verney MSS.*

[15] *Verney MSS.* (partly printed in *Verney Memoirs* (1925 ed.), ii. 74–5).

[16] *Verney Memoirs* (1925 ed.), ii. 75–6.

[17] *Verney MSS.* (partly printed in *Verney Memoirs* (1925 ed.), ii. 77–8).

[18] *Verney MSS.* (partly printed in *Verney Memoirs* (1925 ed.), ii. 78).

[19] *Verney MSS.* (partly printed in *Verney Memoirs* (1925 ed.), ii. 175).

[20] *Verney MSS.* (partly printed in *Verney Memoirs* (1925 ed.), ii. 176).

[21] *Verney MSS.* (partly printed in *Verney Memoirs* (1925 ed.), ii. 179).

[22] *Verney MSS.*

[23] *Verney MSS.*

[24] *Verney MSS.* (partly printed in *Verney Memoirs* (1925 ed.), ii. 366–9).

[25] *Verney MSS.* (partly printed in *Verney Memoirs* (1925 ed.), ii. 290).

CHAPTER V

[1] Lady Newton, *Lyme Letters* (1925), 32.

[2] Lady Newton, *The House of Lyme* (1917), 275–6.

[3] Lady Newton, *Lyme Letters* (1925), 66.

[4] Lady Newton, *The House of Lyme* (1917), 320.

[5] *Hist. MSS. Com.*, *Cowper* (12th Rep., App. II) (1888), ii. 448–9,

[6] *Verney Memoirs* (1925 ed.), ii. 202.

[7] *Verney MSS.* (partly printed in *Verney Memoirs* (1925 ed.), ii. 371).

[8] E. F. Ward, *Christopher Monck, Duke of Albemarle* (1915), 196 (from *Montagu House MSS.*).

[9] *The Correspondence of the Family of Hatton*, ed. E. M. Thompson (Camden Soc. 1878), ii. 244.

[10] *Verney MSS.* (partly printed in *Verney Memoirs* (1925 ed.), ii. 184–5).

[11] *Shakerley MSS.*

[12] *Shakerley MSS.*

[13] *B.M. Harleian MSS.* 7003, f. 261.

[14] *Collected Works of John Wilmot, Earl of Rochester*, ed. John Hayward (Nonesuch Press, 1926), 288.

[15] *Collected Works of John Wilmot, Earl of Rochester*, ed. John Hayward (Nonesuch Press, 1926), 290.

[16] *Collected Works of John Wilmot, Earl of Rochester*, ed. John Hayward (Nonesuch Press, 1926), 293.

[17] H. C. Foxcroft, *Life and Letters of Sir George Savile, Bart., First Marquis of Halifax* (1898), ii. 148–50.

[18] James Ferguson, *Robert Ferguson : the Plotter* (1887), 94–5.

[19] James Ferguson, *Robert Ferguson : the Plotter* (1887), 96–7.

[20] *Four Centuries of English Letters*, ed. W. Baptiste Scoones (1880), 114–15.

[21] *Four Centuries of English Letters*, ed. W. Baptiste Scoones (1880), 115.

CHAPTER VI

[1] *Verney Memoirs* (1925 ed.), ii. 209.

[2] *Verney MSS.* (partly printed in *Verney Memoirs* (1925 ed.), ii. 211).

[3] C. H. Hartmann, *La Belle Stuart* (1924), 137–40.

[4] *Shakerley MSS.*

[5] *Letters and the Second Diary of Samuel Pepys*, ed. R. G. Howarth (1932), 10–11. (*Carte MSS.* 73, f. 190.)

[6] *Verney Letters of the Eighteenth Century*, ed. Margaret Maria, Lady Verney (1930), 41–2.

[7] Lady Newton, *The House of Lyme* (1917), 265–6.

[8] *Shakerley MSS.*

[9] *Shakerley MSS.*
[10] *Shakerley MSS.*
[11] *Shakerley MSS.*
[12] *Shakerley MSS.*
[13] *Shakerley MSS.*
[14] *Shakerley MSS.*
[15] *Shakerley MSS.*
[16] *Shakerley MSS.*
[17] *Shakerley MSS.*
[18] *Shakerley MSS.*
[19] *Shakerley MSS.*
[20] *Shakerley MSS.*
[21] *Verney MSS.* (partly printed in *Verney Memoirs* (1925 ed.), ii. 317–18).

CHAPTER VII

[1] *Hist. MSS. Com., Cowper* (12th Rep., App. II) (1888), ii. 382–3.
[2] *Hist. MSS. Com., Cowper* (12th Rep., App. II) (1888), ii. 383.
[3] *The Correspondence of the Family of Hatton*, ed. E. M. Thompson (Camden Soc. 1878), ii. 196.
[4] *Shakerley MSS.*
[5] *Verney Memoirs* (1925 ed.), ii. 462.
[6] A. L. Cust, *Chronicles of Erthig on the Dyke* (1914), i. 87–8.
[7] *Hist. MSS. Com., Ormonde* (New Series, 1908), v. 74–5.
[8] E. F. Ward, *Christopher Monck, Duke of Albemarle* (1915), 164. (From Montagu House MSS.)
[9] *Shakerley MSS.*
[10] *Four Centuries of English Letters*, ed. W. Baptiste Scoones (1880), 150–1.

CHAPTER VIII

[1] *Letters of Philip, Second Earl of Chesterfield* (1829), 97.
[2] *Letters of Philip, Second Earl of Chesterfield* (1829), 99–100.
[3] *Savile Correspondence*, ed. W. D. Cooper (Camden Soc. 1858), 1–2.
[4] *Savile Correspondence*, ed. W. D. Cooper (Camden Soc. 1858), 86–7.
[5] *Savile Correspondence*, ed. W. D. Cooper (Camden Soc. 1858), 132–3.
[6] *Collected Works of John Wilmot, Earl of Rochester*, ed. John Hayward (Nonesuch Press, 1926), 252–3.
[7] *Hist. MSS. Com., Bath*, ii. (1907), 160–1.
[8] *Hist. MSS. Com., Bath*, ii. (1907), 164–5.
[9] V. de Sola Pinto, *Sir Charles Sedley* (1927), 152–4.
[10] *Letter Book of Sir George Etherege, Minister at Ratisbon, 1685–1688* (*B.M. Add. MSS.* 11513, f. 140). (Printed in Sybil Rosenfeld, *The Letterbook of Sir George Etherege* (1928), 282–3.)

[11] *Letter Book of Sir George Etherege, Minister at Ratisbon,* 1685–1688 (*B.M. Add. MSS.* 11513, f. 154). (Printed in Sybil Rosenfeld, *The Letterbook of Sir George Etherege* (1928), 303–5.)

[12] Sybil Rosenfeld, *The Letterbook of Sir George Etherege* (1928), 416–21 (reprinted from *Miscellaneous Works of G. Duke of Buckingham* (1704), 131).

[13] Mr. Tite's *Collection of Autographs* (*Camden Miscellany,* v. 1864), 25–7.

CHAPTER IX

[1] *The Correspondence of the Family of Hatton,* ed. E. M. Thompson (Camden Soc. 1878), i. 115–16.

[2] *The Correspondence of the Family of Hatton,* ed. E. M. Thompson (Camden Soc. 1878), i. 117.

[3] *Collected Works of John Wilmot, Earl of Rochester,* ed. John Hayward (Nonesuch Press, 1926), 261.

[4] *Cavalier: Letters of William Blundell to his Friends,* ed. Margaret Blundell (1933), 235–6.

[5] *Shakerley MSS.*

[6] *Hist. MSS. Com., Ingilby* (App. to 6th Rep.) (1877), 374.

CHAPTER X

[1] *Verney MSS.*

[2] *Verney Letters of the Eighteenth Century,* ed. Margaret Maria, Lady Verney (1930), 20–1.

[3] *Hist. MSS. Com., Ormonde* (New Series, 1904), iii. 39.

[4] *The Correspondence of the Family of Hatton,* ed. E. M. Thompson (Camden Soc. 1878), i. 140–2.

[5] *The Works of John Dryden,* ed. Sir Walter Scott (rev. by George Saintsbury, 1893), xviii. 144–5.

[6] *The Works of John Dryden,* ed. Sir Walter Scott (rev. by George Saintsbury, 1893), xviii. 156–8.

[7] *Private Correspondence and Miscellaneous Papers of Samuel Pepys,* ed. J. R. Tanner (1926), i. 209–12.

[8] *Private Correspondence and Miscellaneous Papers of Samuel Pepys,* ed. J. R. Tanner (1926), i. 194–5.

[9] *Private Correspondence and Miscellaneous Papers of Samuel Pepys,* ed. J. R. Tanner (1926), i. 196–7.

[10] *Letters and the Second Diary of Samuel Pepys,* ed. R. G. Howarth (1932), 35–6.

[11] *The Works of Sir Thomas Browne,* ed. Geoffrey Keynes (1931), vi. 15.

[12] *Sir Thomas Browne's Works,* ed. Simon Wilkin (1836), i. 74–5.

[13] Lady Newton, *Lyme Letters* (1925), 64.

[14] *Hist. MSS. Com., Fitzherbert* (13th Rep., App. VI) (1893), 11.

[15] *Cavalier: The Letters of William Blundell to his Friends,* ed. Margaret Blundell (1933), 155–6.

CHAPTER XI

1 *Cavalier: Letters of William Blundell to his Friends*, ed. Margaret Blundell (1933), 101–2.

2 *Letters and the Second Diary of Samuel Pepys*, ed. R. G. Howarth (1932), 106–7.

3 *Letters and the Second Diary of Samuel Pepys*, ed. R. G. Howarth (1932), 198.

4 *Letters and the Second Diary of Samuel Pepys*, ed. R. G. Howarth (1932), 198–9.

5 B. Bathurst, *Letters of Two Queens* (1924), 49–50.

6 B. Bathurst, *Letters of Two Queens* (1924), 51.

7 B. Bathurst, *Letters of Two Queens* (1924), 91–2.

8 *Letters and the Second Diary of Samuel Pepys*, ed. R. G. Howarth (1932), 334–5.

CHAPTER XII

1 *Letters of Philip, Second Earl of Chesterfield* (1829), 182.

2 *Letters of Philip, Second Earl of Chesterfield* (1829), 376–9.

3 *Letters of Philip, Second Earl of Chesterfield* (1829), 380.

4 *Savile Correspondence*, ed. W. D. Cooper (Camden Soc. 1858), 137–8.

5 George D'Oyly, *The Life of William Sancroft, Archbishop of Canterbury* (1821), ii. 13–14.

6 *The Works of John Dryden*, ed. Sir Walter Scott (rev. by George Saintsbury, 1893), xviii. 141–2.

7 *The Works of John Dryden*, ed. Sir Walter Scott (rev. by George Saintsbury, 1893), xviii, 147–8.

CHAPTER XIII

1 *Diaries and Letters of Philip Henry*, ed. M. H. Lee (1882), 341–3.

2 *The Works of Sir Thomas Browne*, ed. Geoffrey Keynes (1931), vi. 230–1.

3 *Hist. MSS. Com., Portland* (14th Rep., App. II) (1894), iii. 268–9.

4 *Verney MSS.*

5 *Cavalier: Letters of William Blundell to his Friends*, ed. Margaret Blundell (1933), 107–9.

6 *The Lauderdale Papers*, ed. O. Airy (Camden Soc. 1885), iii. 235–9.

7 Samuel M. Janney, *The Life of William Penn: with selections from his Correspondence and Autobiography* (6th ed. 1882), 66–7.

8 *The Flemings in Oxford*, ed. J. R. Magrath (1904), i. 164–5.

9 *Correspondence of the Family of Hatton*, ed. E. M. Thompson (Camden Soc. 1878), i. 156–7.

10 E. H. Plumptre, *Life of Thomas Ken, D.D., Bishop of Bath and Wells* (1890), ii. 102–3.

11 *Hist. MSS. Com., Portland* (14th Rep., App. II) (1894), iii. 266.

12 *Hist. MSS. Com., Rutland* (12th Rep., App. V) (1889), ii. 158.

CHAPTER XIV

1 *The Works of Sir Thomas Browne*, ed. Geoffrey Keynes (1931), vi. 207–8.

2 *Cavalier: Letters of William Blundell to his Friends*, ed. Margaret Blundell (1933), 226–7.

3 *Shakerley MSS.*

4 *Letters written by Eminent Persons in the Seventeenth and Eighteenth Centuries* (1813), i. 58–9.

5 *The Works of Sir Thomas Browne*, ed. Geoffrey Keynes (1931), vi. 405–6.

6 *Cavalier: Letters of William Blundell to his Friends*, ed. Margaret Blundell (1933), 106–7.

7 *Verney MSS.* (partly printed in *Verney Memoirs* (1925 ed.), ii. 243–4).

8 E. H. Plumptre, *The Life of Thomas Ken, D.D., Bishop of Bath and Wells* (1890), i. 255–6.

9 *Collected Works of John Wilmot, Earl of Rochester*, ed. John Hayward (Nonesuch Press, 1926), 323–4.

10 *Letters of Humphrey Prideaux*, ed. E. M. Thompson (Camden Soc. 1875), 25–6.

11 *The Correspondence of the Family of Hatton*, ed. E. M. Thompson (Camden Soc. 1878), ii. 166–8.

12 *Verney MSS.* (partly printed in *Verney Memoirs* (1925 ed.), ii. 421).

13 *Verney Memoirs* (1925 ed.), ii. 422–3.

14 *Letters of Eminent Men, addressed to Ralph Thoresby, F.R.S.* (1832), i. 202–3.

15 *Petty-Southwell Correspondence 1676–1687*, ed. from Bowood Papers by the Marquis of Lansdowne (1928), 88–90.

16 *Shakerley MSS.*

17 *Hist. MSS. Com., Egmont* (New Series, 1909), ii. 21.

18 *Four Centuries of English Letters*, ed. W. Baptiste Scoones (1880), 105–7.

19 *Hist. MSS. Com., Ormonde* (New Series, 1912), vii. 260–1.

Printed in England at THE BALLANTYNE PRESS *by* SPOTTISWOODE, BALLANTYNE & CO. LTD. *Colchester, London & Eton*